WILLIAM M. A. GRIMALDI, S. J.

STUDIES IN THE PHILOSOPHY OF ARISTOTLE'S RHETORIC

HERMES

ZEITSCHRIFT FÜR KLASSISCHE PHILOLOGIE

EINZELSCHRIFTEN

HERAUSGEGEBEN VON

KARL BÜCHNER · HERMANN GUNDERT

HERBERT NESSELHAUF

HEFT 25

STUDIES IN THE PHILOSOPHY OF ARISTOTLE'S RHETORIC

BY

WILLIAM M. A. GRIMALDI, S.J.

FRANZ STEINER VERLAG GMBH · WIESBADEN

1972

STUDIES IN THE PHILOSOPHY OF ARISTOTLE'S RHETORIC

BY

WILLIAM M. A. GRIMALDI, S. J.

FRANZ STEINER VERLAG GMBH · WIESBADEN
1972

To the memory of
my Mother and Father.

I wish to thank the editors of THE AMERICAN JOURNAL OF PHILOLOGY, THE CLASSICAL JOURNAL, CLASSICAL PHILOLOGY, and TRADITIO for permission to use some material originally published by them.

CONTENTS

INTRODUCTION

Despite the extensive use of Aristotle's *Rhetoric* as a critical document in the study of literature and literary composition a common judgment of the work is fairly well represented in the observation that "Advertising ... is perhaps the best example of an activity that practises what Aristotle preached"[1]. If one were to argue that, on the contrary, the object of Aristotle's treatise on rhetoric is ultimately an analysis of the nature of human discourse in all areas of knowledge, the argument would be received with suspicion. For as an academic discipline rhetoric has long been identified exclusively with the facile manipulation of language. We find this view reflected in every phase of contemporary critical activity. Prose, poetry, painting, politics and philosophy are dismissed as "rhetorical" when the criticism is to underscore concentration on form with little or no reference to content. It should be more than obvious that when the form of language is cultivated without regard to the content of the statement we have the misuse of language. We do not, however, have "rhetoric", and to describe this misuse by the words "rhetoric" or "rhetorical" is at the very least to misunderstand the art of rhetoric as it was developed by the Greeks who gave it their attention. Aristotle, Plato and Isocrates when they spoke of rhetoric and rhetorical study were speaking of the intimate articulation of matter and form in discourse.

This stance on the part of these men becomes more readily understandable when we realize that for the Greeks rhetorical study was a method of education and consequently a responsible activity. To equate this *paideusis*, as has been done, with public relations, advertising, or even with college textbooks on English composition is an admission that we have little or no idea of what the Greeks were about. Certainly Plato in works like the *Phaedrus, Gorgias, Protagoras,* Isocrates in his *Antidosis, Panegyricus, Against the Sophists,* and Aristotle in the *Rhetoric* and *Poetics,* give no indication that they are concerned with the mere surface techniques of speaking and writing. Their attention is centered on the character, nature, and use of language as the vehicle of communication. Isocrates aptly expresses the idea: "the proper use of language is the most substantial index of sound thinking" (*Antidosis* 255; *Nicocles, or the Cyprians* 7). Plato speaks of one who "plants and sows words grounded in

---

[1] R. P. J. CORBETT, Classical Rhetoric for the Modern Student, Oxford University Press 1965, p. 31.

knowledge . . . words which are fruitful and carry a seed from which other words are implanted in other minds" *(Phaedrus* 276e). The study of rhetoric occupied itself with the way in which language was used and it realized quite early that the content of discourse is substantially conditioned by the way in which it is expressed. The only reasonable way to explain the genesis of the study (even if we accept the traditional account of Tisias-Corax and the Sicilian law courts) is a realization on the part of the Greeks that content is inextricably bound in with the medium, that the "what" of one's statement is eminently qualified by the "way-in-which" or "way-by-which" one expresses the statement. Aristotle's *Rhetoric*, for example, occupies itself essentially with the principles which are necessary if one is to make significant statements on any subject in a way which communicates this significance most effectively. This is the simple object of the whole exercise: "Rhetoric is valuable because truth and justice are naturally superior to their opposites; and so, if incorrect judgments are made, truth and justice are worsted through their own fault" (*A* 1, 55a 21—23). At the same time it should be clear that a formal treatise, such as the *Rhetoric* is, will be specified, as any intelligent analysis will, by the concrete historical and cultural context in which the author is working as well as by the commonly accepted understanding of the subject which he is analyzing. One cannot dismiss the background from which it arose. It is not surprising, then, that the dominant tenor of the *Rhetoric* is oral discourse in the field of deliberative, judicial, and epideictic oratory. On the other hand, without attributing to the analysis more than its due, one should not emasculate the work by a reading narrowly limited to its surface statement. For the character of the analysis is a substantially critical study of discourse as men employ it to communicate with their fellow men whether the subject be philosophy, history, literature, political science. In its essential character Aristotle's analysis has much in common with Plato's study of rhetoric in the *Phaedrus* as expressed in the thematic statement at 261a ff.

Herein Aristotle's work reflects its antecedents since the Greeks were of the opinion that when men use language to speak to each other they need rhetoric, for this was the *techne* whose concern is the structure of language as the mode of human communication[2]. For Aristotle, the rhetorical *techne* in-

---

[2] How critically necessary it is to understand this is illustrated by interpretations which criticize the *Rhetoric* for what it is not. To see the work as concerned with a "superficial political science", or "a conventional ethics" (see E. L. HUNT, "Plato and Aristotle on Rhetoric and Rhetoricians", pp. 57 ff., in Historical Studies of Rhetoric and Rhetoricians, ed. R. F. Howes (Ithaca 1961) is to misunderstand it. It is none of these things. Ethics, politics, logic, epistemology, etc. offer the material with which rhetoric works. Rhetoric, like dialectic, is for Aristotle a methodology. But it is a methodology for discourse with others; as a *dynamis* its function is to aid in discovering that structure in discourse on any subject (v. *A* 2, 55b 25—34) which will lead to conviction and belief.

cludes within its ambience any subject which is open to discussion and deliberation. Further, it attends to all the aspects of that subject which admit of verbal presentation and which are necessary to make the subject understandable and acceptable to an other. Dialectic, for example, considers the same general kind of subject for the purpose of rational investigation and speculative discussion. Rhetoric, its counterpart for Aristotle[3], approaches the subject under the formality of communication, that is to say with the intention of presenting the matter to an other in such a way as to make accessible to the other the possibility of reasonable judgment. As the art of language among the Greeks rhetoric recognized the fact that language originates from people and is destined for persons. Consequently it was the study of discourse in order to discover the most effective way in which to present the problematic so that an other person may reach an intelligent decision.

The more common way of saying this when one speaks of rhetoric is to say that "rhetoric effects persuasion", a phrase attributed to Gorgias by Plato (*Gorgias* 453a) and frequently repeated in discussions on rhetoric. This kind of statement certainly does not describe Aristotelian rhetoric. He does not speak of "effecting persuasion", but rather of discovering in the subject those things which are suasive to an other. It is unfortunate that the word "persuasion" somehow or other prejudices the whole undertaking insofar as it has long carried with it an acquired pejorative connotation. To many "persuasion" has always implied the coercion of reason and the distortion of evidence under the pressure of careless or false reasoning and a strong appeal to the emotions. Since both can falsify the truth "persuasion" has been looked upon as unbecoming a man of reason[4]. Persuasion *qua* persuasion was not in-

---

[3] Isocrates, in a way, joins the two when he describes his rhetoric as the faculty whereby "we argue with others on matters open to dispute and investigate for ourselves things unknown" (*Antidosis* 256).

[4] It would be interesting to know how much of this distrust of the art of rhetoric was occasioned by the fact that the 17th century philosophers who developed and strongly influenced modern thought were mainly mathematicians, (e. g. Hobbes, Descartes, Spinoza, Leibniz), interested in a language modeled on the symbolism of mathematics: "words often impede me and I am almost deceived by the terms of ordinary language" (Descartes). As a general attitude of mind, prescinding from philosophical distinctions such as we find in the *Gorgias* of Plato, there was no fundamentally intrinsic opposition between persuasion and truth for the Greeks. As a matter of fact the two could be closely related as we see in Cassandra who was a prophetess of truth, ἀληθόμαντις (*Agam.* 1241), not given to deceiving (1195); but after violating her oath her words had no effect on anyone: ἔπειθον οὐδέν' οὐδέν (they *persuaded* no one). There is the same close relation five centuries later in Longinus, *On the Sublime* 15. 10—11 between factual demonstration and persuasion. Indeed this passage should be compared with BACON's observation: "The duty and office of rhetoric is to apply reason to the imagination for the better moving of the will" (Advancement of Learning, Book II). M. DÉTIENNE says well: "Au même titre que *Pistis*, Peithô est un aspect nécessaire de l'Alétheia . . ." (Les Maîtres de vérité dans la Grèce archaïque, Paris 1967, p. 62). This is the maieutic character of language well used; we see its effect in *Laches* (188 c—d):

terpreted in such an exclusive manner by the Greeks. Furthermore such an attitude of mind is erroneous in itself because of its refusal to acknowledge that persuasion is at the heart of all communication be it in discourse with the self or the other. As soon as man comes into contact with the world of reality (contingent or absolute) and wishes to make a judgment, he puts before himself or others those reasons which not only represent the real facts or real situation insofar as he can apprehend them, but which are also the more convincing to himself or to his auditors. When we say "more convincing", or as Aristotle would say "suasive", we are simply accepting the inescapable fact that in all areas of human living there are large complexes of pre-existing convictions and assumptions within which we must attempt to speak to the other. There is first of all the large area of common-sense judgments in which it is taken for granted that normal, intelligent persons would maintain, for example, that justice is better than injustice. Again there are assumptions made by people as members of a particular kind of society; for example, those who live in a democracy ordinarily assume that it is a better form of government. Then there are the series of convictions developed by diverse sub-cultures such as professional training or the academic disciplines. Each milieu has a way of establishing its own set of convictions, assumptions, basic understandings, out of which the individual works. There is not only a rational foundation for discourse but also a psychological and sociological foundation. Aristotle himself recognizes this when he comments that "With regard to winning credence it is a matter of much importance that the speaker appear to be of a certain character and that the hearers assume that he be somehow disposed toward them, and further, too, that the audience be somehow disposed" (B 1, 77b 25—29). Discourse is meant to convey meaning, but meaning has both a logical and psychological aspect. Discourse occurs within a social and cultural context in which knowledge, belief, attitude, qualify statement. To accept this, as one must, and to work within it is to admit that one speaks to others in different ways in the effort to speak to them with meaning on a problem of common concern. One of the most obvious instances of this in the field of philosophical discourse are the Socratic dialogues. Their dramatic setting is a factor which actually specifies and con-

---

"When I hear a man discourse on *arete*, or on wisdom, one who is truly a man . . . I am deeply delighted as I behold how both the speaker and his words become each other and are suited to each other". B. Muntéano, "Constantes humaines en litérature" in Stil und Formprobleme in der Literatur, (Heidelberg 1959) after rejecting the idea of Aristotle's *Rhetoric* as a mere collection of tricks and commonplaces (p. 69), continues: "C'est que la structure rhétorique du discours n'est autre chose que la cristallisation en principes et préceptes des données foncières de la nature humaine . . . Au centre du système fonctionne le principe moteur de la persuasion, où je crois qu'il convient de voir l'expression même de l'instinct qui engage l'individu à communiquer avec ses semblables . . . C'est à *persuader autrui*, c'est à *communiquer* et même, de quelque manière, à *communier* avec lui . . ."

structs their argumentation, and it represents Plato's effort to use the cultural and social context in articulating critical philosophical problems: "truth is essentially communicable, and it is the first task of the lover, as is emphasized in the *Phaedrus*, to arouse an answering or requiting love in the object of his affection"[5]. As M. POLANYI remarks (Personal Knowledge, Univ. of Chicago 1958, p. 3): "For as human beings, we must inevitably see the universe from a centre lying within ourselves and speak about it in terms of a human knowledge shaped by the exigencies of human intercourse. Any attempt rigorously to eliminate our human perspective from our picture of the world must lead to absurdity".

Aristotle understood this, and to call his *Rhetoric* a "rhetoric of persuasion" with the understanding of "persuasion at any cost" is wrong. He was aware of the fact that person speaks to person, to the "other" in whom resides the tension between self-possession and its possible loss which may be incurred in any decision made toward further growth in understanding. In this matter of "persuasion" Aristotle's thesis is simply that good rhetoric effectively places before the other person all the means necessary for such decision making. At this point the person must exercise his own freedom.

Men are always engaged in converse with the self and with others in an effort to grasp meaning in the world of reality. This is particularly true of all educational effort where one is quite conscious that the burden of language is to express and communicate meaning. In view of the fact that rhetoric held a prominent position in the educational effort of the Greeks, to the extent, indeed, that it was seriously argued over in the fourth century B. C., one may legitimately question whether this prominence resulted from a simple interest in the tricks of persuasion or an interest in the more substantial question of the nature of human discourse.

It is usual to attribute the interest in, and the study of the spoken and written word to very practical and hard-headed motives: power and security. In the emerging development of political structures, particularly democracy, facility with the practical skills of using language was, we are assured, a talisman for self-defense in the courts of law and self-advancement in the body politic. Certainly this interpretation is reasonable and a partial explanation. Yet the nature of Greek education and the place of rhetoric within it would seem to indicate that the purpose of rhetorical study was something more substantial than the study of ways and means to gain one's way in the world.

The purpose of these introductory remarks is to suggest that the study of rhetoric among the Greeks was of a more serious character than is frequently

---

[5] Plato accepts the fact that to teach one must use persuasion, e. g. *Gorg.* 453d; *Crito* 51b—c; *Protag.* 352e; *Apol.* 35c; and this extends to the sciences as well as the humanities, *Gorg.* 454a; see also R. CUSHMAN, Therapeia, Chapel Hill 1958, pp. 219 ff.

suggested, and that Aristotle's *Rhetoric* echoes this original concern and gives it new form. The remarks are somewhat partial in that they do not attend to the "schools" of practical rhetoric, to the technographers of rhetorical handbooks, nor to the criticisms of practical rhetoric found in the major writers. Certainly there were treatises in circulation on what appears to be practical rhetoric (cf. Plato, *Phaedrus* 271c. 266c—269c; Isocrates *Against the Sophists* 19; Aristotle, *Rhetoric A* 1, 54a 12), and there were also teachers of rhetoric usually identified with the Sophists, as is quite clear from Plato, or earlier, Aristophanes. All of this material, however, can be found in any history of Greek rhetoric. Furthermore there is no intent here to dismiss the fact that there were probably rhetoricians who devoted their time exclusively to the practical aspects of technique and verbal expertise. This would be foolish, particularly in view of the fact that one senses the development of such an approach in the strong antagonism in the fourth century between philosophy and rhetoric as the true instrument of education.

It is difficult, however, to accept the study of rhetoric in the schools as vocational training in persuasive speaking when we find the study and the teachers so obviously concentrating on literature and academic subjects. If anything, the evidence supports a concern on their part with language and its structure and its relation to the knowing mind. It is not surprising, then, when we come to the fourth century to find that the men who gave their attention to the problem of rhetoric present us with critiques reflecting the same concern with language and its structure in conjunction with knowledge and understanding. Plato, Isocrates and Aristotle were manifestly exposed to a developing tension between "rhetoric" and "philosophy" as educational methods. But it is certainly an over-simplification to speak, as is done, about "rhetorical education" and the "teachers of rhetoric" in either the fifth or the fourth century, and to describe without qualification the latter (and so the former) as "interested only in the art of persuasion, in rhetorical tricks to arouse the emotions of an audience . . . without regard for morality or truth". If this is true we must conclude that the Greeks, aside from selecting a rather strange method to educate their young people, succeeded in producing a remarkable literature which reveals no significant signs of such an influence, as well as such notable students as Euripides, Pericles, Thucydides, Plato. A side of the coin which is rarely alluded to is the fact that the formal study of rhetoric began and flourished in Greece at a time when there was confidence in the human intellect and in man's ability to formulate his problems. When one examines in this light most of what is dismissed as tricks of the rhetoricians' trade, the common stock dispensed by the teachers of rhetoric, another explanation emerges. Very common techniques, to cite but two, from the teaching of the Sophists, were probability argumentation and the use of antithesis. And yet in the final analysis both are logical methods to open up a question or a problem to all of its implications. They are in fact forms of critical analysis. When we meet the apparent confrontation of rhetorical versus philosophical education in Isocrates and Plato there is still no question of mere verbal expertise and the mechanics of language. Enough has been written on the subject to indicate that neither man would accept rhetoric as a study of the techniques of language manipulation in order to make one's point at any cost and so obtain one's way without regard for fact or truth. The primary concern of these men, and in this they repeat the earlier tradition and were followed by Aristotle, was the ability of the mind to know and to apprehend meaning in the world of reality and to interpret this knowledge to others. Their comments, both formal and informal, on the nature of rhetoric come from within the structure of their philosophical convictions[6]. Aristotle's *Rhetoric*, for example, can be understood correctly, as shall be seen, only when we place it within the context of his philosophy. Plato makes the point well when, speaking in the *Phaedrus* about rhetorical discourse, he asks the aid of those arguments which will prove to Phaedrus that "unless he gets on with his philosophy he will never get on as a speaker on any subject" (269e). Earlier he had remarked that "good discourse demands that the speaker know the truth about the subject of his discourse" (259e), a view reflected in Isocrates' comment that the power of discourse is grounded in the study of philosophy *(Antidosis* 48). It is difficult to escape the conclusion that the interest of these men in rhetoric is with language and its importance as the vehicle of meaning, indeed with form as expressive of meaning[7]. No one questions the fact that the Greeks in their

---

[6] If we look at Isocrates from Plato's position then Isocrates' "philosophy" was no philosophy since for Plato philosophy was concerned with infallible knowledge. Isocrates was quite satisfied with "right opinion" on reality (cf. *Panathenaicus* 9). Yet in Isocrates the word "philosophy" both denotes and connotes the exercise of mind and reason in the effort to grasp the world as experience. It is a serious effort toward the truth insofar as the truth can be known by the mind; it is an effort that accepts a kind of total human understanding from knowledge and experience without demanding a metaphysics. On this matter of the relation of rhetorical theory to philosophical convictions P. A. DUHAMEL notes: "There were as many conceptions of rhetoric in the period usually called "Classical" as there were philosophies, and the rhetoric can be understood only within the commensurable terms of the philosophy. In every observable instance the rhetoric is dependent for its content and orientation upon the more fundamental concepts which are the burden of epistemological or metaphysical discussion. The complete understanding of a system of rhetoric not only entails a scrutiny of the underlying philosophy but the elucidation of those implications is the task of any future historian of the concept of effective expression." ("The Function of Rhetoric as Effective Expression" *JHI* 10, 1949, p. 356).

[7] We find the same concern in the later literary theorists, Dionysius of Halicarnassus and Longinus, in their effort to relate the study of rhetoric to a firm background in literature, philosophy, and the varied branches of learning. They were quite conscious of structure and their work, in the view of W. RHYS ROBERTS, illustrates in many ways the *Rhetoric* of Aristotle (see his Dionysius of Halicarnassus on Literary Composition, London 1910, p. xi).

poetry understood the importance of form to convey meaning, although the same understanding for their prose has been, and continues to be identified with sophistry and charlatanism.

Yet the heart of the problem of rhetorical study as seen in Aristotle is that all significant human discourse is structured language, an organic whole, which communicates effectively man's reflection on, and articulation of, reality. In this he reflects the concern of early rhetorical study for structure, Plato's sense of the power of the *logos* in its capacity to engender in the person an awareness of the self and of the world of the real, and Isocrates' theory that rhetoric as the "source of civilization, of law, and the arts" is a creative entity: ποιητικὸν πρᾶγμα (*Against the Sophists* 12). This phrase, interesting in its recognition that language transforms experience, makes rhetoric the analogue in language of the other arts[8]. Rhetoric is the art which presents man with the structure for language, and, by way of structure, enables language to become an effective medium whereby man apprehends reality.

This is a different view of the art of rhetoric than that which is commonly put forward. While it is certainly true of Aristotle's *Rhetoric* there is reason to believe that the *Rhetoric*, in this respect, gives expression to what was substantially the Greek view. For when we turn to the men who are considered to be the exponents of practical rhetoric, the Sophists, we find sufficient evidence to challenge the view that their interest was confined to the superficial tricks of language expression in order to achieve one's practical aims. In the first place the Sophists were educators and MARROU correctly calls the First Sophistic the movement which "produced the great revolution in teaching which was to put Greek education on the road to maturity"[9]. As educators

---

[8] Oddly enough his teacher Gorgias uses the word *poiesis* of both *logos* and sculpture (*Helen* 9, 18); H. DIELS, Die Fragmente der Vorsokratiker[10], Berlin 1960, 82 B 11 (8 of the *Helen*). In many ways it is difficult to see how the rhetorician is not, as far as Aristotle is concerned, as much a maker as the poet. The rhetorician is making something according to certain definite rules for a definite purpose. In both instances language is the medium; the goal is different in that the object of the poet is knowledge directed toward contemplation, that of the rhetorician knowledge directed toward action. Both arts have to do with the *logos* and H. LAUSBERG (Handbuch der literarischen Rhetorik, Munich 1960, p. 42) is certainly not alone in his judgment of the close relationship of poetic and rhetoric when he writes: "beide . . . sind ja poietische Künste im Bereich der Sprache."

[9] H. I. MARROU, A History of Education in Antiquity (transl. G. LAMB), London 1956, p. 47; A. KOYRÉ, Discovering Plato (transl. L. C. ROSENFIELD), N. Y. 1946, p. 28, n. 12: "Literary criticism, interpretation of classical poets, was one of the main bases of the teaching given by the sophists." R. PFEIFFER, History of Classical Scholarship, Oxford 1968, pp. 16—32, "the sophists . . . were the first to influence by their theories not only prose writing, rhetoric, and dialectic above all, but also contemporary and later poetry . . ." (p. 16). G. M. A. GRUBE, A Greek Critic: Demetrius on Style, Toronto 1961, speaking of the new sophists, e. g. Gorgias, etc., notes that "as the first *theorists* of the art of language, the Sophists did have a very great influence on the development of Greek style" (p. 4). It surely does not seem an over simplification to ask from where precisely came the impetus to the vast amount of competent work in dramatic literature, historiography,

their primary interest was with literature and consequently with the study of language. Their studies, and in particular the kind of literary study found in the *Protagoras* 339a—347a, imply that they were alert to the fact that as a cultural instrument the potential of language is realized in the care with which it is used. As FÉNELON remarked "Chez les grecs tout dépendait du peuple et le peuple dépendait de la parole", and language was the instrument the Sophists exploited in their effort to educate. While their curriculum was catholic in its subject-matter, (e. g. philosophy, music, astronomy, mathematics, dialectic, science, semantics), their education followed the traditional pattern in which literature played a prominent role and in which the common denominator was language[10]. Education for them was a matter of the intellect with emphasis on the study of language as the medium whereby man interpreted reality to himself and to others. The concentration of this education on literature, e. g. Protagoras' comment that the study of poetry is the most important part of all education *(Protag.* 338e), developed a sensitivity to the *logos*, an awareness of the intimate relation between thought and language[11]. Only someone concerned with language and its use could remark as Gorgias did of the *logos:* "The word is a mighty power . . . it can end fear, abolish pain, instil joy, increase pity"[12]. Within this context one can only conclude that rhetorical study as a form of education for the Sophists employed var-

philosophy, and political discourse of the fifth and fourth century if we equate the rhetorical studies of the sophists with mere techniques of writing.

[10] As for the specifically utilitarian character of these studies in the mind of the Sophists the comment of Isocrates merits serious consideration and is quite relevant. Speaking of many of these same subjects he remarks that all of them are of no immediate practical aid *(Antidosis* 262) but do help the student (267) and, like grammar and literature (266), prepare the mind for philosophy, i. e. for an informed and intelligent mind on the critical problems of existence.

[11] MARROU, A History of Education, p. 134 speaking of rhetoric and words has this to say: "These, we said, are inseparable; and this is so because the effort to find the right expression demands and develops a sensitivity of thought, a sense of different shades of meaning, which it is difficult to express in conceptual ideas . . ." There can be little question from the many statements of Isocrates that JAEGER is quite correct in saying that his ideal of culture was *logos* as the union of speech and reason *(Paideia* vol. III, p. 79). E. ARNOLD, Roman Stoicism, Cambridge 1911, pp. 128—154 in setting forth the Stoic doctrine on reason and speech reveals this same idea at work in Stoic concern for the union of language and thought. From the work of the Sophists in the study of the artistic use of language it does not seem correct to attribute the development of literary theory exclusively to the work of Plato and Aristotle as GRUBE does (A Greek Critic, p. 10). Quite clearly the work in rhetoric of Gorgias, Prodicus, Hippias, to mention but three of the Sophists, indicates a body of informed thinking on literary theory. Rhetorical study was directed to the art of language and GRUBE (p. 12) makes the point rather well when he writes: "For we should never forget that *rhêtorikê* was the art of expression as a whole, even if oratory was the art of expression par excellence". The evidence such as it is on "textbooks of rhetoric" and their character ("technical and immoral") is not sufficient to permit firm judgments on their occupation with verbal agility and trickery to the exclusion of substantial theory.

[12] *Helen* 8

ious areas of learning but worked primarily with literature. This apparently continued into the fourth century if the statement of Isocrates (*Panathenaicus* 16—19 with 26) makes any sense.

As a consequence of such an educational process it becomes more easy to comprehend why the Greeks responded readily to language and its effective use, or language in oral and written discourse. When we have an audience educated to be alert to the verbal medium we can understand the large body of distinguished literature which came from them[13], literature, moreover, which demands sensitivity to language as, for example, the plays of Aristophanes with their literary parody, allusion, and criticism. A minimal enjoyment of such parody (which we find also in Plato) requires some knowledge in the audience of the literary manner, form, and substance of the object of the sport.

Doubts about the desire of the Sophists to educate and their use of rhetoric as the method are dispelled by dialogues such as the *Gorgias* and *Protagoras* of Plato. What might remain open to question is how they related the two. For example, Protagoras' solicitude for correctness in diction and in linguistic construction, or Prodicus' attention to the semantics of language (e. g. *Protag.* 340b ff.) can readily read as an interest in the mere mechanics of language, or even in mental gymnastics (as is implied in *Protag.* 339a). It can also represent an interest in language meaning, the philosophy of language, which is usually the role of semantics. Since the Sophists, however, have been so consistently identified with attention to the structure and the artistic use of language it is more likely that their primary concern is with man's ability to express meaning for himself and for others by way of language structure rather than with the mere ability to verbalize with a certain panache. This likelihood is further increased when we recall the variety of academic subjects which they taught as well as their attention to philosophical problems in epistemology, ontology, ethics. The same understanding of rhetoric appears to be at work here as has already been mentioned in the case of Plato, Isocrates, and Aristotle, namely, that rhetoric as the study of the intelligent and artistic use of language in discourse requires knowledge[14].

---

[13] In view of the existence of written works, e. g. *Gorgias* 462b, c, this language study may have been more detailed and precise than we have been accustomed to accept; see also the *Protagoras* 325e ff., and PFEIFFER, History of Classical Scholarship, pp. 14—32.

[14] Protagoras' concept of the *dissoi logoi*, the two opposing views which exist with respect to any aspect of the real, can easily suggest debate topics which exhaust themselves in shallow eristics. Considered, however, as a methodology for educating, it appears to be simply an effort to discriminate and determine where the truth may lie on any problem. For example in the *Dissoi Logoi* (Die Vorsokratiker[10], 90) at the end of the first antinomy the writer remarks (17) that he is not saying what "good" is but attempting to show that it is not the same as "bad". Of this A. E. TAYLOR (Varia Socratica, Oxford 1911, p. 101) notes: "This is precisely the sort of conclusion we get in many of the Platonic dialogues".

Gorgias[15], for example, illustrates both the character and the results of such study in his attempt to construct a theory of the *logos*. A recent account of his work in the area of rhetoric concludes: "The *logos* is no longer only the directive tool of the whole society, the indispensable instrument of communication of the Periclean statesman, but a means of reaching the individual psyche. The emotional conception of the *logos* in Gorgias, moreover, stands in the greatest contrast to the rationalist reaction of Socrates; and the whole system of Plato rests upon the rational force of the *logos* as the antithesis of emotion . . . Thus although Gorgias may not himself have worked out the systematic consequences, psychological and ethical, of his *techne*, nevertheless his rationalistic approach to an area of human activity that did not admit of easy systematization, namely the emotional reaction to art, suggested and stimulated a line of development which proves highly fruitful in the fifth century and culminates as a full-blown 'scientific' theory in the *Poetics* of Aristotle"[16]. Whether or not we could confine this effort to Gorgias alone can be argued. For the work of Hippias on the relation between language and music (*Hippias Maior* 285d; *H. Minor* 368d) implies the same acute perception of the character of the verbal medium. Further, we can add that if these studies reached fulfilment in the fourth century they did so most substantially in Aristotle's *Rhetoric*, his study of language as discourse.

In view of the long tradition on the question, however, it would be difficult to deny that the study of rhetoric, even with the Sophists, did on occasion degenerate into training in verbal skill, or what has been called a rhetoric of "verbal surface". To acknowledge this, however, is not at all to accept the usual thesis that their work in rhetoric and education was rigidly confined to such activity. PFEIFFER's comment, even in the light of the evidence he himself adduces, is far too stringent: "If scholarship were a mere artifice they (the Sophists) would indeed have been its pioneers; for they invented and taught a number of very useful tricks and believed that such technical devices could do everything . . . Still less should they be termed 'humanists'; Sophists concerned themselves not with the values that imbue man's conduct with 'humanitas', but with the usefulness of their doctrine or technique

---

[15] Both H. DIELS, Gorgias und Empedokles, Sitzungsberichte der Akademie der Wissenschaften zu Berlin, 1884, pp. 343—368, and O. GIGON, Gorgias über das Nichtssein, Hermes 71, 1936, pp. 186—213, while disagreeing with the place of science, eleatic philosophy, and rhetoric in the development of Gorgias accept the fact that he worked in each area.

[16] C. P. SEGAL, Gorgias and the Psychology of the Logos, Harvard Studies in Classical Philology 66, 1962, pp. 133—134. See also, R. KASSEL, Untersuchungen zur griechischen und römischen Konsolationsliteratur, Munich 1958, on Gorgias (pp. 7 ff.) and the question of the correlation between the effect of *logos* on the psyche and medicine on the body, and H. KOLLER, Die Mimesis in der Antike, Bern 1954, pp. 157—162 on Gorgias' use of the Pythagorean theory of music in his rhetorical study. A passage like the *Theaetetus* (167a) indicates that the *logos* is not simply a logical symbol and implies that it is polysemantic in character.

for the individual man, especially in political life"[17]. This appears to be ten-
dentious and to be occasioned by the conviction that the educational effort of
the Sophists was utilitarian and pragmatic. This kind of criticism is also directed without justification against Isocrates, possibly one of the most distinguished pupils of the Sophistic movement. In this regard one can reasonably
question whether the effort of the Sophists was as exclusively utilitarian as it
is constantly made out to be[18]. The presence of a practical aspect to their education should neither be surprising nor a cause for condemnation. We must
recognize the possibility that the practical aspect of Sophistic teaching was
part, as it was with Isocrates, of a larger whole which was humanistic, namely, to make men better. When Isocrates in the *Antidosis* 261—305 (or Protagoras in the *Protagoras* 320d—328d) sets forth his program of study with emphasis on its object to make men who are responsible and of use to the *polis*
he is only stating what is, by and large, the general object of any educational
effort. Indeed, Plato notwithstanding, one might justifiably ask whether or
not the Greeks of the fifth century did not expect this of the arts, particularly
literature. Faced with the strictures thrust upon him by Aristophanes Euripides
instructively responds that he makes men better and teaches them to live better *(Frogs* 1009 f.; 971—977)[19]. The Sophists and Isocrates in this matter can

[17] History of Classical Scholarship, p. 17, in which he takes issue with the judgments of JAEGER,
Paideia and FORBES, 'Greek Pioneers in Philology and Grammar', Classical Review 47 (1933).
The difficulty in a judgment like PFEIFFER's is brought into focus by the kind of statement found
in Segal ("Gorgias"): "It is again not necessary to assume that Gorgias ever wrote a full-blown
treatise systematizing ontology, epistemology, and aesthetics into a unified theory; but the *Helen*,
after all, contains an encomium on the *logos* which seems to present at least the basis of a theory of
poiesis, and other fragments, too, seem to fit into a framework consistent with that theory . . ."
(109), "Thus his rhetoric, though concerned primarily with a technique of verbal elaboration, rests
ultimately upon a psychology of literary experience." (110).

[18] Some scepticism of the ordinary value judgments in these areas seems in place, or the consequences of these judgments must be accepted. For example one is puzzled when one reads this not
untypical judgment of Isocrates' work: "the total effect . . . is one of deadly monotony. His contemporary influence, however, was very great (greater than that of the Academy or Lyceum); his
posthumous influence was no less . . ." (GRUBE, A Greek Critic, p. 11). One is constrained to ask:
were so many Greeks completely impervious to the stultifying? is there any evidence that his oral
style as a teacher (PFEIFFER calls him a pedagogical genius comparable with Melanchthon) differed
vastly from his written style on which the judgment is made? do not Isocrates' comments imply
that if there was a difference it would be in favor of his written style, (e. g. *Panath.* 9, 10 (I was
born lacking an adequate voice and self-assurance), *Phil.* 81, *Epp.* 1. 9; 8. 7). When we also read
that "He was the teacher of most of the great Athenians of his day" we must agree that the Athenians were eminently able to transcend their educational experience or that the content of their education distinctly differed from the corpus of Isocrates' work. While the former is possible there is
no adequate evidence for the latter.

[19] W. H. THOMPSON, The Gorgias of Plato, London 1871, commenting on 502b has this to say:
"The censure which follows is too sweeping even from Plato's point of view, for Euripides at any
rate aimed at a moral purpose of one sort or another . . . As a criticism of Sophocles and Aeschylus
it is, to modern comprehension, still more deplorable".

be more correctly understood from the viewpoint set forth by E. CARR which reflects indeed the tenor of Isocrates' argument in the *Panathenaicus* 30 ff.: "Educators at all levels are nowadays more and more consciously concerned to make their contribution to the shaping of society in a particular mould, and to inculcate in the rising generation the attitudes, loyalties, and opinions appropriate to that type of society; educational policy is an integral part of any rationally planned social policy. The primary function of reason, as applied to man in society, is no longer merely to investigate but to transform; and this heightened consciousness of the power of man to improve the management of his social, economic, and political affairs by the application of rational processes seems to me one of the major aspects of the twentieth century revolution" (What is History?, N. Y. 1962, p. 190). This seems to be an insight as accessible to a Greek of the fifth and fourth century as to men of the twentieth.

On this question of the study of rhetoric Isocrates in many ways is an appropriate summation of the work of the Sophists, and an introduction to that of Aristotle. The program of this student of the Sophists shows rather well what was meant by rhetorical study as a method of education. Quite clearly it was not the commonly understood training in verbal and linguistic skills. Isocrates dismisses such study as false education *(Against the Sophists* 9), adding for good measure that no expositors of prose composition will teach anyone to speak intelligently and with meaning[20]. He continually describes his own manner of educating as ἡ τῶν λόγων παιδεία *(Antidosis* 180) and it is this which he calls his philosophy *(Antidosis* 175 ff.). This stress on philology (love of the word) to specify his philosophy (love of wisdom) points to the fact that Isocrates did not view language as the instrument which simply expressed man's thinking, but that he looked upon thinking itself as a function of language. Thus we find the *logos* placed at the center of man's culture in so far as culture is the expression of the thinking man. This union of *logos* and *nous* is strengthened in the *Panegyricus* 47—50[21]. What at first appears to be a distinction between *logos* and philosophy fuses here into a statement whose main theme is the importance of the *logos* to the cultivated mind. This idea is similar to that expressed in the *Charmides* of Plato (157a) where we read that *kaloi logoi* "engender *sophrosyne* in the soul".

Education for Isocrates is always an education engaged with language, e. g. τὴν περὶ τοὺς λόγους παίδευσιν *(Busiris* 49)[22]. The phrase has been in-

---

[20] From his work Isocrates was clearly concerned with both writing and speaking; he says in *Against the Sophists* 15—16 that his instruction includes writing as well as speaking.

[21] See also *Antid.* 244; NC 5—9. It is the task of educators and philosophers to impart the ability to bring the two together.

[22] *Ep. 5 To Alexander* 4—5 explains this τὴν παιδείαν τὴν περὶ τοὺς λόγους in the ideas of *Panegyricus* (47—50) and NC (5—9).

terpreted as "rhetorical education". If that is understood in the large sense as the study of language for significant discourse it describes both the endeavor of Isocrates and of rhetorical study in general. If it is understood in the more usual and restricted sense of training in public speaking it does not conform to Isocrates' usage. For him the word "rhetorical" is a rare occurence, and, when it appears, he means by it "public speaking"[23]. The word he uses for his work is "logos" in various phrases, and it denotes his concern with rhetoric as the study and use of language in discourse, e. g. *Nicocles, or the Cyprians* 5—10. This interest in the study of language as rational discourse reveals itself in a number of ways. In the first place it appears to be the point of the close connection he maintains between discourse and philosophy in *NC* 1: "there are people who are ill-disposed toward discourse ($\lambda \acute{o} \gamma o \upsilon \varsigma$) and find great fault with those who pursue knowledge ($\varphi \iota \lambda o \sigma o \varphi o \tilde{\upsilon} \nu \tau a \varsigma$)". Secondly, he informs us that he welcomes discourse in all branches of learning *(NC* 10; *Against the Soph.* 16), and, as a background for such work, he tells us that his *paideusis* requires of the student knowledge and understanding in literature and philosophy and is also open to eristics, geometry, astronomy, grammar *(Nicocles* 13; *Antid.* 261)[24]. He admits that the types of discourse are quite varied and recognizes specifically theological, philosophical, and historical discourse as well as critical studies of the poets *(Antid.* 45—46). At the same time he finds that his own particular preferences incline him to discourse upon ethics, political science, international affairs *(Antid.* 46—50; *Panath.* 1—11; *NC* 10; *Against the Soph.* 21). From his criticism of those who train men solely in the techniques of eloquence and in the making of speeches *(Helen* 7 ff.; *Against the Soph.* 9—10) it is clear that his kind of education used language study in a much more substantial manner. The goal of his effort in education, as he tells us in the *Panathenaicus* (30 ff.), is the cultivated, informed and responsible mind, or, as he calls it in the *Antidosis* (272): *phronesis*. This is a far remove from mere technical skill and facility with language (Plato's "verbal sport", *Rep.* 539b; *Euthyd.* 271c—272a) and Isocrates makes this obvious when he sums up his educational effort: "I would clearly be found to be more happy with my students who are held in esteem for their lives and their deeds than for those reputed to be excellent speakers" *(Panathenaicus* 87)[25].

---

[23] $\dot{\rho}\eta\tau o\rho\iota\kappa\acute{o}\varsigma$ used at *Antid.* 256 in a passage repeated again at *NC* 8; $\dot{\rho}\eta\tau o\rho\epsilon\acute{\iota}a$: *Against the Soph.* 21, *Philip* 26, *Panath.* 2, *Nicocles* 5—9.

[24] Clearly he accepts as valid criticism of any discourse the observation of Socrates that the first discourse of Lysias was poorly written since Lysias does not know what he is speaking about *(Phaedrus* 234—235).

[25] "The things that Isocrates tried to foster in his disciples were — ability to make decisions, an intuitive grasp of the complexity of human affairs, and a perception of all the imponderable factors which help to direct one's "opinion" and make it a just one. Literature — the art (not the science)

In general, then, this is the background out of which Aristotle's *Rhetoric* came, and in terms of which it should be evaluated. The work must obviously speak for itself. It is uncritical, however, to assay its statement apart from its provenance, as well as apart from Aristotle's other works. The treatise has run the gamut of appraisals. It has been described as a mishmash of half-baked logic, psychology, and ethics. Aristotle unquestionably speaks on occasion and at sufficient length in a manner to justify at times the judgment that his critique is nothing but a collection of handbook techniques on practical speaking and writing. Yet others, among whom was Voltaire (who certainly possessed a fine sense of the role of language in discourse), have called it an excellent exposition of the art, "a remarkable product", as Rhys Roberts says (Dionysius of Halicarnassus on Literary Composition, London 1910, p. xi), "of its great author's maturity, in reading which constant reference should be made to Aristotle's other works, to the writings of his predecessors, and to those later Greek and Roman critics who illustrate it in so many ways . . . Aristotle . . . looks at rhetoric with the breadth of a lover of wisdom".

The cause of the highly divergent interpretation of the *Rhetoric* is frequently the stance the interpreter takes in the presence of a work which is more complex than it appears to be. When Aristotle studied the art of rhetoric he did not one, but two things. As the first to engage in a formal analysis of the nature of discourse he directed his attention, as Isocrates and Plato did not, to the principles involved as well as to their application. Thus he attempted to found the art on a set of solid and reasonable principles rooted in his philosophical convictions. He also made a serious effort to spell out in some detail the practical applications of these general principles. In reading the treatise the conflict which arises between the philosophy of rhetoric *(theoria)* and applied methodology *(praxis)* has been sufficient to cause careful students of the text to question the unity of the work, the authenticity of the third book, the arrangement of the material in the books, and the consistency of Aristotle's thinking on major themes of his work like the *enthymeme, ethos, pathos*. Each of these problems will be considered in the chapters which follow. To understand them, however, we must recognize that Aristotle is trying to establish a theory of discourse and to give it a ground in philosophy. Relatively little, for example, is said in the pages which follow of the third book of the *Rhetoric*. Yet, if Aristotle's analysis of the organic character of discourse in the first two books is valid, the third book despite its technical character is obviously an integral part of the work. For his study there of the various technical aspects of *lexis* (language) and *taxis* (arrangement)

of speech — is the best instrument for sharpening the faculty of judgment" Marrou, A History of Education, p. 134.

clearly recognizes that language itself and its organization substantially contribute to the organic character of discourse. It is difficult to see that his view
in the third book differs from that of COLERIDGE: "Be it observed, however,
that I include in the *meaning* of a word not only its correspondent object, but
likewise all the associations which it recalls. For language is framed to convey not the object alone, but likewise the character, mood and intentions of
the person who is representing it."[26]

The most obvious area in which Aristotle has introduced a theory of discourse to rhetorical study is with the enthymeme, the syllogism of rhetoric.
He calls the enthymeme the center of the rhetorical art and the following
pages develop entirely about the effort to understand the enthymeme.
Among other things the enthymeme introduces Aristotelian logic to rhetoric, i. e. the ways of inference and the axiomatic principles which for Aristotle are the tools enabling the mind to apprehend the true. It makes rhetoric,
among other things, the study of reasoned statement. Furthermore in bringing the syllogism into rhetoric Aristotle acknowledges that there is an epistemology of the probable, namely, that the mind can know and use the probable as well as the unconditioned in its attempt to understand the world of
reality. At the same time Aristotle also displays a sharp awareness that reason
alone does not necessarily speak to the other, something which discourse in
its effort to communicate must do. Reason does not posses the power of persuasion. Thus Aristotle introduces into the syllogism, the instrument of reason, his psychology of human action. The enthymeme as the main instrument of rhetorical argument incorporates the interplay of reason and emotion in discourse.

When we see the enthymeme as the integrating structure of rhetorical discourse the *Rhetoric* is found to be a unified whole and to be developed in a se-
quential manner which can be readily explained. The enthymeme now ceases
to be the instrument of reason alone, or "rational proof" as it has been so
consistently interpreted by the commentators who strictly separate it from
proof by *ethos*, and proof by *pathos*. On the contrary enthymeme is the syllogism of rhetoric precisely because, as the form of deductive demonstration, it
incorporates in its argument all of the elements demanded by language as the

---

[26] Biographia Literaria c. xxii (vol. 2, p. 115 in 1967 ed. of J. SHAWCROSS, Oxford). C. FRANKE-
NA, "Some Aspects of Language" in Language, Thought and Culture, ed. P. HENLE, Ann Arbor
1958, pp. 121—172, after setting up nine aspects found in linguistic utterance among which are
"emotions and conative attitudes", "emotional tone", "propositional attitudes" goes on to remark (p. 139): "It would seem, then, that we are justified in holding that all kinds of sentence-ut-
terances, with the relatively trivial exceptions just noted (e. g. hurrah, damn etc.) involve the nine
factors we have distinguished". Aristotle's concern with simile, metaphor, rhythm, choice of language, types of style, etc. in the third book would clearly define his awareness that the verbal medium cannot be simply referential or stenographic but contains within itself organizations of
meaning which it communicates to the whole person: mind, emotions, feelings.

vehicle of discourse with another: *reason, ethos, pathos*[27]. The enthymeme
brings together the logical and psychological reasons which convey meaning
to an auditor, and thus Aristotle recognizes that person speaks to person not
only with the mind but with the emotions and feelings as well.

At the heart of Aristotle's theory of rhetoric the enthymeme brings meaning to the assumed conflict in the *Rhetoric* between reason and *ethos-pathos*.
The enthymeme also serves as the integrating factor whereby Aristotle is
able to introduce his *Dialectics* to the art of rhetoric. For the enthymeme explains the methodology of the topics as we find it in the *Rhetoric*. The topics
are the source material for argumentation by enthymeme, e. g., (a) the particular topics provide material for intelligent and significant presentation of the
subject of discourse as well as a presentation relevant to the auditor; (b) the
general topics are axiomatic in character and provide modes of inference, i. e.
forms of deductive reasoning which the enthymeme can assume in its effort
to speak most convincingly to a particular audience. Finally the enthymeme
as the instrument for reasoned discourse makes the third book a perfectly
logical conclusion to the work. An analysis which emphasizes the organic
nature of discourse must obviously study the medium which articulates such
discourse and is also constitutive of it. Like the metaphor in poetry the enthymeme in rhetoric fuses knowing in the person, makes the act of knowing
a total perception of intellect, emotions, feelings.

In his *Rhetoric* Aristotle developed the work of the Sophists and Isocrates
into an analysis of the underlying principles of discourse bringing about the
one thing of concern to Plato: a union of rhetoric and philosophy. He
worked out a theory of discourse which is far removed from the activities of
advertising or the simple techniques of language composition. As his treatise
reveals he perceived that at the center of discourse, as discourse is used when
person speaks to person, is a use of the verbal medium in a manner which
brings together reason and emotion.

---

[27] Although this point is the subject of an extended argument in c. 2 a preliminary note of a
more general character seems in order. Those who accept that Aristotle gave us three distinct
modes of rhetorical proof, i. e. *enthymeme* (rational), *ethos* (ethical), *pathos* (emotional) never ask
why Aristotle gave his attention to a formal discussion of the misuse of rational proof, namely his
discussion of apparent enthymeme in book *B*, but never bothered to discuss formally or informally
the misuse of ethical proof or emotional proof. There is certainly an equal demand for such a discussion, particularly in view of the extended discussion of *pathos* in book *B*. It is difficult to understand on what grounds the omission can be justified.

CHAPTER I

THE UNITY OF THE *RHETORIC*

Any effort to understand Aristotle's *Art of Rhetoric* must begin with its place within his philosophy. For rhetoric functions as a method of communication, spoken or written, between people as they seek to determine truth or fallacy in real situations. To engage in a critical analysis of such communication implicates one's convictions about the nature of reality, the ability of the mind to know it, the nature of language, and in particular the nature of the human persons who use the method. Thus the meaning of "rhetoric" is very largely dependent upon the epistemology, psychology, and metaphysics of the philosophical system in which it occurs[1]. This would seem to be a natural conclusion when rhetoric is subjected to critical analysis as an activity of reasoning man and as an art, and is not considered as a mere collection of technological tricks with which to overwhelm an opponent.

In the cultural context of the Platonic and Isocratean tradition it would have been difficult for Aristotle to dismiss rhetoric as a serious discipline. That he does not do so is obvious from the opening words of his study in which he relates rhetoric to his theory of dialectic and from the substantial study he devotes to the subject. To underline, as it were, the significance of this discipline Aristotle insists from the outset upon showing the relation of his comments to his work on dialectic, epistemology, ethics, and even metaphysics. Thus it is that the relation of rhetoric to its own philosophical system is nowhere more evident than in the *Rhetoric*. Throughout the analysis his constant explicit and implicit reference to his philosophical works clearly reveals that he was working with his own philosophical system in mind, and yet this has been consistently overlooked in much Aristotelian criticism. Here the tendency has been to characterize his analysis as exclusively logical with the result that we have a misreading of his work to say nothing of misunderstanding. Once we subscribe to the common belief that Aristotle committed himself to a purely intellectual theory of rhetoric in which reason and the tools of reason were presumably to play a dominant, indeed an exclusive, role, we meet with the problem that has faced many commentators: open

---

[1] See P. DUHAMEL, "The Function of Rhetoric as Effective Expression" The Journal of the History of Ideas 10, 1949, pp. 344—56; E. MADDEN, "The Enthymeme; Crossroads of Logic, Rhetoric, and Metaphysics" The Philosophical Review 61, 1952, pp. 368—76; R. McKEON, "Rhetoric in the Middle Ages" Speculum 17, 1942, pp. 1—32. J. GEFFCKEN, Griechische Literaturgeschichte, vol. 2, Heidelberg 1934, pp. 230, 233 ff.

contradiction in the opening statement of his study and inconsistency in the subsequent analysis. For Aristotle's ready acceptance and careful study of the psychological aspect of rhetoric, specifically *ethos* and *pathos*, after an apparently absolute rejection of these elements, seems inexplicable[2]. Even his more sympathetic readers, convinced as they are that Aristotle had in mind a theory of rhetoric which was essentially intellectual, would reason away this study of *ethos* and *pathos* in the *Rhetoric* as sheer accommodation on Aristotle's part to the very real exigencies of a fourth-century audience: a sacrifice, in brief, of theory to expediency[3].

Thus we find that the character of most interpretation of the *Rhetoric* is a concentrated effort on the role of the mind and reason in human discourse. In this reading of our text Aristotle is concerned exclusively with rhetoric as a purely intellectual discipline. His effort, in other words, was to free rhetoric from what is called the demagoguery of the Sophists with their crude appeal to the emotional (and irrational) in man and to dignify it as a discipline of the mind which is so much more becoming to the rational man. Aristotle would thus carry to substantial fulfilment part of the promise of the Platonic *Phaedrus*. As a partial interpretation this is correct but it falls short of the full answer and in doing so it creates further problems. Placing Aristotle's analysis of rhetoric in the neat category of the thinking, rational mind with its concern for logic and order, and setting it apart from man's emotive life and the whole range of his emotional drives and dynamic energies creates a problem which rightly offends many of his commentators. It creates a division within the psyche which is absolute in character and which neither Aristotle nor Plato would recognize. More disturbing still, as has been said, it condemns this admittedly rather careful thinker to an inescapable contradiction in the very opening chapters of his treatise.

As soon as we accept the common interpretation that Aristotle was committed to a purely intellectual theory of rhetoric in which the rational mind plays a dominant, indeed exclusive, role, we are confronted with the con-

---

[2] Cf. *A* 1, 54a 1 — 55b 24 and *A* 2, 56a 1 ff. (References are to the edition of ROEMER, Teubner, 1923). See D. ALLAN, The Philosophy of Aristotle, Oxford 1952, p. 200; T. GOMPERZ, Griechische Denker, vol. 3—4, Berlin 1931, pp. 367—68; E. HAVET, Etude sur la Rhétorique d'Aristote, Paris 1846, pp. 27—31; W. SÜSS, Ethos, Berlin 1910, p. 126; F. SOLMSEN, Die Entwicklung der aristotelischen Logik und Rhetorik, Berlin 1929, pp. 208—209; E. M. COPE, An Introduction to Aristotle's Rhetoric, London 1867, p. 4, and his commentary, Cambridge 1877, passim under the text numbers cited above; MARX, Aristoteles' Rhetorik, BSG 52, 1900, p. 301. GEFFCKEN, op. cit., p. 231.

[3] J. VATER, Animadversiones ad Aristotelis Librum Primum Rhetoricum, Saxony 1794, p. 10, and L. SPENGEL, Aristotelis Ars Rhetorica I—II, Leipzig 1867, under 1354b 18. J. RUSSO, La Filosofia della Retorica in Aristotele, Naples 1962, p. 82: "E la critica moderna è caduta talora in strane contraddizioni proprio su questo punto: dopo aver scoperto che la *Rhetorica* aristotelica è un opera filsofica, e non già un manuale o empirica indagine sullo stile . . ."

tradiction which has troubled his commentators: after an apparent rejection
of the psychological and emotional elements of rhetoric Aristotle engages
quite readily in a careful study of these very factors in his extensive analysis
of *ethos* and *pathos* in books *A* and *B*.

Those commentators who are rather concerned about this obvious *volte-
face* attempt to explain it away. Since they remain convinced that Aristotle
definitely intended a theory of rhetoric essentially intellectualistic they argue
that the study of *ethos* and *pathos* in the *Rhetoric* is either the result of a careless
combination of various stages of Aristotle's study of rhetoric, or a ready accommodation on his part to the practical requirements of the concrete human
situation in which the art of rhetoric takes place. In the latter instance Aristotle quickly discovered that his theory was not commensurate with human
nature or with the practice of rhetoric. This, of course, would be an example
of notoriously lax and careless writing and thinking by Aristotle on a substantial point of doctrine in a treatise. No advocates of this thesis advance by
way of confirmation other examples of such carelessness on his part and this
should give one pause. With respect to the combination of earlier and later
theories of rhetoric and a consequent confusion of materials the position is
possible but not at all a necessary or convincing solution. It is not necessary
since Aristotle's analysis can be shown to be consistent as it stands; it is not
convincing since, as we shall see, it demands radical revisions in a text which
can be read as an intelligently consistent and consecutive development of a
theory of rhetoric.

Such interpretation glosses two rather significant facts. In the first place
when Aristotle presumably refuses to situate the art of rhetoric within anything remotely resembling a non-logical environment he is engaged in an
obvious polemic. The polemic character of the chapters has never been denied. In his first chapter (A 1, 54a 11—55a 3) he takes preceding technographers to task for their exclusive concern with extraneous emotional appeals
and for the fact that they are totally unconcerned with the logical demonstration of the subject under discussion. Actually the criticism is directed against
a theory of rhetoric which had become somewhat current and was frequently
identified, as is familiar to any reader of the *Gorgias* and *Protagoras* of
Plato, with the Sophists[4]. Indeed it was a theory which was growing in
strength, and the constant criticism of it has conferred upon the word "rhetoric" in all its forms the pejorative meaning so constantly met in critical literature. Against this position Aristotle urges the need for the logical demonstration of the subject-matter and connects this demonstration with the
syllogism of rhetoric which he calls the enthymeme (A 2, 56b 4—5). In so
doing he conveys the impression that the art of rhetoric for him pertains ex-

---

[4] For example cf. SOLMSEN, op. cit., pp. 199 f., 202, 226.

clusively to the intellect and concerns itself quite simply with merely the logical proof of the subject under discussion[5]. Any polemic tends toward emphatic statement, but particularly does it do so when the subject concerns a strongly felt issue. Consequently when immediately following upon the first chapter Aristotle admits *ethos* and *pathos* as elements co-equal with reason in the art of rhetoric (A 2, 56a 1 ff.) it would seem that we would more reasonably inquire whether or not this position is possible for him.

To accuse him of contradicting himself and thus compromising his presumed intention to present a theory of rhetoric grounded exclusively in the intellect and reason is to give too much weight to a brief passage of arms in the opening chapter and to ignore the rest of his study. The opening remarks are obviously directed against an existing situation. Of far more importance is the fact that they must be viewed within the context of the whole *Rhetoric*.

Rather than assume that the rest of the study is at odds with the programmatic statement of the opening chapters it would appear more correct, on the part of those who would interpret the *Rhetoric*, to ask whether or not the opening chapters (which, in fact, encapsulate all of Aristotle's major theoretic statements on rhetoric) are consonant with his general thinking. Certainly the work cannot be studied in isolation when there is in it a frequent cross-reference in the first three chapters alone to his other writings, and when major ideas are introduced for whose full solution assistance must be sought outside the *Rhetoric* itself. It is not a matter of seeking or not seeking this assistance, of asking or not asking the questions of the *Rhetoric* and the other treatises. The *Rhetoric* forces one to ask the questions and to seek the assistance. Because the questions have not been asked the work finds itself saddled with charges of inconsistency and incoherence, e. g. "a curious jumble of literary criticism and second-rate logic".

No one challenges the fact that Aristotle is attempting a scientific analysis of rhetoric similar to the effort of Plato in the *Phaedrus*[6]. The fairly common references within the *Rhetoric* to the *Organon* and the *Ethics* make manifest that he is doing the analysis within the context of philosophical ideas and principles which he considers himself to have established and to be important to his present analysis (e. g. *A* 1, 55b 8—9, *A* 2, 56b 6—11, *A* 11, 72a 1—2). It is in the light of these principles that he makes his major break with Plato. Both men considered rhetoric to be an art *(techne)* in every sense of the

---

[5] See note 2 above and also K. BARWICK, Die Gliederung der rhetorischen TECHNE und die horazische Epistula ad Pisones, Hermes 57, 1922, pp. 16—18.

[6] GEFFCKEN, op. cit., pp. 229—237 with all of his reservations on the work makes this eminently clear. GOMPERZ, op. cit., p. 367: "Hierzu ward A. wohl in erster Linie durch das platonische im 'Phaidros' verfochtene Ideal jener Kunst vermocht ... die neue Darstellung der Rhetorik so scharf als möglich von ihrer älteren, der bloß empirischen oder routinemäßigen Behandlung zu scheiden."

word, and an art which played an important role in the life of the *polis*. The major difference between the two was the subject-matter of the art, certainly not the constituent elements of the art. After the extended exposition (257b—279c) in the *Phaedrus* it would be difficult to deny that Plato recognized the role of *pathos* and *ethos* (cf. 270b—272b) as well as the intellect in the rhetorical art. The *logos* at every level of communication is the expression of the whole person. However, Plato (even with his acceptance of ὀρθὴ δόξα in the *Meno*) did not recognize the area of contingent reality and probable knowledge as absolutely valid ground for real knowledge. Consequently, while it is impossible to escape the fact that Plato admits the legitimacy of an art of language in the *Phaedrus* the burden of his argument would appear to restrict its legitimate exercise to the object of the speculative intellect: the knowledge of ultimate, unchanging reality. There can be no art of rhetoric without *episteme*. The fact remains, however, that even the speculative intellect, as any perceptive reading of a Platonic dialogue will reveal, works closely with the emotional and psychological structure of those engaged in such discourse of the mind[7]. This rather enigmatic divorce in Plato between theory and practise was even recognized in antiquity: *"cuius tum Athenis cum Charmada diligentius legi Gorgiam ; quo in libro hoc maxime admirabar Platonem, quod mihi [in] oratoribus inridendis ipse esse orator summus videbatur"* (Cicero, *de orat.* 1. 47).

Aristotle admitted the fact of contingent reality and, consequently, probable knowledge[8]. Obviously this is an area of reality which is at a level defin-

---

[7] The deliberately human context within which the rational argument is built in a dialogue represents one conditioning aspect. Another phase of it is the intellectual problem proposed; for example the whole argument of the *Phaedo* on immortality ultimately rests upon that reason which is "the best and the most difficult to refute" (85d). This kind of intellectual problem demands choice, as does also the method of hypothesis in which a series of relevant and plausible hypotheses are considered in order to choose the one which possesses the maximum of truth. In the choice more than intellect is involved. BACON who said that "the duty and science of Rhetoric is, to apply reason to imagination for the better moving of the will" has clearly analyzed the weakness in Plato's theoretical attitude: "it was great injustice in Plato . . . to esteem of rhetoric but as a voluptuary art . . . And therefore as Plato said elegantly 'That Virtue, if she could be seen, would move great love and affection'; so seeing that she cannot be showed to the senses by corporal shape, the next degree is to show her to the imagination in lively representation: for to show her to reason only in subtilty of argument, was a thing ever derided in Chrysippus and many of the Stoics; who thought to thrust virtue upon men by sharp disputations and conclusions, which have no sympathy with the will of man." (Advancement of Learning, Book II).

[8] Aristotle not only admitted this knowledge, it was an inevitable admission. To say that there is only knowledge of the universal surely has as its corollary that there is only *episteme* of the necessary. Granted that the only true *episteme* for Aristotle is knowledge of the cause, the universal, and the necessary, he could then ask himself just as well as we ask ourselves: what knowledge do we have of the world of things as we apprehend them (*An. Post.* 88b 30 — 89b 6). His response was direct: that which we find in reality which is constant, but not necessary, can be the object of a kind of knowledge, and it also leads one to seek out the cause, the universal, and the necessary, or

itely below Plato's world of forms and Aristotle's metaphysics. In this area of reality the human person is faced not with incontrovertible and unchanged absolutes but with factual problems, questions, situations which are subject to change and which while grounded in reality are yet limited by the very nature of this reality. The constitutive elements of this environment admit neither absolute knowledge nor absolute assertion since their very contingency asserts that change is possible and that this very fact of change may very well condition what can be known or said about them. Such factual evidence and such contingent situations admit a probable knowledge about themselves, and they demand deliberation and considered discussion consequent upon which we are able to assent to their probable truth.

Quite clearly this is the area in which the intelligent and prudential course of responsible action (i. e. action most conformable to the existential reality and to truth) will be determined in each instance by the specific evidence which carries the greatest validity. It is primarily and almost exclusively at this level that Aristotle makes his analysis of the rhetorical art. Writing so clearly in terms of his own philosophical commitments Aristotle causes a series of questions to arise in the mind of anyone who would interpret the *Rhetoric*, questions occasioned by the text and its statements. When we find him saying (*A* 1, 55a 24—25): "not even if we should possess the most precise knowledge would it be easy to win conviction with its help" (i. e. the idea of the *De Anima* 433a 1 ff. that intellect alone is not sufficient for action), we ask whether or not in the area of the probable, and in a discipline directed toward winning judgment, he could divorce intellect from the emotions or the appetitive element in man. Indeed even in the quest for truth about absolute and unchanging reality it would be difficult to demonstrate such divorce much less tolerate it. Plato's insight in the *Phaedrus* was to perceive that the complex of intellect, emotions, and psychological attitudes must be put to work in the search for absolute, unchanging truth. There is nothing to indicate that Aristotle would not concur entirely. And strictly speaking there is no evidence in the *Rhetoric* that Aristotle could permit such a separation in the realm of contingent reality.

---

truly legitimate *episteme*. *Doxa*, as this knowledge is called, is, in the last analysis, the only valid way to know things which come to be and cease to be, and which, as a consequence, are contingent by the very fact that they are. Indeed it would be otherwise difficult to understand Aristotle's efforts in ethics, poetics, rhetoric (all called *technai* by him) and politics, as well as the object of his inductive methodology. *Doxa* is the manner of knowing in which sensible reality presents itself authentically to man. Weil's comment on the *Topics* is to the point (La place de la logique dans la pensée aristotelicienne, Rev. de Metaphysique et Morale 56, 1951, p. 299): "La topique n'est pas une logique du vraisemblable, du plausible, de l'opinion; elle constitue une technique pour extraire du discours le vrai discursif, plus précisément pour en éliminer le faux, à partir de ces connaissances préalables sans lesquelles aucune science ne se conçoit pour Aristote".

Thus our immediate concern is this: considering that Aristotle located the primary activity of rhetoric in the area of the contingent and probable is it possible, from what he says in the *Rhetoric* and elsewhere, that he dismissed the whole psychological complex of human action in his study of the art of rhetoric? The answer is that it is not possible. A series of statements in his introduction (*A* 1, 55a 1 — *A* 3, 59a 29) make it more than apparent that for Aristotle the very essence of the rhetorical art is constituted by an intimate fusion of the intellectual and appetitive elements in man. *Pathos* and *ethos* are by no means expedient additions or a feeble retreat from a purely intellectualistic position. On the contrary they form with the intellect (*nous*) the integrated act which is the exercise of the art of rhetoric. *Ethos* and *pathos* are not accidental nor epiphenomenal, they are substantial components of the art.

Let us begin where Aristotle begins and follow somewhat carefully the import of his comments. A study of the introduction reveals that Aristotle in rather rapid shorthand sets down what he considers to be the critical elements of the art. Each of his statements implicates the concurring presence of *intellect*, *ethos* and *pathos* in the use of the art. First of all he posits as the general object of the art of rhetoric the whole area of human activity[9]. Here no absolute certitude is possible since we are working with contingent reality, reality which is subject to change. Such changeable and generally non-predictable subject-matter obviously requires study and deliberation before one is able to make any assertion about it with security. Aristotle indeed makes this more emphatically clear by declaring that the proper activity (*ergon*) of rhetoric is directed to subject-matter which requires deliberation (*A* 2, 57a 1—7; 23 ff.). And lest there be any doubt he follows this with an analysis of the nature of rhetoric and the kinds of rhetoric[10] in which the dominant idea is the role of the audience as judge (*krites*). As judge the hearer must first deliberate and then exercise an act of judgment on the evidence as

___

[9] *A* 2, 57a 1—5: That about which men deliberate; and men deliberate about all things which are problematic, i. e. appear open to other possibilities (φαινομένων ἐνδέχεσθαι ἀμφοτέρως ἔχειν). The phrase: καὶ τέχνας μὴ ἔχομεν means that there is no systematic body of knowledge which would facilitate a resolution of the problem. Yet even in this last instance, as we see at *A* 2, 55b 27—34, rhetoric still has the facility to discern those elements in any subject of deliberation which are particularly apt to secure a response from the auditor.

[10] *A* 3, 58a 36 — 59a 5: This analysis is central to the *Rhetoric* and also to the whole domain of human discourse. For it does not simply specify the object of the study of rhetoric and present us with a threefold genus around which the *techne* revolves but it also embraces the major areas of human discourse with which rhetoric as the art of discourse is concerned. Rhetoric, as he tells us at *A* 2, 55b 25—26, is the "*dynamis* (faculty, power) to perceive and grasp the possibly suasive in any given subject, and this is the function of no other *techne*." As such a *dynamis* it clearly finds its completion and fulfilment in its object as presented here. The "possibly suasive" are those elements within any given subject which are likely to bring about a state of mind open to the speaker's thesis. There should be no need to say that for Aristotle in the *Rhetoric* this means an openness to the truth in so far as it can be discerned in a given situation.

presented[11]. It might be well to note that the concept of the audience as judge is underlined throughout the *Rhetoric* by frequent references to the fact that all rhetoric is directed toward *krisis*, or judgment, as its final goal[12].

Reflection upon these statements and their inescapable implication in terms of Aristotle's philosophy clearly reveals that Aristotle could not have devised a rhetoric whose primary and proper nature would be the mere logical demonstration of one's proposition. The moment Aristotle decided that the art of rhetoric directs its major effort upon the world of contingent reality and the area of the probable, and calls into play deliberation and judgment he places it under the domain of what he calls the practical intellect rather than the speculative intellect[13].

This is an essential point insofar as the difference between the activity of the two intellects is crucial. The difference is specified by the different object of each intellect. The speculative intellect moves toward Being, or ultimate reality, in itself whereas the practical intellect moves toward Being, or reality, insofar as this Being is to issue in human action[14]. Owing to this difference one might say that the role of the appetitive (i. e. *ethos* and *pathos)* is comparatively negligible in, but not absent from, the activity of the speculative intellect compared with its role in the action of the practical intellect. There can be no question that in the effort to grasp and comprehend the nature of ontological reality (or what Aristotle would call the subject-matter of first philosophy, and Plato the world of Forms), the speculative intellect must receive an initial assist from the appetite. Indeed we could go further, although it is neither to the point nor necessary to the argument, and maintain that in any effort to reason to, and understand the nature of, ontological reality the appetitive element works concomitantly with the rational. The practical intellect, however, *demands* the appetitive element in the psyche as an essential component for its activity: "... the intellect taken in itself tends uniquely to grasp Being; and it is only as permeated in one way or another by the movement of the appetite towards its own ends that the intellect concerns itself not with Being to be grasped, but with action to be brought about"[15].

---

[11] A very explicit statement on the ultimate *telos* of rhetoric is found at *B* 18, 91b 8—18.

[12] The whole first chapter is much concerned with this fact. In particular see *A* 1, 55a 14—24; *A* 2, 56a 15 ff., 57a 2—b4; *B* 1, 77b 21; *B* 18, 91b 8 ff.; *B* 25, 02b 31 ff.

[13] From a statement such as *EN* 1139a 3 ff. we are forced to conclude that rhetoric must include that part of the soul which Aristotle calls *to logistikon* as opposed to *to epistemonikon*, that is to say, that it involves *dianoia praktike* rather than *nous theoretikos;* see Ross, Aristotle, op. cit., p. 215, or COPLESTON, A History of Philosophy vol. I, London 1951, p. 328.

[14] See *Metaph.* 993b 21—23. Aristotle states their objects as truth and action. And I would note that he remarks that the practical intellect does not necessarily neglect truth but is concerned with its immediate and relative application to human action.

[15] J. MARITAIN, Creative Intuition in Art and Poetry, New York 1953, p. 47; 44—7 clearly expresses the point Aristotle is making in the introductory chapters.

In the *EN* 1109b 30—1115a 3 Aristotle attempts to determine the nature of voluntary action, that which man does responsibly and deliberately. It is to this kind of action that the practical intellect directs itself. The important factors in his effort are *proairesis* (choice) 1111b 4—1112a 16, and *bouleusis* (deliberation) 1112a 17—1113a 14. The passage on deliberation, which explains at much greater length Aristotle's brief comments in the *Rhetoric* (A 2, 57a 1—7), definitely establishes that deliberation involves the area of the contingent, of practical action (i. e. things man can do), and it further indicates that with respect to the things about which man deliberates reason alone is not adequate. This last is implicit in the denial that there is any deliberation about the unchangeable, or absolutely regular, and becomes more explicit in the statement on the role of *proairesis* in deliberation at 1113a 2—14. When men deliberate and decide (1113a 4, 12—3) as a result of deliberation, then they desire (ὀρεγόμεθα) in accord with the deliberation (12). But the thing they desire after deliberation is the *proaireton* (9—10). Thus deliberation completes itself by the act of *proairesis*, e. g. 9—11: the *proaireton* is one of the things within our power which is desired after deliberation. Deliberation is not complete without *proairesis*. But *proairesis*, or the act of choosing, is only effected in the human person by the activity of both reason (1112a 15—16: μετὰ λόγου καὶ διανοίας) and appetition. In 1111b 4—1112a 17 the place of the appetitive element is expressed negatively when we are told that *proairesis* is *not simply* ἐπιθυμία, θυμός, or βούλησις. In 1113a 9—13 we find that *proairesis* is βουλευτικὴ ὄρεξις, a deliberate desire, and the word *orexis*, of course, introduces into the notion of *proairesis* the appetitive element in the soul. At 1139 a 3—b 13 we are presented with a more detailed account of this activity. In a rather succinct summary at 1139b 4 we are told that *proairesis* is either "desireful reason" or "reasonable desire". This phrase would seem to leave no doubt about Aristotle's mind on the unified and integrated action of the two faculties. As a matter of fact Aristotle leads up to this statement by demonstrating that the appetitive element must enter into *proairesis* since choice has its origin in both desire and reason (1139a 32—33), for reason by itself will not cause action (1139a 35—36).

When Aristotle, then, in his introductory analysis of the nature of rhetoric finds that its primary object is discourse about the contingent, changing reality of human existence wherein man must exercise both deliberation and judgment he automatically locates the art under the activity of the practical intellect. Rhetoric becomes an activity of what he calls the "logistic" soul. In other words rhetoric by its nature is an activity of the *nous logistikos*, or the intellect working together with the appetitive element in the soul as man moves toward a judgment, *krisis*. Thus rhetoric for Aristotle must give careful and detailed consideration to rational demonstration and to *ethos* and *pathos*. In effect we have here the very *psychagogia*, or appeal to the whole person in his intellectual and emotional life, which Plato discussed in his *Phaedrus*.

To overlook this fact is to study the *Rhetoric* in a rather strange vacuum and to neglect in the whole process some fundamental Aristotelian ideas on the dianoetic (i. e. reasoning) activity in its relation to human action.

By way of final confirmation of the author's intent in his introductory analysis of rhetoric let us look at his comments on the reason why men engage in this art. He points out that the ultimate goal of rhetorical activity is the effort to perceive in a given subject, or problem, or situation, those elements in it which may effect persuasion. The act of rhetoric seeks out those factors which lead a reasonable mind to accept the subject or the problem (*A* 2, 55b 8—14). This is the proper activity of rhetoric and there it rests[16]. It does not effect persuasion as some of the technographers said (*A* 1, 55b 10; *Topics* 101b 5—10), nor does it, as far as Aristotle is concerned, make persuasion in the same sense as the artist makes his object. Rather it creates an attitude in another's mind, a sense of the reasonableness of the position proposed, whereby the auditor may make his own decision. The art, or technique, of rhetoric is the ability to perceive and to present evidence which makes decision, and a definite decision, possible; but to stop with the presentation. "Its purpose is not to persuade but to discern the possibly suasive in a subject" (*A* 1, 55b 10—11), at which point the auditor must step forward to accept or reject, to make his particular judgment to act or not to act.

Rhetoric, then, is preparatory for judgment and action. To understand the character of the preparation it does help, somewhat, to look at his analysis of the human person in action as seen in the *Poetics*. For there is an inner coherence between his study of rhetoric and drama: the movement of rhetoric is to dispose the person for action *(praxis)*, the movement of drama ordinarily is the person-in-act[17]. In the *Poetics* human action is the act of the whole person, the intellectual and appetitive part of man engages totally in the specific human act[18]. It should not, then, appear strange that when Aristotle studies

---

[16] It would be well to recall the analogy Aristotle draws between medicine and rhetoric; *A* 1, 55b 12 ff.

[17] See *Poet.* 1449b 35 ff. where drama is defined as an imitation of *praxis* and postulates the causes of *praxis: ethos* and *dianoia*. There is far more that can be made of this relationship between the *Poetics* and the *Rhetoric* than has been done; in this respect GEFFCKEN, op cit., p. 230 correctly calls them complementary to each other.

[18] See, for example, J. VAHLEN, Aristoteles' Lehre von der Rangfolge der Theile der Tragödie, Symbola Philologorum Bonnensium, Lipsiae 1867, p. 172, n. 43, and S. BUTCHER, Aristotle's Theory of Fine Art and Poetry[3], London 1902, p. 347. It is true that Aristotle speaks of *ethos* only in the *Poetics*; *ethos* ultimately, however, is nothing more nor less than an established attitude with respect to one's dominant emotional reactions *(EN* 1098a 3 ff.; 1102a 27 ff.; 1105b 19 ff.; 1139a 17 ff. are a few places which indicate this), or a firm disposition of the appetitive part of the soul with respect to all the elements which make up this part of the soul. Chief among these elements

the art which is directed to pre-disposing the person to action he would consider the art as affecting the whole person: *intellect, ethos, pathos.*

Philosophically no other approach would seem possible for Aristotle. Rhetoric incorporated as integral components *reason, ethos* and *pathos* and addressed itself to the whole man. There could be no division nor separation between reason and purely logical demonstration on one side and the emotions and appetitive dynamism on the other. If rhetoric is to work within the terms of Aristotle's philosophical commitments reason and appetite must cooperate.

Within the framework of this commitment the preceding analysis can stand by itself. If we re-examine the structure of the three books of the *Rhetoric*, however, we discover that there is a highly developed coherence within the work which independently confirms the position taken here. Yet this unity has been consistently challenged even though the most convinced critics do not question Aristotelian authorship of the substantials, as well as most of the accidentals, of the rhetorical theory contained within the work. Insofar as it is correct to say that most of the difficulties on the unity of the treatise ultimately arise in the apparent contradiction which has just been discussed, namely the presumed accommodation by Aristotle of his new theory of rhetoric to an older theory grounded in the play upon the emotions and feelings of the audience, it seems appropriate to consider this problem of unity now.

The logical coherence of the treatise as it has come down to us, and indeed in places actual Aristotelian authorship, has been denied for a number of reasons: the seemingly obvious accommodation just mentioned, textual inconsistencies, repetitions, contradictions, obscurity of statement, as well as the apparent failure of the author to follow out in detail programmatic statements which give the organization of the work. It would be foolish not to admit that difficulties are present within the text. It is hardly folly to inquire whether these difficulties require the radical surgery on the text which has been proposed. Certainly many of the difficulties introduced as supporting evidence for the disorganization of the work from Aristotle's original composition are not convincing. If one adds to this the fact that frequently a difficult text passage gives rise to an interpretation (for example the polemic against *pathos* as indicative of an accommodation of two theories of rhetoric) which interpretation is then the source for finding problems with other text passages, it is possible to understand the confusion which can arise. Furthermore some

---

are the *pathe*. As a matter of fact the very close interrelation between reason and emotion which exists within the soul as it is presented to us by Aristotle can be seen in the study of the *pathe* (*Rhet. B* 1, 78a 20 ff.). These *pathe* are in reality affective dispositions of the mind and as such they are intimately associated with both mental and appetitive activity.

of the problems proposed demand from Aristotle a highly systematized and remarkably detailed organization which is never justified on critical grounds by parallel references to precisely such organization in other works of the *corpus*. It is encouraging to know that Aristotle is held in such high esteem, but it is not particularly helpful to be told rather frequently that a textual statement is "entirely unthinkable", "totally impossible"[19] for Aristotle, or to read[20]: "Scriptorem diligentissimum qualem novimus Aristotelem, hoc modo promisso suo stetisse num cuiquam credibile est? Minime! Ergo haec omnia, quae hic promisit Aristoteles, tractaverat, at deleta sunt et sublata a librario vel redactore minime religioso . . ." Yet the evidence offered, detailed and intricate as it frequently is, does not constrain one to agree[21].

To argue for unity is neither to deny development in Aristotle's thought nor the possibility of contradictory statements in the text. It would be simple-minded to say that there are no real problems in the text, particularly in view of the fact that difficulties have been perceived since the time of VICTORIUS. In more recent times SPENGEL and VAHLEN[22] called attention to a number of them. ROEMER picked these up and enlarged upon them in his introduction to the Teubner edition of the *Rhetoric*. He concluded that our text results from the efforts of one or two *librarii* working with two copies of the treatise, one of which was in an abbreviated form. MARX in his attempt to further the work of ROEMER created a new series of problems, the most substantial of which is that we are asked to accept our present *Rhetoric* as the result of an unknown editor's reorganization of a student's notes ("Schulheft", pp. 295, 313 f.) of Aristotle's original work. Solmsen developed the twofold enthymeme idea mentioned by MARX, and MAIER (Die Syllogistik des Aristoteles, Tübingen 1900), into an earlier and later *Rhetoric* which are united in our present work.

It is pointless to attempt here a detailed reply to the criticisms proposed by these men. If it can be shown that a correct understanding of the enthymeme, which is so clearly central to Aristotle's theory and admitted by all of them to be such, permits the treatise in its traditional form to evolve as an integral and rational whole, then, at the very least, a re-consideration of the in-

[19] F. MARX, Aristoteles' Rhetorik, BSG 52, 1900, pp. 270 ff.

[20] A. ROEMER, Aristotelis Ars Rhetorica, Leipzig 1923, p. liv.

[21] SOLMSEN who has pursued the work of SPENGEL, VAHLEN, ROEMER and MARX, and who has devised his own theory of our *Rhetoric* as a combination of an earlier and later Aristotelian theory, has this to say: "es war wahrscheinlich nicht einmal Aristoteles' Absicht, die *Rhetorik* mit der Konsequenz und ἀκρίβεια zu einer gedanklichen Einheit zu gestalten, wie sie diesem Stoffgebiet gar nicht gemäß war . . ." Die Entwicklung der aristotelischen Logik und Rhetorik, Berlin 1929, p. 225.

[22] L. SPENGEL, Aristotelis Ars Rhetorica I—II, Leipzig 1867, passim; Über die Rhetorik des Aristoteles, ABA 6, 1851, pp. 455—513. J. VAHLEN, Zur Kritik aristotelischer Schriften (Poetik und Rhetorik), SAWW 38, 1861, 59—148.

dividual arguments against unity is demanded. Since the demonstration here and throughout this study eventually involves many, if not all, of the passages discussed by these scholars it is in its own way a reply to the attack on the unity.

In view of the fact that the whole thrust of most scholarship on this problem is such that the mildest criticism leveled against the *Rhetoric* is that it surely represents an amalgam of earlier and later Aristotelian views of rhetoric it may seem rather temerarious to move in the opposite direction toward a judgment such as that of BRANDIS[23]: "Among all the writings of Aristotle preserved for us there has been none more completely, harmoniously and consistently executed than the *Rhetoric*, none in which thought and expression correspond better with each other. It is a perfect whole". On the other hand the alternatives are unsatisfying. The kind of freedom represented by the following rather typical comments does not encourage one to dismiss unity in the work too readily[24].

> Transcripsit autem, quisquis erat, vel idem vel alter librarius in exemplar brevius et decurtatum supplementa sua, ut supra demonstrare conati sumus, parum ratione habita aut textus iam ex breviore exemplari exarati aut loci, quibus additamenta adnectenda erant . . .
>
> (ROEMER)

> Daß Aristoteles jenen Satz so nicht geschrieben haben kann, bedarf keines Beweises.
>
> (MARX)

> Es ist nun wohl dem Leser klargeworden, warum wir nicht die gekennzeichneten Einschübe einem Redaktor zutrauen können, warum wir mit so großer Sicherheit behaupten, sie stammten von Aristoteles selbst: weil sie nur aus seiner Entwicklung heraus verständlich werden.
>
> (GOHLKE)

A slight uneasiness is experienced when we further learn that one such study would suggest a re-organization of the following character: start the treatise with *A* 15, and then follow with *B* 12—17, 1—11, 20—21, *A* 3, 2, 4 etc.[25]. This uneasiness remains even though we apparently have a remarkably facile and subtle editor of Aristotle's original work as is revealed by the clever piece of re-writing done at *B* 26, 03a 34 — *Γ* 1, b 23[26]. This disquiet is intensified by a number of further problems:

[23] C. A. BRANDIS, Über Aristoteles' Rhetorik und die griechischen Ausleger derselben, Philologus 4, 1849, p. 1.

[24] ROEMER, op. cit., p. Lxix; MARX, op. cit., p. 289; P. GOHLKE, Die Entstehung der aristotelischen Ethik, Politik, Rhetorik, Wien 1944, p. 123.

[25] MARX, op. cit., p. 287, and see pp. 301—02.

[26] MARX, op. cit., p. 255. This passage will illustrate the whole endeavor. GOHLKE who accepts it as genuine (op. cit., p. 130 f.) uses it (p. 133) to rearrange part of Book *B*. MARX who finds problems in Book *Γ* demands, as a consequence, a rearrangement of Book *B* at this point. SOLMSEN, (op. cit., p. 32) says of it that it is "extremely unlikely that a later editor manufactured the transition in order to link the first two books to the third".

a) SPENGEL suspects his own suggested order (i. e. *A* 4—15, *B* 18—26, *B* 1—17) because he believes that *B* 26, 03a 35 — b 1 is genuine; and so he admits (p. 494 of "Über die Rhetorik . . .") that we could have: A 4—15, *B* 1—17, 18—26. BARWICK'S comment on this is that it demonstrates how difficult it is to show that the present arrangement of the text does not go back to Aristotle[27].

b) Everyone argues for a reorganization by a *librarius* or an editor, but no one has yet explained why any editor experienced the need for, or freely undertook, such a radical reorganization of three books.

The problem on the unity of the *Rhetoric* may be outlined in general in the following manner:

1. the work is fundamentally unified and from the hand of Aristotle,
2. the work is a conflation made by Aristotle of an earlier and later study in which he did not resolve these conflicting theories of rhetoric,
3. the work is a conflation but possesses a unified structure which is Aristotelian in origin,
4. the work, while Aristotelian in character, has been so changed by others that it is not unified, nor intelligible as it stands.

The argument here is for (1). There is no convincing evidence either external or internal for (4). The argument here can accept (3) without difficulty; but the evidence for an Aristotelian conflation is neither firm nor convincing. This last, together with the evidence which will be discussed in what follows, makes (2) unacceptable. For once we locate the importance of the enthymeme in the *Rhetoric* there is a coherent and convincing unity in the treatise.

Resolving the problem of unity at this point is necessary to an intelligent understanding of the following chapters in this book. Unfortunately it also assumes a knowledge of the material discussed in those chapters, for example, the centrality of the enthymeme to the *Rhetoric* (c. 2) and the meaning of "topics", both particular and general, in the *Rhetoric* (c. 4). For the purpose of analyzing what the text says, however, there does not appear to be a more satisfying solution. The attacks on the unified structure of the *Rhetoric* weaken in a very effective way every attempt to understand the statement of the text itself.

Of the passages offered in evidence for the disunity of the *Rhetoric* the largest and most critical involves the section between cc. 18 and 22 in book *B*.

---

[27] BARWICK, Die Gliederung . . ., op. cit., p. 16. Of course if one begins with a short and long exemplar of the *Rhetoric*, as ROEMER suggests, there is room to operate. Unfortunately no one alludes to the fact that the content of each such exemplar (if it existed) is unknown; the existence of each depends upon the reconstruction of each interpreter. The general problem has been discussed more recently by V. BUCHHEIT, Untersuchungen zur Theorie des Genos Epideiktikon von Gorgias bis Aristoteles, Munich 1960.

This section was first challenged by Spengel who argued that *B* 18—26 should follow immediately after *A* 4—15 because of its study of the enthymeme as syllogism. In actual fact this is really an interpretation determined by the conviction that the *"enthymeme"* is really the third *pistis* from among the three *pisteis* of *A* 2, 56a 1—20, namely, the logical proof of one's thesis. In turn *B* 18—26 should be followed by *B* 1—17 which discussed the other two *pisteis*, *ethos* and *pathos*: e. g. *A* 4—15, *B* 18—26, 1—17. VAHLEN agreed with this, as did MARX. ROEMER took up the matter with some qualifications, and SOLMSEN, while he disagreed, has used this section as a further confirmation of his argument for a double enthymeme theory[28].

Chapters 18—22 are a critical passage but they appear perfectly placed in Aristotle's total exposition. They can be read not only quite reasonably and correctly here without any need for a radical shift, but they also provide an important bridge to cc. 23—26. Aristotle's study is centered on the enthymeme. By book *B* 17 (91b 7) Aristotle has finished the presentation of the particular aspects of the theory. The general aspects of the theory, however, remain to be considered. At *B* 17 we are clearly at the end of one phase of the development and Aristotle is about to proceed to another. A reading of *B* 18 makes it difficult to understand how this can be overlooked, or with what justification MARX can say: "Aber die größte Unklarheit und Verwirrung herrscht in den darauf folgenden Kapiteln 18—22, welche zu der Darlegung der τόποι überführen". Chapters 18—22 are transitional; before going on to discuss the general aspects of his theory of the enthymeme Aristotle makes a summation at cc. 18—22. They are in great part parallel to, and a restatement of, many of the ideas in the programmatic statement in *A*, cc. 1—3.

At the end of c. 17 of book *B* Aristotle has come to the conclusion of his analysis of the way whereby one can obtain relevant and specific material for enthymematic statement in rhetorical discourse. Such material demands a knowledge of the subject of discourse in each kind of rhetoric, and a consideration of *pathos* and *ethos* so that this knowledge can be conveyed to others in a meaningful and persuasive way. It was the burden of *A* 4 — *B* 17 to place this material before the student. As he tells us at the beginning of book *B* (77b 16 ff.) where he will begin the analysis of *pathos* and *ethos* and their place in discourse: "These, then, are the materials from which one must exhort and dissuade, praise and blame, accuse and defend, and these are the general probabilities and premises useful for the proofs in each case. For the enthymeme implicates these elements and comes from them if we take, so to speak, each kind of discourse by itself. But since rhetoric is directed to judgment . . . it is necessary for the speaker not only to look to the discourse that

---

[28] ROEMER, op. cit., pp. xcvii—cii; SOLMSEN, op. cit., pp. 223 ff.; for SPENGEL (Über die Rhetorik . . .) and VAHLEN see note 22 above; MARX, op. cit., pp. 290—300; MARX, pp. 280 ff. also discusses a double enthymeme theory, and see also GOHLKE, op. cit., p. 117 f., 130 ff.

it be probative and convincing, but also to develop a certain character in himself and in the one deciding . . ." This close co-relation of *A* 4—14 with *B* 1—17, in Aristotle's mind, is further revealed by remarks such as those in book *A* 10 at 69a 28—31, and b 14—15 where he says that *ethos* and *pathos* will be separately discussed later on in the treatise. Moreover we can see the importance of *ethos* and *pathos* for judgment and decision as far as Aristotle is concerned at *A* 10, 68b 3—4. In brief, from *A* 4 to *B* 17 the particular aspects of argument by rhetorical syllogism were presented as promised at *A* 3, 59a 27—28: διαιρετέον ἰδίᾳ περὶ ἑκάστου τούτων.

Then at c. 18 of book *B* we are told (91b 28) that περὶ τούτων διώρισται, namely, that he has discussed: (b 24—28) the particular materials for each kind of rhetoric as well as *ethos*[29]. He continues: there remains to be discussed the *koina;* when these have been defined there remains the discussion of enthymeme in general and example in order that "we may fulfil our initial proposal" (92a 4). This study of enthymeme in general (i. e. its general topics c. 23, the apparent enthymeme c. 24, refutation c. 25) is made almost exclusively in terms of the enthymeme as an inferential form.

However, before turning to this presentation of the enthymeme as inference Aristotle makes a resumé of a number of the major concepts of his theory of rhetoric which he first presented in cc. 1—3 of book *A*. Pedagogically the summary is quite wise here for it recalls these ideas which were first broached in *A* and which being important to his theory are naturally necessary for an understanding of the discussion on general argumentation by enthymeme. It may be of help here to show how *B* 18—22 repeat the major thematic statements of *A* 1—3[30].

c.18	91b 8—23	relation of persuasive speech to *krisis*	*c.3*	58a 36—b 7
	b 24—29	*doxai* and *protaseis* for *telos* of each genre	*c.3* *c.3*	59a 6—10 *protaseis* 58b 20—30 *telos*
	b 29—92a1	the *koina* (explained in *B* 19 and in text below)	*c.3*	59a 11—27
	92a 1—4	the program for cc.18—26 (this should be compared with:	*c.3*	59a 27—29)

[29] He does not mention *pathos*. A discussion of this and SPENGEL's reaction can be read in ROEMER, op. cit., pp. xcvii—ci. The omission may be unhappy, but scarcely critical; BARWICK, Die Gliederung . . ., op. cit., pp. 19—20 speaking of this passage believes that πάθη are readily thought of in relation to ἤθη, and cites examples thereof.

[30] I would call attention to the way in which Aristotle follows a schema here: after "example" in c. 20 he takes up *gnome* (maxim) in c. 21 which he has already told us (*B* 20, 93a 25) is part of enthymeme. *Gnome* leads him on to c. 22 and to the enthymeme as a syllogism, i. e. a form of inference. It is in speaking of enthymeme as syllogism that he reviews the particular topics and then moves on in c. 23 to its general topics.

	92a 4—7	introduction to c.19. (preferably it should be the beginning of 19 and not the end of 18)		
c.19	92a 8—b14	possible-impossible	*c.3*	59a 11—27
	b 15—93a8	past-future	,,	,,
	93a 9—18	more-less	,,	,,
	a 19—21	conclusion to above.		
c.20	93a 22—27	the two common proofs of rhetoric. (compare 93a 24—25 with 56b 6—7) (*gnome* mentioned here *as part of* enthymeme.)	*c.2*	56a 35—b 27
			- - -	- - - -
	93a 28—94a 19	*paradeigma* (example)	*c.2*	57b 26—36
c.21	94a 19—95b 20	*gnome* (which is very closely related to enthymeme: 94a 26—29)	nothing	
c.22	95b 20—96a 4	enthymeme as syllogism	*c.2*	56b 3—21 57a 7—12; 22—33
	96a 4—b 19	particular topics (a more detailed statement of 58a 17—28 and a recapitulation of *A* 4—14, not of *B* 1—17, but see below: 96b 28—97a 6)	*c.2*	58a 17—28
	96b 20—22	transition to *stoicheia* of enthymemes, i. e. general topics.	- -	- - - -
	b 22—28	two kinds of enthymeme: demonstrative, refutative		no mention formally of such a distinction save indirectly, *c.1* 55a 30—33
	96b 28—97a 6	summary statement on work done on particular methodology for enthymeme, i. e. both *A* 4—14 and *B* 1—17; followed by a transition to general methodology;	*c.2*	58a 2—35
		concluding with statement on rest of program: apparent enthymeme (c. 24) and refutation (c. 25)	*c.2*	56b 2—4 nothing, but see above under 96b 22—28

In addition to the above there are two critical passages which confirm the fact that in 18—22 we have a general summation of the work thus far

achieved and a bridge between the study of the particular sources of the enthymeme (*A* 4—*B* 17) and the study of the enthymeme in general and its
general sources. A correct understanding of what Aristotle is saying in these
two passages would appear to remove the need for radically changing the
text about. The two passages are at 91b 29 (c. 18) and 96b 29 (c. 22). Both
passages are among the major cruces for those who argue against the unity
of the work.

The first passage involves the meaning of κοινῶν. Marx was so troubled
with it (op. cit. 284—295) that he concluded that the passage is another proof
"daß wir nur ein Schulheft . . . nicht ein Originalwerk des Philosophen in
der *Rhetorik* erhalten haben" (295). The second passage which is concerned
with the exact meaning of εἰδῶν makes it quite obvious, when we see the
meaning of the word, that these chapters are a recapitulation of the work
thus far achieved in the treatise, a recapitulation in the form of a transition
to the final part of the analysis of the enthymeme.

We will begin with the passage at 91b 29: λοιπὸν ἡμῖν διελθεῖν περὶ τῶν
κοινῶν; from Spengel's comment the phrase obviously demands elucidation[31]. Although the word κοινῶν stands by itself Aristotle does indicate at
once its referents: "the possible and impossible, the past and future, the
great and small" (b 30—33). In the usual interpretation of the word, however, such a limited meaning is not attributed to it. It is much more common to
accept it in a very large sense, but one which causes confusion. In this broad
sense the word is understood to include not merely the possible and impossible, past and future, great and small, but also the κοιναὶ πίστεις and the
κοινοὶ τόποι. In the edition of Jebb-Sandys (Cambridge 1909) we read, for
example, this translation of our passage: "it remains for us to discuss the *general* appliances", to which the note is appended: "κοινῶν i. e. both the
κοινοὶ τόποι and the κοιναὶ πίστεις".

---

[31] Spengel, Ars Rhetorica, op. cit., *ad* 1393a 22. In cc. 18—26 κοινόν appears a number of
times; it may be of some help toward an understanding of the word to look at all of the instances
in which it occurs:

a) 91b 29 cf. analysis in text.
   b 32 same as b29, i. e. *megethos* is "common to all speech" like possible, impossible, etc.
   92a 4 same as 91b 29
b) 92a 2 the adverb: "in a general way" as opposed to: "in particular"
   95a 10—11 "common", "general"
   96b 11—12 "common", "general"
   93a 23—24 the *koinai pisteis* i. e. the general proofs, enthymeme and example, as opposed
   apparently to what we can call the *idiai pisteis*: ἦθος, πάθος, πρᾶγμα which he says he has
   discussed: ἐπεί περ εἴρηται περὶ τῶν ἰδίων. This is another confirmation of the shift from
   the particular to the general presentation.
c) 01a 20 *to koinonikon*
   21 means "common" but the expression is a proverbial one here.

In terms of our text, however, when Aristotle uses the word here he apparently means to refer to the possible and impossible, past and future, great and small, and in doing this he is speaking about concepts which are well-known to the reader (e. g. *A* 1, 54 a 26—30, b 13—15; *A* 2, 57a 4—7; *A* 3, 58b 2—20, 59a 11—26; *A* 6, 62a 15—16, 37—b 2; *A* 7, 63b 5—65b 21; *A* 8, 66a 17—18; *A* 12, 72a 9—10, etc.) by the time he has reached *B* 18 of the treatise. Consequently it does not seem correct, and SPENGEL would appear to agree, to extend the meaning to include the κοιναὶ πίστεις of *B* 20, 93a 23[32]. These are, as a matter of fact, clearly identified in the *Rhetoric* as enthymeme and example[33].

Further, the word as Aristotle is using it here cannot mean τόποι or κοινοὶ τόποι as VAHLEN and COPE suggest[34], and as it is often interpreted. Speaking of the great and small at *B* 26, 03a 20—25 Aristotle explicitly denies to this phrase any title to the term τόπος as he understands this term in the *Rhetoric*. And if this is so for the great and small it is also true of the possible and impossible, and the past and future. As he well says: the great and small, the good, the just, etc. are those aspects of a subject *with which* rhetorical argumentation is concerned (*B* 26, 03a 23). But the τόποι are always that *from which* rhetorical argumentation is derived: τοὺς τόπους ἐξ ὧν at *A* 2, 58a 30 is the common phrase[35].

To understand what Aristotle may have in mind when he uses κοινῶν of the possible and impossible, past and future, great and small, we must turn to *A* 3, 59a 11—29 and *B* 18, 91b 24 — *B* 19, 93a 21. These passages present a formal study of the part played in the rhetorical *techne* by the possible and impossible, past and future, great and small; and the second passage is, in fact, a restatement and explanation of the first.

An analysis of both passages reveals the following (I anticipate my conclusion by using the form κοινά):

1. Aristotle does not use the word τόποι of these κοινά. In no place where they are mentioned are they so termed. Nor is COPE (Comm. II, p. 173) correct in attributing such an identification to SPENGEL in his "Über die Rhetorik des Aristoteles".

---

[32] SPENGEL, ibid.; VAHLEN apparently identifies them not merely with the πίστεις but also with the τόποι as well as with δυνατόν, γεγονός, αὔξησις, op. cit., pp. 122, 124—25, 128; SOLMSEN, Die Entwicklung, op. cit., p. 225 calls them κοιναὶ προτάσεις; MARX, op. cit. would find *B* 18, 91b 24—92a 7 more appropriately located at the end of *A* 3. ROEMER in a note to *B* 19, 93a 21 in his apparatus locates the problem as Spengel saw it.   [33] See c. 3.

[34] VAHLEN, see note 32 above; COPE, An Introduction, op. cit., pp. 128 ff. where he cites them as four in number; he cites them more correctly as three in the Commentary, op. cit., I, pp. 55—56, and II, p. 175.

[35] "The great and the small" are not "the more and the less" or variations thereof. "The more and the less" is a *koinos topos*: *B* 23, 97b 12 ff. This distinction is often overlooked with consequent confusion.

2. These κοινά are first introduced in connection with the three ἴδια τέλη of the three kinds of rhetoric (*A* 3, 58a 36—59a 5), and are then specified in both of our passages as *common to* these three ends: e. g. *A* 3, 59a 16—21 and *B* 18, 91b 24—92a 1.

3. We are told that the τέλη are the three specific goals of rhetoric, some one of which an orator must have in mind as he attempts to bring about a judgment on the part of his audience: *A* 3, 58b 2—5 and *B* 18, 91b 8—23. The κοινά are necessary to the orator for achieving this goal: *A* 3, 59a 11—26 and *B* 18, 91b 29—92a 1. (n. b. *A* 3, 58b 2—5 mentions only "past and future" but the whole discussion of the τέλη leads right into the κοινά.)

4. Finally, in the two passages of a more general character in which Aristotle gives a summary presentation of what he means by enthymeme, by example, by the particular topics, and by the general topics, he also discusses the κοινά as part of these structural blocks of his rhetorical theory, e. g. *A* 2, 56a 35—58a 35 (the programmatic statement at the beginning of the work) and *B* 19, 92a 8—*B* 22, 96b 19 (the recapitulation of the major ideas before the concluding section on the enthymeme in general). These two passages present us with general synopses of a series of key concepts of his rhetoric as we possess it in the first two books. The κοινά are included in each section.

From a study of these passages it appears that what has been missed in the discussion of these κοινά is their particular character and the place which they occupy in Aristotle's rhetorical analysis. From the passages cited above (particularly if we read *A* 2, 57 together with *A* 3, 59) it becomes quite clear that in Aristotle's mind men engage in the practice of rhetoric[36] when faced with a problem which calls for thoughtful consideration. Or as he expresses it himself (*A* 2, 57a 1) rhetoric is concerned with matters about which men usually deliberate since a judgment is required. In the real situation it is obvious that such matters range over a wide area of contingencies and circumstances. But the fact remains that the scope within which the art of rhetoric operates is that wherein there is both the possibility and necessity for deliberation. By the same token, however, men initiate the whole activity of rhetorical discussion only when there is question of a possible matter (δυνατόν) past, present, future (γεγονός — ἐσόμενον) that is of significance to them (μέγεθος — μικρότης). And their deliberation is ordinarily directed toward establishing a subject which is thus qualified as expedient or injurious (deliberative rhetoric), just or unjust (judicial), or honorable or dishonorable (epideictic), that is, one or other of the three ἴδια τέλη τοῦ λόγου.

---

[36] To avoid misunderstanding, it might be well to remark here that it is clear from the tenor of Aristotle's words that he is writing with both the speaker and the audience in mind.

These κοινά, then, qualify the ends, which is to say that the three special ends of rhetoric can only be such under one or all of these common aspects[37]. Aristotle in both of our passages says as much when he states quite absolutely that it is necessary (ἀναγκαῖον *A* 3, 59a 14, *B* 18, 91b 30) for every speaker to know whether the matter of his discussion is possible or impossible, whether it has happened, is happening, or will take place, and what is its relative importance. From a reading of the text in both passages it is clear that this necessity does not arise from the fact that this is what speakers usually do. Rather it is discovered that this necessity derives from the actual character of the rhetorical *techne* as Aristotle has analyzed it. In this analysis Aristotle has determined the nature of rhetoric in terms of the speaker and the audience as an art concerned with deliberation and directed toward specific judgment in three general areas of human endeavor. When he has established this, namely that there are three kinds of rhetoric, each with its own particular end and each calling for deliberation and judgment, he goes on to make one final determination with respect to the general nature of rhetoric. This last determination sets forth those elements which are ultimately demanded before the whole rhetorical process can begin. These elements are the κοινά, which, in short, represent the common and basic requisites postulated with respect to any subject in order that it may become an object of the rhetorical *techne*. They represent categories within which a subject must fall before it can be used by the orator. Prior to the attempt to demonstrate any one of the three peculiar ends for any subject the orator must know and be able to show for that subject its possibility (or impossibility), its actuality (present—past) or potential actuality (future), and its general significance (great—small). This is clearly set forth at *A* 3, 59a 11—29; it is restated at *B* 18—19, 91b 24—93a 21 as a part of a general summation of what has been thus far achieved in the *Rhetoric* before Aristotle moves on to his discussion of the κοινοὶ τόποι. And not only is this true, but this meaning and use of the κοινά has been employed throughout the first book in the analysis of the three kinds of rhetoric (cf. *supra* pp. 36-37).

The κοινά are in many ways analogous to the concept of the four *organa* in the *Topics* (I. cc. 13—18) but they are more sharply delineated and explained. The *koina* are as critical to the process of rhetorical discourse as the *organa* are to topical methodology for without each there can presumably be neither rhetorical discourse nor topical investigation. It would be satisfying to determine these *koina* more definitely by having the noun to which they apply[38],

---

[37] Aristotle indicates a close relationship between the ἴδια τέλη and one or the other of the κοινά in at least three different places: *A* 2, 57a 1—7, *A* 3, 58b 2—8, and *B* 26, 03a 20—25. In the 57a 1 ff. passage men deliberate about "the possible" not the "impossible".

[38] Süss, who appears to have caught the character of these κοινά ("Schließlich gibt es auch gemeinsame Instanzen dieser Art, ohne die kein Genus auskommen kann", op. cit., p. 131) calls

but Aristotle apparently felt no need for one since he never suggests one. His failure to do so, however, hardly gives us the right to reduce them to an amorphous concept capable of any extension in its referents.

The passage at *B* 22, 96b 28—97a 1, "multum vexatus a viris doctis", and one which in GOHLKE'S words "schon viel Kopfzerbrechen gemacht hat," contains the phrase (96b 29): τῶν εἰδῶν τῶν χρησίμων καὶ ἀναγκαίων. Most, if not all, of the interpretations of these words are quite attractive and seemingly correct.

It does not appear, however, in the light of the text and context, that εἰδῶν here can be interpreted as "special topics" or "special subjects"[39] as practically all understand it[40]. Up to this point in the *Rhetoric* it is true that the meaning "special topics" is both acceptable to Aristotle and has received some prominence[41]. Furthermore the word here occurs in a chapter (22) which forms a transition from the discussion of these particular topics (εἴδη) to a discussion of the general topics (κοινοὶ τόποι). It may well be that the confusion has arisen from these circumstances.

And yet εἰδῶν here would appear to refer to the three kinds (γένη) of rhetoric: deliberative, judicial, and epideictic, and not to any such thing as "special topics", or "special subjects."

First of all the use of εἶδος for γένος need occasion no difficulty since Aristotle has already used εἶδος a number of times for "type" or "kind" where we might have expected him to use γένος[42]. Indeed the use here of εἴδη rather than of the more usual γένη (for which compare *A* 2, 58a 33 τὰ γένη τῆς

them εἴδη on one occasion (133) but also appears to consider them as τέλη (168). The closest we get is *eidon* describing *auxesis* at *A* 9, 68a 26—27: ὅλως δὲ τῶν κοινῶν εἰδῶν ἅπασι τοῖς λόγοις ἡ μὲν αὔξησις...

[39] "Special subjects" within the context of the passage, and in the light of the use of εἶδος in the *Rhetoric* is a strange interpretation of the word. And to translate the term as "special topics" results in the meaningless jumble of "the topic of the topics". No modern commentator to my knowledge has referred the word to the two kinds of enthymeme just mentioned in the text. Such reference would seem to have more point but still does not appear to be correct. SPENGEL does not discuss εἰδῶν in his commentary here, but at 1396b 33 has a comment from which we might conclude that he understands the term to refer the three γένη: "exposuit εἴδη (de quibus vid. I, 2 finem), h. e. τὸ ἀγαθὸν καὶ κακόν, τὸ καλὸν καὶ αἰσχρόν, τὸ δίκαιον καὶ ἄδικον..."

[40] See COPE, Commentary II, p. 233, and the more recent translations of RHYS ROBERTS, Oxford 1924; JEBB-SANDYS, Cambridge 1909; FREESE, London 1926; LANE COOPER, New York 1932. Since these interpretations echo fairly consistently the older translations, there is no need to cite the latter. It is possible, however, to find some older works which interpret εἰδῶν as the three kinds of rhetoric. Thus T. GOULSTON in his 1619 edition Aristotelis "De Rhetorica" has: "Ac fere quidem de generibus singulis quae oratori commodata sunt", and his note on the text indicates that he means by "generibus" the three γένη.   [41] See c. 4 on the topics.

[42] In the immediate vicinity of our text: *B* 20, 93a 28, 94a 17 (on example); *B* 21, 94b 26, 95b 18 (on maxim); *B* 22, 96b 24 (on enthymeme). See also *B* 2, 78b 14, *B* 4, 81b 33, *Γ* 2, 05a 3, *Γ* 14, 15a 24.

ρητορικῆς, and *A* 3, 58b 7 τρία γένη) should not be too surprising in the light of *A* 3, 58a 36 ἔστιν δὲ τῆς ῥητορικῆς εἴδη τρία. SPENGEL in a note on this passage, although he brackets τῆς ῥητορικῆς εἴδη remarks: "Commutantur haec verba [namely εἴδη and γένη] saepius apud auctorem nostrum." And ROEMER in defense of his reading at *A* 3, 58a 36, which I have just cited, comments: "nihil tamen mutare audeo cum et alibi et 1396b, 29 περὶ ἕκαστον τῶν εἰδῶν i. e. γενῶν nisi fallor, dicatur".

Furthermore, both the general context of the passage and the specific text of *B* 22, 96b 28—33 appear to indicate that εἰδῶν refers to the three types of rhetorical discourse and not to "special topics".

The general context of c. 22: In this chapter we have a transitional chapter in which Aristotle is preparing the ground for his discussion (c. 23) of the rhetorical syllogism in terms of the general topics (κοινοὶ τόποι). Before doing so he restates a number of general principles: 1) he reviews briefly the nature of the syllogism or enthymeme (95b 20 — 96a 4), the mode of demonstration common to each kind of rhetoric; 2) he recalls to our attention that it is the use of the particular topics (εἴδη) proper to one's subject that makes the orator's rhetorical syllogisms pertinent and apposite to the *telos* of the type of rhetoric in which he is engaged[43]. And he exemplifies his meaning at once for *each of the three* genres (96a 4 — b 19); 3) he notes further that the use of these particular topics as a source of enthymemes is one way in which to develop rhetorical syllogisms (96b 20), and he continues with the remark (at 96b 28—34) that at this point in the treatise he has given the topics for the *subject-matter*, *ethos* and *pathos* which fill this role. If we stop and ask what *topoi* (96b 30), what sources from which to form enthymemes (b31—2), we possess at this juncture in the treatise (i. e. from *A* 4, 59b 19 to *B* 17, 91b 7) we discover without much search that we have only the particular topics for *the three kinds* of rhetoric, for *ethos*, and *pathos*[44].

Aristotle then goes on at 96b 34 — 97a 6 to say that there is another method, a general method: ἔτι δὲ ἄλλον τρόπον καθόλου περὶ ἁπάντων for obtaining enthymemes, and that he now proposes to consider it. This general method is something different from the particular method of the particular topics which has been the major subject of the study up to *B* 17 (91 b 7). In Aristotle's words we are told at 97a 1 that there is an ἄλλος τρόπος καθόλου; obviously this "method" is being set in contrast to 96b 20: εἷς μὲν οὖν τρόπος τῆς ἐκλογῆς πρῶτος.

Like the first method which is "topical" (96b 20) the second method is also a "topical" method as was promised at 95b 21: μετὰ ταῦτα τοὺς τόπους,

---

[43] See *B* 22, 96a 4 — b19 which is a summary of his study of the particular topics for each kind of rhetoric, a study that has been the burden of his work from *A* 4 to *B* 17. In chapter 4 there is a detailed consideration of these εἴδη, or what Aristotle calls in the passage here ἴδια (96b 15).

[44] On the ἕξεις see GOHLKE, op. cit., pp. 133 ff.; SPENGEL's commentary *ad* 1396 b33.

and as is eminently clear from c. 23 which immediately follows and begins: ἔστι δὲ εἷς μὲν τόπος. The first topical method is particular and specific to each of the three genres as far as the subject-matter is concerned, and specific to the audience and speaker *(ethos* and *pathos)* depending upon the circumstances. The second topical method is obviously general (97a 1: καθόλου περὶ ἁπάντων) and, as a method, provides ways which enable one to argue by rhetorical syllogism, and ways which also are not restricted *to any one kind* of rhetoric but are equally valid for rhetorical argumentation in *any of the three* genres (cf. the analysis of 96b 28 ff. which follows). From the context, then, it is obvious that Aristotle is speaking throughout the whole passage (i. e. from 96a 4 to b 19) with the three kinds of rhetoric continually in mind.

The text: 96b 28—33: Here we are told that at this point in the treatise we have the topics περὶ ἕκαστον τῶν εἰδῶν (29)[45]. It is difficult to understand what else the phrase could mean other than: each of the three kinds of rhetoric. First of all a reason which partly repeats our phrase is immediately given by Aristotle to explain his statement ἐξειλεγμέναι γὰρ αἱ προτάσεις περὶ ἕκαστον (b 30—31)[46]. And in answer to the query: Each what? Aristotle replies at once: each of the three γένη (b 31—33)[47]. The close logical correlation of the whole statement would seem almost inescapable. And a reading of *B* 18, 91b 24—29 and *B* 1, 77b 16—20 which are parallel to our passage strengthens this meaning.

---

[45] The significance of the qualifying adjectives τῶν χρησίμων καὶ ἀναγκαίων modifying εἰδῶν is difficult to understand in any of the proposed interpretations of this word. Some take καί as copulative, some as corrective, and both meanings appear possible as is indicated in the interpretation offered in this chapter. As for the qualifying adjectives I do not pretend here to make them any less problematic, but merely to show that for Aristotle they would not be any less probable or possible as attributes of εἰδῶν understood as the three kinds of rhetoric. Aristotle remarks at *A* 3, 58b 6 f. that the rhetorical *techne* as he understands it is "of necessity" made up of three kinds of rhetorical discourse: ὥστ' ἐξ ἀνάγκης ἂν εἴη τρία γένη τῶν λόγων τῶν ῥητορικῶν. This would appear to mean that if anyone is to make use of this art he must of necessity owing to the nature of rhetoric engage in one or other of the three kinds of rhetoric. In this sense, then, ἀναγκαίων is quite legitimate as an attribute of εἰδῶν. It would also seem quite legitimate to conclude that, since the art of rhetoric realizes itself fully in these three kinds of discourse, what is said of rhetoric may also be said of them; namely that for intelligent action in society they are helpful and useful: cf. *A* 1,55a 21 ff.: χρήσιμος δέ ἐστιν ἡ ῥητορική . . .

[46] These premises are *derived from* particular topics: *B* 1, 77b 16—20, *Γ* 1, 03b 13—14, *A* 4, 60b 1—3, *A* 6, 62b 29—30. They are not topics in themselves.

[47] Aristotle does not use the word γένη in the text, but it is more than clear from a comparison of *A* 3, 58b 20—28 with the text here, and also from his usual mode of expression in the *Rhetoric*, that he specifically means γένη to be understood here. Thus in our text when he speaks of τόπων περὶ ἀγαθοῦ ἢ κακοῦ he obviously means deliberative rhetoric (cf. *A* 4, 59a 30—31), while καλοῦ ἢ αἰσχροῦ is epideictic (cf. *A* 9, 66a 23—24), and δικαίου ἢ ἀδίκου is judicial (cf. *A* 10, 68b 1—5). The rest of the sentence is additive and is a summation of the particular topics presented in *B* 1—17.

Our passage, then, would be translated: "Now, then, practically all the topics concerning each of the kinds of rhetoric which are useful or (and) necessary are in our possession; for propositions with respect to each kind have been selected so that now we have the topics from which one is to present enthymemes[48] on good or evil, the honorable or dishonorable, the just or unjust . . ."

On this interpretation the transitional sentence to the discussion of the general topics (97a 1) takes on new meaning. For ἁπάντων in this line must mean the three kinds of rhetoric[49], and since it also clearly appears to refer back to εἰδῶν at 96b 29 we would seem to have further confirmation that εἰδῶν must mean the three kinds of rhetoric.

We would then translate the whole passage: "Now then practically all the topics concerning each of the kinds of rhetoric which are useful or (and) necessary are in our possession . . . But further let us now take up another method, a general one, with respect to all three kinds of rhetoric."

And with this general summation of his achievement thus far he starts upon his presentation of the general topics which brings to a logical conclusion the program proposed in the opening chapters. Actually this parallelism in subject-matter between *B* 18—22 and *A* 1—3 inclines one to accept our present disposition of the text. Chapters 18—22 restate in more detail a number of the fundamentally new concepts which Aristotle introduced into the study of rhetoric in the opening chapters. Further, they make this restatement at a place in the study which is rather critical. Aristotle has just finished an extended analysis of the particular elements essential to deliberative, judicial, and epideictic oratory (*A* 4 to *B* 17), and he is about to pass on to an analysis of the general elements common to all oratory. Before doing so he recapitulates what has thus far been achieved in his work, and at the same time he recalls to the reader's attention the key ideas of his analysis of rhetoric (the role of judgment, the kinds of rhetorical discourse, the *koina*, enthymeme, and example). With this done he is prepared to pass from the analysis of the method of rhetorical argumentation in particular to an analysis of it in general.

If we now move back to the beginning of the *Rhetoric* and take an overview of the work we find an intelligently organized presentation of Aristotle's theory of rhetoric. Chapters 1—3 contain the programmatic statement for the work incorporating the new ideas which Aristotle wishes to introduce to the study of rhetoric.

---

[48] And one makes enthymemes from propositions (*A* 3, 59a 6 ff.), and these propositions both in content and form are derived from the topics both particular and general.

[49] SPENGEL seems to want to say this (commentary *ad* 1397a 1): "Locos non uni alterive generi, hos enim singulos iam exposuit, sed omnibus tribus communes enumerare vult . . ." The comment of COPE (Comm. II, p. 236) may mean the same.

Chapter 1: 1354a 1 — 1355b 24: The very first assertion correlates rhetoric with dialectic (54a 1) which at once makes the art of the *logos* a rational and reasonable endeavor, an activity of the intellect. This correlation (which runs through the second chapter also) is underlined a number of times in this first chapter at 55a 8—10, 28, 34—35, b 8—10, 16. The relation between rhetoric and reason is strengthened at once by calling rhetoric a *techne* and so subject to the direction of reason (54a 10—11). The most obvious instance of its *techne* quality, we are told, are the *pisteis*, a word which is itself explained by the word *enthymeme*, 54a 13—15: " the *pisteis* alone come within the province of *techne* . . . but they [the technographers] say nothing about *enthymemes* which are the body of *pistis*". Aristotle makes this statement more specific at 54b 21—22 where he speaks of the *pisteis entechnoi*, the use of which makes one "master of the *enthymeme*", or, (from what he will eventually say) "master of the way of reasoning in rhetorical discourse". For, as we are told at 55a 3—8, a rhetorical methodology which is subject to reason and rules (ἔντεχνος μέθοδος) involves the *pisteis* and the rhetorical *pistis, par excellence,* is the *enthymeme:* the syllogism of rhetoric. With this specification of the *enthymeme* as a form of syllogism Aristotle at once takes the opportunity to repeat again the rational and reasoned aspect of rhetoric by commenting that to know the *enthymeme* one must know the syllogism which, of course, is the proper study of the *Analytics* (55a 8—14; this is picked up a number of times in c. 2, e. g. 57a 28—31, b 24—25). This last statement is followed at once (55a 14—18 and 21—24) by two others which make a close connection between truth and rhetoric; they, in turn, repeat a statement at 54b 10 which implicitly connects rhetoric with truth. All of these introductory statements with reference to dialectic, *techne*, the *Analytics*, truth, emphasize Aristotle's intention to stress from the beginning that rhetoric is an activity of the mind concerned with communicating in a reasoned way to an other the truth in so far as it can be known.

Running as a counter motif to this proposition, and thereby accentuating the thematic announcement of rhetoric as reasoned activity, is the polemic against an emotional rhetoric (54a 15 — 55a 3) which Aristotle finds in the current handbooks. Although I can accept this statement for what it obviously is, namely, an attack on the ill-conceived use of emotion, an attack, however, in no way at odds with his later statements on the place of *pathos* and *ethos* in rhetoric, some corrective remarks seem in place in view of the way in which the polemic is usually read. As we have already seen these statements of Aristotle in c. 1 are taken as his rejection of *pathos* and *ethos* in rhetoric and consequently in direct conflict with c. 2 (it can only be c. 2 since the question does not arise in c. 3).

The very first statement by Aristotle on the subject at 54a 11—13 acknowledges in its very criticism of the misuse of emotion by the technogra-

phers that *pathos* is a part of the rhetorical *techne:* αὐτῆς μόριον (54a 13). It is
the non-organic and restricted view of emotion that Aristotle is criticizing
when he says that these technographers have "constructed a small portion of
the art". Indeed Aristotle is directing his remarks here to something which is
usually never noticed, namely, the *practise in judicial rhetoric:* 54b 26—28, 55a
19—20. Obviously, from what he says, the emotions in this branch of rhetoric can be orchestrated for or against the litigant without any regard at all for
the real situation at issue. He indicates at 54b 22—33 precisely what he is
thinking about. When he speaks of the attention of these technographers to
τὰ ἔξω τοῦ πράγματος (54a 15—16) the only correct interpretation of the
phrase from the explanation which he gives in the text is "irrelevancies".
Certainly one cannot claim that Aristotle is arguing simply for the logical
and rational proof of the case. The statement at 55a 24—26 should raise
doubts about that: ἔτι δὲ πρὸς ἐνίους οὐδ' εἰ τὴν ἀκριβεστάτην ἔχοιμεν
ἐπιστήμην, ῥᾴδιον ἀπ' ἐκείνης πεῖσαι λέγοντας. The point he is making is
that the technographers treat of matters that are in no way directed to stating the case (54b 30—31) but to awakening a response in the audience (54a
16—18). I believe that RADERMACHER puts the target of these comments in
sight for us in an observation he makes on a text of Anaximenes (Artium
Scriptores, Wien 1951, p. 216): "Vereor autem, ne antiquissima Graecorum
oratio apud iudices habita nihil fere continuerit praeter testimonia, ius iuran-
dum, calumnias, preces, donec quinto a Chr. saeculo incepere argumenta ex
ratiocinatione ducere. Semper autem si quis in iudicium prodierat, ei veren-
dum erat ne vitae examen (ἔλεγχον τοῦ βίου) esset subiturus. Inde specialiter
διαβολή vocatur, quidquid ἔξω τοῦ πράγματος profertur." According to Aristotle these technographers do not realize that the focal point of rhetoric as
an art is in the *pisteis* (54a 13); and since he says further (14—15) that the *enthymeme* embodies *pistis* one must conclude from his words that the art of rhetoric ultimately resides in the *enthymeme*. He continues his criticism of the
technographers, however, and does not return to these *pisteis* until 54b 21—22
where they are now called the *pisteis entechnoi* whose control makes one master of the *enthymeme*. These *pisteis entechnoi* are identified for us for the first
time at the beginning of c. 2: 55b 35—56a 4 where we find that they are ἦθος,
πάθος and ἐν αὐτῷ τῷ λόγῳ. Unless one has independently decided upon a
complete discontinuity between c. 1 and c. 2 there is no reason at all why the
passage in c. 2 cannot be used toward an understanding of the phrase in c. 1.
This is particularly true since the expression *pisteis entechnoi* is used for the
first time after *A* 1, 54b 21—22 at *A* 2, 55b 35, and there is no clear reason
from cc. 1 and 2 to think that the phrase is used in a substantially different
way. The whole point of this observation is this: since the *pisteis entechnoi* in
c. 2 (55b 35 — 56a 4) include *ethos* and *pathos* one could argue without any
difficulty being caused by the text that by the use of this expression at 54b

21—22 Aristotle acknowledges the place of *ethos* and *pathos* in the first chapter. Further the way in which he speaks of *pisteis* and *enthymeme* in c. 1 (54a 13—15 and b 21—22) indicates quite clearly that the *enthymeme* is not identified with any one *pistis;* if anything it has something to do with all three. This is quite critical in any exegesis of these opening chapters, and in c. 2 of this study I will discuss the various meanings of *pistis* in the *Rhetoric* as well as the fact that there is no evidence to identify the *enthymeme* with any one of the three *pisteis.*

Chapter 1 concludes (55b 8—24) with a return to its opening statement on the correlation between rhetoric and dialectic. It also emphasizes further that the art of rhetoric applies to every kind of subject (55b 8, which is picked up again in the definition of rhetoric at the very beginning of c. 2, i. e. 55b 25: περὶ ἕκαστον [see also 55b 31—34, and especially 56a 33]), and that its object is not to persuade but to find those elements in each and every subject which make the subject acceptable: (55b 10—11) τὸ ἰδεῖν τὰ ὑπάρχοντα πιθανὰ περὶ ἕκαστον.

Chapter 2: 1355b 25 — 1358a 35: The re-statement at the end of c. 1 (55b 16—24) of the correlation between rhetoric and dialectic leads to the definition of rhetoric as a *dynamis*, an ability "to perceive the possibly suasive in any subject" which opens c. 2: (55b 25—26) περὶ ἕκαστον τοῦ θεωρῆσαι τὸ ἐνδεχόμενον πιθανόν. The ἐνδεχόμενον πιθανόν here picks up τὰ ὑπάρχοντα πιθανά of 55b 10—11. We should note that the "suasive" in each text is neutral as far as the subject-matter is concerned. Its "suasive" character is determined by the person as Aristotle says at 56b 28. Therefore the "suasive" can be something absolute or contingent, certain or merely probable. Rhetoric as the art of language for effective discourse is interested in it in so far as it "speaks to" the auditor be it absolute or contingent, certain or generally probable. These *pithana* are, of necessity, related in some way to the subject of discussion whatever it may be. The *techne* of rhetoric, as opposed to other *technai* (55b 27—34), is the ability of the rhetorical art to discern these *pithana* for any subject. Nothing, at the moment, is said directly about what the ἐνδεχόμενον πιθανὸν περὶ ἕκαστον (55b 25—26) is, for it is obviously the task of a treatise on rhetoric to explain it. But when Aristotle takes up the question of rhetorical proof, *pistis* (55b 35—56a 20), he leads into an explanation indirectly. For the material of such proof *(pistis)*, when it is ἔντεχνον, must be the *pithana* in any and every subject. (This problem is discussed at greater length in c. 4 of this study on the sources of rhetorical argumentation.)

We now learn (55b 35 — 56a 20) that there are two kinds of rhetorical *pistis:* artistic *(entechnic)*, and non-artistic *(atechnic:* this last is explained in c. 15 of *A*). The artistic, i. e. *entechnic* because they are the result of method, are ἦθος, πάθος, and ἐν αὐτῷ τῷ λόγῳ which I call πρᾶγμα. (I give my reasons for

this word in c. 2; indeed, the terminology is not unknown to students of
the *Rhetoric*. BARWICK, for example, speaks without any hesitation of
"*πραγματικαὶ πίστεις*" (see "Die Gliederung . . .", Hermes 57, 1922, pp.
15 ff.). In the course of this explanation Aristotle mentions two things worthy
of note to one interested in the coherence of our present text: (a) he refers
back again to c. 1 and the writers of *technai* and remarks (56a 11—13, 16—17)
that they assign no value to *ethos* and give all of their attention to *pathos;* (b)
he refers forward (56a 18—19) to his treatment of *pathos* in *B* 1—11. Since
the *entechnic pisteis* are such as he has described Aristotle notes (56a 20—35)
that one who is to use them must be able to reason, and to handle *ethos* and
pathos in an intelligent way. This twofold demand of the art makes rhetoric
an "offshoot", as it were, of Dialectic and Ethics. He qualifies this, however:
i. e. despite misunderstanding on the part of some about rhetoric's relation
to Ethics (56a 27—30), rhetoric is, in fact, as was stated at the outset (i. e. c.
1: 54a 1—6), a part of, and like to Dialectic; for rhetoric and dialectic are:
(56a 33) *δυνάμεις τινὲς τοῦ πορίσαι λόγους.*

Aristotle continues this parallel (56a 35 — b 26) as he turns to the method
of rhetorical demonstration. Rhetoric, like dialectic, uses deduction and induction, i. e. *enthymeme* and example *(paradeigma)*. Here (56b 9—10) Aristotle introduces quite explicitly into rhetoric his general system of deductive
and inductive reasoning from the *Analytics*. (This passage on the *enthymeme*
as syllogism will be studied in c. 3 of this work). Aristotle's promise (56b
25—26) to compare the nature of *enthymeme* and example is realized in cc.
20—24 of book *B* as most, if not all, commentators note.

Now that he has introduced the method of rhetorical demonstration Aristotle takes up (56b 28—30) the general subject-matter of rhetoric: that which
is persuasive (the *pithana* of 55b 10—11, 26) in the subject under discussion.
He demonstrates (a) why, in fact, it is the subject of rhetorical discourse:
(57a 1—7) "the function *(ergon)* of rhetoric is to attend to those matters
about which we are wont to deliberate and for which we have no systems of
rules . . . but we only deliberate about matters which appear capable of being
one thing or another"; and, (b) 57a 8—21: the place of a reasoned method of
argument for such subjects through the use of *enthymeme* and example.

As soon as Aristotle speaks of reasoning by *enthymeme* or example he is involved with sources for these two methods (e. g. 57a 8, 9, 12—13: *ἐκ* or *ἐξ*).
Consequently at 57a 22 — b 25 he takes up the sources for enthymemes, e. g.
57a 30: *ἐξ ὧν τὰ ἐνθυμήματα λέγεται.* These sources will usually be contingent in character, but can also be necessary, and they are called by the more
specific name of *eikota* and *semeia* (57a 30—33). (This passage is discussed in
detail in c. 4 of this work.) This particular section on the enthymeme and its
source material closes with a few words on the other method of reasoning,
example *(paradeigma* 57b 26—36), in which Aristotle indicates what kind of

inductive reasoning is implied by *paradeigma*. At 58a 1—2 he draws this section to a conclusion and notes that he has told us now the sources of the *pisteis apodeiktikai*. It should not be necessary to call attention to the fact that these *pisteis apodeiktikai*, even though obviously entechnic in their own right, are not the *pisteis entechnoi* of which Aristotle has been talking (see above pp. 44—46). Indeed, in the light of both the text immediately preceding (57a 22 — b 36) and the earlier statement at 56b 6—8 the *pisteis apodeiktikai* can only be *enthymeme* and *paradeigma*.

Aristotle then singles out the *enthymeme* for special consideration (as should be clear the attention he gives to *paradeigma* in the work is minimal). He introduces his remarks with these words: "an extremely important distinction among *enthymemes*, a distinction particularly ignored almost universally, is one which also applies to the dialectic method of syllogisms" (58a 2—4). Substantially the difference, as explained at 58a 4—35 (the end of c. 2), is that some *enthymemes* in their enunciation are general in form and as such can be used without change for disciplines specifically different (58a 12—17); other *enthymemes* are particular and specific in their enunciation and can only be used with a specific discipline (58a 18—21).

This is the critical passage which, in a treatise centered as it is on the *enthymeme* as the heart of the rhetorical process, states quite clearly that *enthymemes* can be analyzed in particular and in general. The passage also gives the ground for a division which is taken for granted in the treatise. Thus it is possible, as we have already seen, for Aristotle to say in book *B* at 22, 96b 34—5 that he will now take up the general method of *enthymemes*, after telling us at *B* 22, 96b 20 that the first method is the particular method. Both methods are "topical" in character: (58a 11—12) "by rhetorical syllogisms I mean those which have to do with the topics"; both methods have their sources in the *topoi*, either particular or general topics. (This material on the topics is discussed at length in c. 4 of this work.) The important point for us at the moment is that here we are given a clear division of the study of the *enthymeme* as it will be developed in the treatise which is to follow. It is a division which reaches its final achievement in cc. 23—26 of book *B* beginning at 22, 96b 34 and following upon the resumé in cc. 18—22 of the programmatic material of *A* 1—3. Furthermore, this is not a division which should come as a total surprise to one who has read the first two chapters of the work with attention. Aristotle has indicated from the beginning that rhetoric is the art of language which applies to all subjects, *but at the same time* must be able to use the language of somewhat specialized knowledge if it is to use language with any intelligence; to cite a few instances: *A* 1, 54a 1—3, *A* 1, 55b 8—11, *A* 2, 55b 25—34 read against *A* 1, 54a 21 — 55a 3 (where the whole point of the argument is that you must speak to the subject), or again *A* 2, 56a 19—20.

Aristotle concludes c. 2 with a statement (58a 32—35) that his intent is to discuss "first the particular topics; but before doing so let us take up the kinds of rhetoric in order that, after determining the kinds, we may take up separately the substantial characteristics and the propositions for each kind"[50].

Chapter 3: 1358a 36 — 1359a 29: This brings him in c. 3 (58a 36 — 59 a 5) to his threefold division of rhetoric and his observation that we must obviously have propositions for these three divisions (59a 6—7), and that these premises (59a 8—10) will be the *eikota* and *semeia* of 57a 22 — b 25: "for, universally speaking, a syllogism is formed from premises and the *enthymeme* is a syllogism formed from the premises mentioned" (59a 8—10) (compare 59a 7—10 with *A* 2, 57a 32—33). The word *protaseis* in this passage (59a 6—10) is simply an explanation that the *enthymeme*, as a syllogism, must have *protaseis*, i. e. premises, and that the *eikota* and *semeia* if they are to be used in an *enthymeme* must be in the form of a propositional statement. We see this use at *A* 2, 58a 17—25, 31—32; and *A* 2, 58a 30 suggests that the topics, both particular and general, give *protaseis*. There is no contradiction here. The topics are the ultimate sources to which the rhetorician goes for his *eikota* and *semeia*. (This is discussed in c. 4 of this work.)

Aristotle closes c. 3 with a short, but necessary, statement on the *koina* (59a 11—27) which specify rhetorical discourse and without which such discourse would not begin on any subject. His final statement in c. 3 (59a 27—29) is: "Next we must make a separate analysis concerning each of these [the three classes of rhetoric], that is to say, concerning the subject-matter of deliberative, epideictic, and judicial rhetoric". Thus with c. 4 he begins and continues through c. 14 of book *A* an analysis of source material (and thus material for *protaseis)* for the three kinds of rhetoric. Indeed at the end of it he describes the whole process (*B* 1, 77b 16—20) as an "account of the δόξαι (i. e. *eikota* and *semeia* in general) καὶ προτάσεις" for each kind of rhetoric. But he appends at once to this (77b 21—29) that one must not only look to the rational account of the subject-matter (πρὸς τὸν λόγον (b 23) — what I call *pragma)* but also to *ethos* and *pathos*. And certainly a legitimate inference from the text at *B* 1, 77b 16—29 is that if the λόγος gives one δόξαι καὶ προτάσεις so, too, will *ethos* and *pathos*. Thus we are back again at the idea that throughout *A* 4 to *B* 17 we are being told by Aristotle how to seek enthymematic argumentation in a particular way with reference to the subject-matter, the audience, the speaker. Thus *B* cc. 1—17 continues the presentation of particular aspects of enthymematic argumentation which are relevant to *ethos* and *pathos*. *Ethos* and *pathos* are not peculiar to any one kind of rheto-

---

[50] I. e. the discussion of the substantial characteristics of each kind of rhetoric — στοιχεῖα —, (this word is needlessly confused by some critics, e. g. MARX, op. cit., p. 282) and the selection of propositional statements for each kind which runs through *A* 4—14.

ric, as *pragma* is, but common to all three, for *ethos* and *pathos* are determined by the audience and the speaker, not the subject-matter. Thus there is no division according to the three kinds of rhetoric.

At chapter 18 of book *B* Aristotle begins the general summation (cc. 18—22) discussed earlier. It serves as a transition to the material which occupies itself with *the general method of reasoning by enthymeme* (see *B* 22, 97a 1—6). And so we have the general topics for inference by *enthymeme*, c. 23; the apparent *enthymeme*, or fallacious reasoning in rhetoric, c. 24; the method to refute rhetorical argumentation, c. 25. The intent of these chapters is more readily discernible when it is understood that rhetorical discourse is discussed here more in terms of the methodology of inference. This is to say that we are given a method which is applicable to all subject-matter to construct, or criticize, discourse in its inferential form. Considered in this way rhetorical discourse is more obviously methodological. In this respect it is like dialectic which was the analogy stressed at the very opening of the treatise.

The final chapter (26) is a brief statement in which Aristotle attempts to clarify two points about the *enthymeme*:

(a) In the first comment he says that "amplification and depreciation" (αὔξειν καὶ μειοῦν) is not a *stoicheion* of *enthymemes*, i. e. not one of the general *topoi* which he took up in c. 23. Since one of these general topics was the "more and less" (*B* 23, 97b 12 ff.) Aristotle may feel that there is need for a clarification. The μᾶλλον καὶ ἧττον is a general *topos*, an axiomatic principle upon which enthymematic argumentation can be built, or as he says here: εἰς ὃ πολλὰ ἐνθυμήματα ἐμπίπτει (03a 19). Such *topoi* are *stoicheia* as he also says here (03a 17) and earlier at *B* 22, 96b 21—22. But the purpose of αὔξειν καὶ μειοῦν is to underline the importance or insignificance of the subject-matter under discussion (and here I read with Spengel and Roemer in excluding ἐνθυμήματα at 03a20, and I believe quite correctly so in the light of *A*9, 68a 26—27, cf. note 38 *supra*). It fulfils the function of one of the *koina* (cf. pp. 35—39), or as he says at *B* 18, 91b 29—92a 1: "For all men in their discourses must make use of the possible and impossible, and attempt to show, some that a thing will be, others that it has been. Further, the matter of magnitude is common to all discourses, for all men use depreciation and amplification (τῷ μειοῦν καὶ αὔξειν) in deliberation, in praising or blaming, accusing or defending". At *B*19, 93a 15 he calls the procedure τὰς αὐξήσεις.

(b) The second comment notes that refutative *enthymeme* is not a class distinct from constructive *enthymeme*. The only possible reason for insisting on this, as far as I can see, is his fear that his discussion of refutation in c. 25 may have left this unclear (cf. his comment at *Γ*17, 18b 5—6).

With the conclusion of the second book Aristotle has clearly made his magisterial contribution toward a new theory of rhetoric. It is manifest, however, that any study which so intimately involves the *logos* and its artistic (i. e. intelligently ordered) use would be incomplete without a discussion of language and the structuring of language.

It is neither my intention, nor necessary for the purpose of this study, to examine in any detail book *Γ* of the *Rhetoric*. I would like to suggest, however, some general reasons why the book is part of Aristotle's treatise, and some particular points within the book which can be understood best if the work is taken as a part of the whole treatise. Any effort to construct a theory of discourse, no matter how it begins, but most certainly if it begins as Aristotle always began such studies by an analysis of the artistic *synolon*, would be totally impossible without a study of language. From this standpoint there can be no question that such a book should be part of a study of rhetorical theory, nor would the close relation of such a book to books *A* and *B* be surprising. Thus it is that, by and large, neither the presence of this book nor its arrangement is challenged[51]. MARX does deny its unity and argues that it was put together by an editor from two existing works of Aristotle, a περὶ λέξεως (seen now in cc. 1—12) and a μέρη τοῦ λόγου (cc. 13—19), and attached to the first two books.

The study on language which we find in the third book was not only relevant to any theory of rhetoric but was a practise within the whole tradition from the 5th century onward. Furthermore, any person who, like Aristotle, is going to place such emphasis on rhetoric as the art of human discourse, and to locate its core in a mode of inference (the *enthymeme*) which, precisely by reason of the careful use of language, carries meaning to the whole person (intellect, will, emotions) must obviously give his attention to language and its structure. Primarily because of the strictures of MARX I have reexamined the third book and offer the following brief comments as indicative of its coherence with, and close relation of the first two books.

It can be said of the third book that, while it might possibly stand by itself, it makes sense only in terms of what has preceded it. Chapter 17 (and also 18) with its constant reminiscences would be a mystery without the first two books. Chapters 1—7 with their stress on the persuasive (τὸ πιθανόν) make but small sense without a knowledge from book *A* of the place of the *pithana* in Aristotle's theory. Statements on *ethos*, *pathos*, and *reason*, and the interrelation of all three both in *lexis*, and in the structuring of *lexis* (cc. 7, 8, 10, 11, 14—16) bear slight meaning apart from *A* and *B*. A study of the thematic development which underlies much of the prescriptive advice in this book confirms this view.

Following the initial statement that we must not only know what we are to say but also how to say it we discover that *lexis* (i. e. language in itself and in composition, cc. 1—12) is ἔντεχνος (Γ1, 04a 16) just as the theory of argumentation in *A—B* was. Further we learn that language is instrumental and important for developing *ethos* (Γ1, 03b 14—18), and that its purpose is simply effective communication with another person *via intellect, ethos, emotions*: Γ 1, 04a 1—11. This, of course, is a resumption of the idea of the three

---

[51] COPE, An Introduction to Aristotle's Rhetoric, London 1867, pp. 277—400 has an analysis and study of this book.

proofs of *A* and *B* and of the transition at *Γ* 1, 03b 9—10. Throughout cc. 1—12 *lexis* is being analyzed constantly with the expressed purpose of rhetoric in mind: ἰδεῖν τὰ ὑπάρχοντα πιϑανά (*A* 1, 55b 10—11). The dominant factor in this analysis (cc. 2—6) is the audience as it was in his analysis of the nature of rhetoric (*A* cc. 2—3). Next there follows a more explicit statement (c. 7) that *lexis* must integrate *ethos*, *pathos*, and *pragma* (this last, *pragma*, is what I would call the rational analogue, i. e. the statement of the subject as reason apprehends it). Indeed this matter of integration (see c. 7, 08a 10—11) in order to communicate more effectively lies at the heart of the analysis of cc. 1 through 12. In c. 8 the discussion of rhythm is predicated on the need for *lexis* to capture the attention of, and give pleasure to the hearer, to speak to the whole person and not merely to his reason (see c. 8, 08b 27—30, 35—36). Chapters 9—11 stress the rational aspect of *lexis* and emphasize that it must speak to the mind for understanding[52], and that it should be like *enthymeme* in conferring quick insight and understanding (c. 10, 10b 20—21). This section concludes (c. 12) with an account of the *lexis* proper to each kind of rhetoric as these kinds were analyzed in *A* and *B*.

The section on *taxis* (cc. 13—19) is unambiguous and somewhat tedious in its prescriptive character, a section someone might wish to give over to non-Aristotelian authorship[53]. The major thematic concern of these chapters is that the *logos* receive a hearing, since the whole analysis of rhetoric up to this point is meaningless if the *logos* is not received by the audience. Thus in cc. 14—16 Aristotle makes very clear the independent role which *ethos* and *pathos* can have toward this end. It is done almost by way of contrast with logical explanation. Aristotle is fully aware (cc. 14—15) of the part which *ethos* and *pathos* can, and at times must, play by themselves. His comment at c. 14, 15b 5, as well as his stress on logical explanation, however, reveals that he is not happy in saying this. In c. 14 it is possible to see the problem which confronted Aristotle in his effort to make the rational and appetitive side of man the complete object of rhetorical discourse; a problem reflected in the polemic of *A* 1. Here in c. 14 he acknowledges by his statements that *ethos* and *pathos* can come into play independently in rhetorical discourse (surely also one of the reasons behind all of *B* 1—17). But his fear of a return to a purely

---

[52] Yet this section with its emphasis on intellectual apprehension contains a continuous undercurrent of the role of *pathos* (*ethos* only indirectly) in such apprehension. It is quite interesting to find the integration of *ethos, pathos, pragma* which is proposed in this study for the enthymeme demanded by Aristotle for *lexis* throughout cc. 1—12.

[53] On the other hand its initial statements on the importance of *apodeixis* (c. 13) are Aristotelian and are a direct return to *A* cc. 1—2. Even MARX, who is most critical of the whole book and who maintains that something new is being introduced here, must say: "Ein neues rhetorisches System, eine neue Theorie ist zudem in der Lehre von der Beweisführung im zweiten Teil des dritten Buches erkenntlich, deren Grundlagen freilich bereits in den beiden ersten Büchern vorhanden sind, deren Bestand aber erst im dritten Buch als bekannt vorausgesetzt wird." op. cit., p. 247.

4*

emotional, non-logical form of rhetoric as a perversion of the art of language is reflected in phrases like those at c. 14, 15a 21—23, 37. The most satisfying use of *ethos* and *pathos* for him is as an integral part of logical demonstration (see c. 16, 16b 23—29, 17a 3—5; c. 17, 18a 38—39). Yet if rhetoric is to exist there must be a hearer and a hearer disposed toward listening. Thus Aristotle admits that this can be achieved by *ethos* and/or *pathos* (see c. 14, 15a 37—b 4, and passim). Logical demonstration is the burden of cc. 17—18 and the work concludes somewhat abruptly with a discussion of the last element in *taxis* the epilogue, which in the tenor of its statements resumes the ideas of c. 13.

In conclusion, then, it must be said that the early chapters of the *Rhetoric* studied in the context of the work itself and Aristotle's philosophy indicate, as does also the analysis of the three books, a unified structure open to no major contradictions. This is not to claim that all problems are fully resolved. It does suggest, however, that our choice of options is limited when we are faced with the kind of problem in the text which has made commentators challenge Aristotelian authorship in part, or Aristotelian organization of the whole work. It does not seem possible that we can readily accept the solution of an "earlier" and "later" rhetorical theory brought into incomplete harmony in our present work. Aside from the fact that the evidence for the content and character of this earlier treatise is neither strong nor convincing the coherence of the *Rhetoric* makes such a solution questionable. The same can be said for those who postulate, as a resolution for the problems they see, a long and short version of the original work which have been brought together inadequately in order to form our present text. The existence of such exemplars is mainly conjectural, and their content is constructed by conjecture in an effort to resolve the problems their authors find in our present text. Yet, as has been seen, these problems are not intractable and do submit to a reasonable explanation as elements in a coherent development of Aristotle's theory of rhetoric. There are possibly *lacunae* in the text (e. g. book Γ), and there are possibly interpolations and editings which have entered the text in the course of time as can be expected in any classical text. The argument, however, that such incursions have affected the substantive parts of Aristotle's rhetorical theory does not stand firm. When we attend to what Aristotle treats as the central principle of his theory, the *enthymeme*, we find a logically consistent development of the theory. In so far as a central principle usually carries with it the ground of unity for all the parts, and confers meaning and significance upon all the elements which form the whole, this could be expected. A study of the *enthymeme* in an effort to discover its meaning as presented by Aristotle oddly enough reveals that not only can we accept the text as received, but also that text statements which appear to militate against the unity and coherence of the text are susceptible to interpretation which makes them both intelligible and acceptable as essential expressions of Aristotle's rhetorical theory.

CHAPTER II

THE CENTRALITY OF THE ENTHYMEME

As soon as it is understood that rhetoric for Aristotle is an activity which engages the whole person in the effort to communicate meaning by way of language a major obstacle toward understanding the *Rhetoric* is removed. We find him where we could, more or less, expect to find him: in the mainstream of Greek rhetorical theory. In any discussion of theory three names are preeminent among the Greeks: Isocrates, Plato, Aristotle. For all of them rhetoric was not a technique but an art, the art of the *logos*. Rhetoric transcended specific intellectual disciplines and was used by man in each discipline in his effort to articulate the world of reality for himself and others by means of language. Although their views have been set in opposition their ultimate observations on the nature of language as the medium whereby man discourses with man are essentially consonant. Each one considered rhetoric as the art of language even though Plato admittedly had his difficulties with it.

Without minimizing their differing attitudes we can say that all three recognized that rhetoric played a central role in the life of man and the polis. When Plato came to write the *Phaedrus* he acknowledged the importance of rhetoric as the art of language, for there can be but small doubt that it is around this subject that the dialogue unfolds. He does insist that the only true rhetoric has its roots in dialectic, and that the only true rhetorician is the philosopher. At the same time his thoughtful reconsideration of the art in the *Phaedrus* would seem to indicate his realization (see the tentative suggestions at 260d, 262c, 269b, d) that rhetoric could indeed serve dialectic which alone has the power to open man on the world of the truly real and knowable. As ROBIN remarks (Platon Oeuvres Complètes IV 3ᵉ partie Phèdre, Paris 1947, p. xxxviii): "Enfin dans la dernière section, à cette rhétorique de fait Platon oppose ce qu' on pourrait appeler une rhétorique de droit, rhétorique philosophique qui n' est autre chose qu' une mise en oeuvre pratique de sa dialectique". There can be little question of Isocrates' convictions on the importance of the art. Aristotle made his own position strikingly clear with the opening words of his treatise: "rhetoric is the correlative of dialectic", — as the art of dialectic came into play in the exercise of the intellectual disciplines so did the rhetorical art.

It does not seem to be an exaggeration to say that for all of these men rhetoric, as the art of the *logos*, could bring together the results of the activity of the speculative intellect and those of the practical intellect (the *pragmateia eth-ike kai politike*) and make them accessible to all for more responsible every-day living in the polis[1]. Rhetoric was certainly not mere speech-making for any one of them; rather it was the heart of the process by which man tried to interpret and make meaningful for himself and others the world of the real. As Aristotle says so well: "Rhetoric is, as it were, a constitutive part of dia-lectic and is similar to dialectic, as I said at the beginning, insofar as neither rhetoric nor dialectic is a science *(episteme)* concerned with the specific and determinate nature of any subject-matter. They are rather faculties *(dyna-meis)*, so to speak, for providing reasonable explanations" (*A* 2, 56a 30—33).

In other words from what Aristotle says, not formally but certainly expli-citly in this passage, rhetoric is general and touches all areas of human knowledge wherein man attempts to convey understanding to another whether it be philosophy, literature, or the physical sciences. This meaning of rhetoric is readily acknowledged in Isocrates, and it is found in the *Phae-drus* when Plato sets down the norms acceptable for an "art" of rhetoric (cf. 277b—c: "whether one is to *expound* or persuade"). Further, it is a meaning clearly at work in all of Plato's dialogues although, strangely enough, never acknowledged there[2].

A study of the enthymeme in the *Rhetoric* makes it clear that Aristotle's point of departure on the nature of rhetoric begins with the idea that rhetoric is quite simply the art of language. Indeed it does not seem possible to ac-quire an intelligent grasp of his analysis of rhetoric without an understand-ing of what he calls the enthymeme and which he considers also in the *Ana-lytics*. In the first place he locates the enthymeme at the very center of the rhe-torical process when he says quite explicitly that rhetoric, in the final analy-

---

[1] We have the evidence of Socrates' extended concern in the *Apology* with the substantial prob-lem of ἡ ἐπιμέλεια τῆς ψυχῆς clothed in the concrete terms of his own life; or Demosthenes' anal-ysis of the implications of the idea of freedom *(eleutheria)* for the city-state in his *Crown Speech* 53 ff.; or Pericles' discussion of the responsibilities of citizenship *(politeia)* in his funeral oration: "for the Athens I have celebrated is only what the heroism of these and their like have made her" (Thucydides 2. 42). In the *Politicus* 304d f. Plato assigns to the true statesman just such a control of the art of rhetoric; and in the *Phaedo* 89d—90d he speaks of the unfortunate and harmful conse-quences of misology as a result of which men blame discourse rather than their own inabilities and their lack of trained skill with language. The consequence is that such men "continue to spend their lives hating and reviling discourse and deprive themselves of truth and knowledge concern-ing reality".

[2] This question deserves more attention than it has apparently received. It would not be diffi-cult to sustain the thesis that Plato's work demonstrates in detail the philosophical analysis of the *logos* which we have in the *Rhetoric*. There is a limited admission of this, for example, in G. E. Morrow, Plato's Conception of Persuasion, The Philosophical Review 62, 1953, pp. 234—250. Morrow argues that Plato intended to use the 'philosophical rhetoric' which he outlined in the *Phaedrus*, and did in fact make use of it, particularly in the educational theory of the *Republic* and the *Laws*.

sis, directs itself to *pistis* and that the enthymeme incorporates *pistis:* "It is obvious, then, that the *entechnic* method is concerned with the *pisteis*" (*A* 1, 55a 3—4), "enthymeme is the corporeal frame for *pistis*" (*A* 1, 54a 15).

This study is predicated on the fact that once we understand the enthymeme, as Aristotle presents it in the *Rhetoric*, we can come to an informed knowledge of what he means by rhetoric. In actual fact the exegesis of the meaning of ἐνθύμημα in the text not only reveals the specific nature of rhetoric as a *dynamis*, namely something which transcends all particular disciplines, but also the complete relevance and importance of ἦθος and πάθος and the whole complex of *psychagogia* in his theory of rhetoric. With the enthymeme as the foundation block one can discern more readily how rhetoric is the analogue of dialectic and in its own right is a methodology, namely, the artful use of language in the various disciplines, to achieve effective communication, or what Plato has in mind when he writes: καθ' ὅσον πέφυκε μεταχειρισθῆναι τὸ λόγων γένος . . . πρὸς τὸ διδάξαι . . . πρὸς τὸ πεῖσαι (*Phaedr.* 277c).

Few scholars would admit this. A far more typical comment on the *Rhetoric* is that which we find in Ross[3]: "The *Rhetoric* may seem at first sight to be a curious jumble of literary criticism with second rate logic, ethics, politics, and jurisprudence, mixed by the cunning of one who knows well how the weaknesses of the human heart are to be played upon." Most students of the *Rhetoric* would concur with Ross' statement and the attitude finds its way into more general studies. Geffcken, while in general agreement, is still constrained to say more correctly that with the *Rhetoric* we have "eine vollkommen neue Grundlage, einen trotz Aristoteles' Verleugnung der Redekunst als Wissenschaft doch wissenschaftlichen Sinn[4]."

The cause of this general misunderstanding arises in the opening chapters of the *Rhetoric* when Aristotle sets down the theme of his study, and it consists in a misreading of the relationship between πίστις and ἐνθύμημα. The misunderstanding consequent upon this is substantial enough to cause commentators to accuse Aristotle of open contradiction, and even to suspect strongly that the *Rhetoric* is very likely a conflation of two (or more) different treatises.

While it is possible to understand how the mistake arose it is quite difficult to comprehend its long life. There can be no question that for Aristotle the enthymeme was the focal point of his analysis of rhetoric. This inescapable fact is the very thing which has caused dismay among his commentators, and led to the somewhat ambivalent observations already noted. The eminently clear statement of the opening (*A* 1, 54a 1—15) in which we are told that the essence of the whole rhetorical art resides in the *pisteis* and that all *pistis* is in-

---

[3] W. D. Ross, Aristotle, London 1953, p. 275.

[4] J. Geffcken, Griechische Literaturgeschichte, Heidelberg 1934, vol. 2, pp. 232, 234.

corporated in the enthymeme becomes immediately muddied — or so it would seem to many. These remarks of Aristotle in *A* 1 have caused commentators to believe that the ideal is logical demonstration by enthymeme which is the syllogism of rhetoric. Enthymeme is *pistis* in a preeminent way, but, somehow or other, *ethos* and *pathos* (the emotional aspect which appears to have been rejected: *A* 1, 54a 16—55a 3) are equally *pisteis* as we discover at the beginning of c. 2 (56a 1 ff.).

However, if we restore the enthymeme to the critical center of his analysis where it was placed by Aristotle we discover that there is neither open contradiction in the introduction, nor a lack of unity in the work, and that, least of all, is there cynicism or sophism in Aristotle's theory. It is somewhat surprising that the enthymeme has not been studied with more attention for it was obviously important to Aristotle who made it a subject of study in both the *Analytics* and the *Rhetoric*, and apparently found it of value in philosophy and literature. It is more than clear that it was not understood by those who followed. In the maze of philosophical and rhetorical speculation from the latter quarter of the 4th century onward it came to be catalogued in a rather cavalier fashion as an abbreviated syllogism, an interpretation still common. A reflection of the insignificance to which it was relegated may be found in Roman rhetorical study and Cicero's description of it as a rhetorical device: *"illa ex repugnantibus sententiis communis conclusio, quae . . . a rhetoribus ἐνθύμημα nuncupatur"*[5]. The lack of any formal study of the concept in more modern literature is further surprising, and this absence contributes, it seems, to the persistent misunderstanding of the *Rhetoric*[6]. In many ways Aristotle's commentators are in a position similar to that of the scholars of his time: "They say nothing about enthymeme" (*A* 1, 54a 14 f.).

The confusion arises with Aristotle's comments on the *pisteis* and the insistence of his commentators in identifying enthymeme as one of the three *pisteis entechnoi* of *A* 2, 55b 35. By way of introduction it can be said that nowhere in the *Rhetoric*, or indeed elsewhere in his writings, is such an identification made by Aristotle.

The introduction of the *pisteis* at the beginning of his work is quite understandable since Aristotle considers that part of the effort of rhetoric is to elicit in another a correct judgment in instances where the act of judgment is totally free and unconstrained. The *pisteis*, as *A* 1—2, 54a 1—56b 27 demon-

---

[5] Cicero, *Topica*, 14. 56 (ed. BORNECQUE, Paris, "Les belles lettres" 1960); see also Demetrius περὶ ἑρμηνείας, no. 30 (Rhetores Graeci, ed. SPENGEL, Teubner 1856, vol. III).

[6] In the most recent study of Aristotle by G. E. R. LLOYD, Aristotle: The Growth and Structure of His Thought, Cambridge 1968, p. 273, the *Rhetoric* is dismissed with a series of inconsequential observations of which the following is typical: "Just as in the *Sophistici Elenchi*, for example, he considers how to deceive your opponent in argument . . . so too in the *Rhetoric* he discusses the tricks of the trade, the various devices the public speaker may use to win his case."

strates, are the principal sources which can cause this act of judgment to be made. It is the task of the commentator, as has ordinarily been recognized, to come forward with a rather precise and determinate meaning of this term πίστις if at all possible. Traditional exegesis has identified the term with the three artistic proofs, the *pisteis entechnoi*. It then makes the further move of identifying the three *pisteis entechnoi* as *ethos*, *pathos* (thus the contradiction often talked about), and *enthymeme*[7]. These three, then, become the means, or modes of proving or demonstrating.

The identification is partially, but not fully, justified by the text of Aristotle. Nowhere does Aristotle explicitly identify enthymeme with the *pisteis entechnoi*, as he does identify *ethos* and *pathos* with them. This point should be kept in mind. Without difficulty one can show Aristotle's clear reference of *ethos* and *pathos* to these *pisteis* (*A* 2, 56a 1—19). There is no such clear conjunction of *enthymeme* with *pistis* where *pistis* means one of the three *pisteis entechnoi*, and there is no clear evidence that the third of the three *pisteis entechnoi* is the *enthymeme*.

In actual fact the word πίστις in Aristotle's text will not sustain the univocal interpretation (i. e. proof, way of proving) which has been imposed upon it. The assumption of such a univocal meaning has generated some of the difficulties about the coherence and unity of the text. In reality the word *pistis* has a number of meanings in the text, and it is necessary to discriminate among them for an understanding of the text and the meaning of enthymeme.

A few comments by way of preface are necessary. First of all the word *pistis* occurs within the text 41 times (22 times in *A*, 7 in *B*, 12 in *Γ*) and offers sufficient evidence within the text for its exegesis. Secondly, it is essential to recognize that the interpretation of *pistis* presented here is the direct consequent of an effort to determine the meaning of enthymeme which Aristotle makes the key concept of his rhetorical analysis. This problem of the meaning of enthymeme arises in the text and its solution is sought there. In this attempt no pre-conceptions about any theories of language were brought to the text. The only question put to the text was: what is meant by enthymeme? In the absence of any formal studies of the enthymeme the interpreta-

---

[7] These proofs are called the "non-logical" *(ethos* and *pathos)* and the "logical" *(enthymeme)* methods of proving. The inconsistency of Aristotle damning "non-logical" *pistis* in the opening pages A 1, 54a—b, and shortly later incorporating it with "logical" (*A* 2, 56a 1 ff.), is so obvious that one does not have to subscribe to the inerrancy of Aristotle in refusing to believe that he was incapable of recognizing what many commentators over the centuries have perceived. See COPE, An Introduction to Aristotle's Rhetoric, London 1867, pp. 90 ff., 140 ff., and his Commentary, Cambridge 1877; E. HAVET, Étude sur la Rhétorique d'Aristote, Paris 1846, pp. 27—31; J. S. VATER, Animadversiones ad Aristotelis Librum Primum Rhetoricum, Saxony 1794, pp. 10—13 is more circumspect but does not remove the problem, nor does Spengel in his commentary (Lipsiae 1867): see *sub* 1354b 18.

tions offered either raised problems with the text, or reduced the enthymeme to a truncated syllogism. Both were possibilities. However, the more Aristotle's text, together with its many interpretations, was studied, the more it began to emerge that the text became tractable and understandable with the explanation offered here, even though this explanation with its strongly organic theory of language may sound to some more modern than ancient. Aristotle's text conveys the strong impression of a theory of discourse which asserts that discourse in all areas, but particularly in the area of the probable and contingent, is never purely logical and notional. It must attend also to the audience and to the confrontation of speaker and audience *(ethos* and *pathos)*. The notional exposition of the subject is insufficient in the sense that "demonstrations have no power of persuasion". In the text one is continually aware of the fact that persuasive discourse must be alert to the attitudes, convictions, beliefs of the auditor and speaker. This theory of the integral character of persuasive discourse is contained in Aristotle's statements on the *pisteis* where he directs our attention to those qualities which must be considered in the presentation of a subject, namely, the logical and emotive aspects. The causes of persuasion and conviction reside not only in the rational explanation of the subject (the *pisteis pragmatikai)*, but also in the character of the audience and speaker and in their emotional resonance with the subject (the *pisteis ethikai* and *pathetikai)*. While the *rational explanation*, or *ethos*, or *pathos*, may be used independently to win assent or conviction (cf. pp. 51-52 above), Aristotle appears to affirm clearly that their effective and proper use is by being brought together in deductive and inductive argumentation.

When we discriminate among Aristotle's various uses of *pistis* his understanding of the nature of language in discourse reveals itself. Basically there are five meanings of the word in the work. Two of them can be put aside fairly quickly. Both are technical expressions. One occurs at *A* 14, 75a 10 and means "pledge" or "word of honor". The other appears in the third book where he discusses the various "parts" of speech. Aristotle uses *pistis* as the technical term for that part of a speech wherein one formally demonstrates one's thesis or proposition. The clear instances of this all appear in the singular, e. g. *Γ* 13, 14a 35, b 8, 9; *Γ* 17, 18a 18. There are a few instances which are not as clear and can be questioned as will be seen below, p. 60.

This leaves us with the three critical meanings of *pistis* which are first met in the opening chapters of the work. These meanings are: (1) *pistis* as a state of mind, i. e. belief or conviction, which results when a person accepts a proof or demonstration; (2) *pistis* as the logical instrument of the reasoning process in deduction or induction; (3) *pistis* as source material, material which comes from the *logical analysis* of the subject, from the study of the *character* of the speaker or audience, and from the study of the *emotional context* potentially present for this audience in this subject and situation. As the source of conviction *pistis* in each meaning — which is *ethos, pathos,* and not enthymeme but what I call *pragma,* the logical aspect of the subject — carries probative force either in itself, or most effectively when it is organized in a form of deductive or inductive inference.

1) *Pistis* is used to represent the state of mind, namely, conviction or belief, at which the auditor arrives when the correctly chosen aspects of the subject-matter are placed before him in an effective manner. In the opening chapters this meaning usually appears in a verb form, *A* 1, 55a 5; 2, 56a 6,19 (or later on 8, 66a 11). The noun is found in this sense at *A* 9, 67b 29; *B* 1, 77b 25. The use at *B* 20, 94a 10 is to my mind questionable, see p. 60 below.

2) In its second meaning *pistis* is the word used for a methodological technique, illustrated best perhaps by Aristotle's comment at *A* 2, 56b 6—8: "all men make their proofs (τὰς πίστεις ποιοῦνται) in a demonstrative way either with examples or enthymemes; aside from these two there is nothing else". In this sense *pistis* means the logical instrument used by the mind to marshal the material into a reasoning process. It is a method which gives the matter a logical form, so to speak, and thus produces that state of mind in the auditor which is called belief, *pistis.* For, as Aristotle remarks (*A* 1, 55a 5—6), belief or conviction is the result of some kind of a demonstrative process. It is this meaning of *pistis* which is applicable primarily to *enthymeme,* but also to *paradeigma* (example). For in rhetoric *enthymeme* (the process of deduction) and *paradeigma* (the inductive process) are the logical instruments which one is to use in constructing argumentation directed toward *krisis,* or judgment, on the part of another (*A* 2, 56a 34—b 27).

At *A* 1, 55a 4 Aristotle speaks of *pisteis* which very probably are the *entechnic pisteis* (see p 64), and then explains that *pistis* is a kind of proof or demonstration: "For it is clear that the entechnic methodology is concerned with the *pisteis* and that *pistis* is a kind of demonstration". This specification of *pistis* as a kind of proof, demonstration, is compatible with the idea of *pistis* as deduction or induction (the second meaning) and also as the source of conviction (the third meaning, see p. 60). However, it exemplifies the somewhat casual way in which Aristotle uses *pistis.* For he continues (55a 5—6) with an explanation of "kind of proof, demonstration" which says that the ἀπόδειξις ῥητορική is the enthymeme and that the enthymeme is a συλλογισμός τις (8). In effect he is saying that *pistis* as rhetorical *apodeixis* is enthymeme, the syllogism of rhetoric. He uses *pistis* in this same way as a technique for inference at *A* 2, 56b 6—7 where he joins enthymeme (deduction) and *paradeigma* (induction) as the only two ways to demonstrate. At *A* 2, 58a 1 enthymeme and *paradeigma* are quite clearly contained in the phrase *pisteis apodeiktikai,* just as they are called the *koinai pisteis* at *B* 20, 93a 23—24. (I believe that πίστεων at *A* 1, 55a 7 also refers to enthymeme and *paradeigma,*

but it could be a more generic use of the word.) *Pistis* at *B* 20, 94a 10 with
the explicit reference to enthymeme and *paradeigma* as the forms of *apodeixis*
is probably used in this meaning of logical instrument: "for the ways of
proving are by means of these [i. e. enthymeme and paradeigma]". In the
same way *pisteis* at *B* 1, 77b 19 with its close correlation to, and explanation
by *enthymemata* can be taken in this sense.

In the third book there are a number of instances of the use of the plural
form, *pisteis*, which, while they occur in the section on the parts of a speech,
do not appear to be the technical use of *pistis* to denote a part of the speech.
These appear at *Γ* 13, 14b 10—11; *Γ* 17, 17b 21, 18b 6, 8, 23. A comparison
of 14b 10—11 and 18b 6, 8 with the text at *B* 22, 96b 23—28, *B* 25, 02a
31—35 and *B* 26, 03a 16—31 makes it clear from the similarity of language
that Aristotle is talking about refutative or demonstrative enthymemes.
Furthermore the whole context of c. 17 is concerned with the use of *paradeigmata* and *enthymemes* so that it would seem reasonable to conclude that *pisteis*
at 17b 21 and 18b 23 also refer to these two logical instruments. (c. 17 is discussed in the final chapter of this study.)

This leaves six instances of *pistis* in this second meaning of logical instrument which could be argued, i. e. *A* 6, 63b 4; *A* 7, 65b 20; *A* 8, 66a 18; *B* 12,
88b 30; *B* 18, 91b 26; *Γ* 16, 16b 34. In each of the first five instances which
occur at the conclusion of a list of particular topics we are told that it is from
these topics (ἐξ ὧν) that one is to take his πίστεις. But we also know that the
sources of argumentation by enthymeme are the topics (cf. *A* 2, 58a 10 ff.). If
this is so, *pisteis* in these instances can refer to *enthymeme* and by extension to
paradeigma which is the second form of proof, namely, that by induction. It is
possible, however, that πίστεις in these instances and also at *Γ* 16, 16b 34 refer
to the third meaning, the sources which induce a state of belief or conviction.

3) In its third meaning *pistis* signifies source material, that which can induce in the auditor, if properly used, a state of mind which is called belief, or
conviction. In this meaning Aristotle is not saying the same thing as he does
in his use of *pistis* in meaning (2). These sources of belief, however, are called
pistis by the same kind of intrinsic denomination by which he has used this
word to indicate belief itself (meaning (1)), and the inferential method to establish belief (meaning (2)). That which can induce conviction in an other,
the *endechomenon pithanon* (A 2, 55b 26) which is possibly suasive to an other
(*A* 2, 56b 28), he calls *pistis* also, and he uses the word of both the *entechnic
pisteis* (*A* 1, 54b 21; *A* 2, 55b 35) and the *atechnic pisteis* (55b 35). In the art of
rhetoric as subject to reason Aristotle locates the sources of belief or conviction in three general areas: *ethos, pathos, logos*. These he calls the *entechnic pisteis* and *pistis* in this sense of source material is to be found *in* each of these
categories: ἐν τῷ ἤθει κτλ. (*A* 2, 56a 2—3). They are the sources. Insofar as
any *ethos, pathos, logos* results in each instance from a whole set of constituent

elements which make the particular *ethos, pathos, logos,* each of the three cannot be conceived independently of its parts. A particular *ethos,* for example, consists of the elements which constitute it. Further, insofar as these elements (which Aristotle investigates between *A* 4 and *B* 17) are simply the material to be used to construct the particular *ethos, pathos, logos* and thus help to establish credibility and eventually win belief or conviction from an other, when Aristotle calls *ethos, pathos, logos* the *pisteis entechnoi* he is obviously using *pistis* in a meaning different from the other two uses. *Pistis* is now used to specify the sources of conviction or belief in three general categories. As he says at *A* 2, 56a 5: *ethos* makes the speaker ἀξιόπιστον, is the source of his credibility. At *A* 9, 66a 23—28 Aristotle repeats the idea: "We must next speak about virtue and vice and of the honorable and dishonorable insofar as these are the *telos* of one who praises or blames. For at the same time that we speak on these subjects we also happen to reveal those qualities *from which* we will be accepted as of a certain nature with respect to *ethos* which was the second *pistis.* As a matter of fact *from the same sources* we will be able to make ourselves and another worthy of belief in relation to *arete.*"

What may cause confusion in this use of *pistis* is contained in the very nature of anything which is a source of credibility or conviction. In a passive sense it is that which makes a person credible (ἀξιόπιστος), the source of the credibility. But once acquired such a source can, in an active sense, operate as that which causes belief in the other. In any particular subject-matter of discourse these sources are varied and frequently indifferent. The art of rhetoric is, in part, the intelligent selection of these sources in each area *(ethos, pathos, logos)* for a particular subject, and this is precisely what Aristotle attempts to illustrate through *A* 4—*B* 17. If they are chosen with reason and care there is no question that by themselves they can lose their passive character and can, in an active sense, effectively contribute to belief or conviction in the auditor without further organization into deductive or inductive argument. Indeed, Aristotle is not precise in the way he uses *pistis* in this meaning and frequently it seems to carry this active sense (cf. the uses of *pistis* through pages 58—66). However, Aristotle definitely expresses the view that in every subject of discourse there is material which can lead an other to belief, and it is to be sought in the way in which the subject is presented by the speaker, his *ethos* (attention is also given to the *ethos* of the auditor); in the tonal resonance within the subject, its emotional ambience for the auditor, *pathos;* and in the factual evidence of its own truth which the subject offers, its *logos.* These are called the three *entechnic pisteis.*

Before proceeding it is necessary to determine these *entechnic pisteis* because much of the confusion in interpreting the *Rhetoric* arises here. In Aristotle's words the *entechnic,* or artistic *pisteis* are (*A* 2, 56a 1—4): ἐν τῷ ἤθει τοῦ λέγοντος . . . ἐν τῷ τὸν ἀκροατὴν διαθεῖναί πως . . . ἐν αὐτῷ τῷ λόγῳ διὰ τοῦ δεικνύναι ἢ φαίνεσθαι δεικνύναι. The accepted way of interpreting this is to call the *entechnic pisteis* ἦθος, πάθος, ἐνθύμημα. The identification of the last is the problem. There does not seem to be any way in which this phrase can be specified as *"enthymema"*. Any effort to argue that interpretation from the phrase itself would have to work from *logos* and *deiknunai*. If we take *deiknunai* and argue from the parallel use of the word at *A* 2, 56a 35—b 8 we would then have to interpret the expression in our passage not only by *enthymema* but also by *paradeigma*. There is no reason why the word at 56a 4 and 20 should be interpreted to mean exclusively inference by syllogism, and so enthymeme the syllogism of rhetoric. *(deiknunai*, for example, at *A* 13, 74a 9; *B* 5, 83a 10, 7, 85a 31 which are the only three times it occurs between *A* 4 and *B* 17 means mostly "show, show forth, prove", or in Bonitz' explanation "universe demonstrandi, exponendi, explicandi vim habet".) There may be some point in arguing from *logos* at 56a 4 since the Greek text makes it coequal with τῷ ἤθει and τῷ . . . διαθεῖναί πως. Owing to this correlation of *logos* with the other two *pisteis* it appears to be something independent and it does seem that *logos* here (and quite likely at 56a 19) has not quite the same meaning as it has in the immediate text when used with *ethos* 56a 5, 9 (διὰ τοῦ λόγου), and *pathos* a14 (ὑπὸ τοῦ λόγου) where it apparently signifies "speech, spoken word, discourse"[8]. However, in contradistinction to the *ethos* of the speaker which is revealed by his speech, and to affecting the auditor in a certain manner which is done by the use of speech, *logos* at a4 seems to mean something like "the explanation, the factual evidence of the subject", the subject viewed in its logical aspect, its internal, rational coherence and significance. At *B* 22, 96b 3 which in its expression is similar to our statement at 56a 4 *logos* appears to have this meaning. We are told that we cannot set forth a subject by *logos* without the *hyparchonta* of the subject (96b 8) which are highly defined (8) and most particular to the subject (9), indeed, in the example Aristotle offers here the *hyparchonta* must be ἴδια (15), all of which mean specific facts which explain the subject.

Thus it is that the phrase ἐν αὐτῷ τῷ λόγῳ should be called something like τὸ πρᾶγμα, and signify the subject of discourse in its purely logical character which speaks to the intellect of the auditor, just as *ethos* and *pathos* are aspects connected with the subject which transmit significance to his emotions, feelings, and will[9]. There is no textual evidence for calling this third *pistis* (ἐν

---

[8] At *A* 8, 66a 9—10 I would take *logos* in δι' ἀποδεικτικοῦ λόγου as rational explanation (i. e. *logos* at 56a 4, 19) since *apodeiktikos* can be a synonym of *didaskalikos*, cf. *Met.* 1073a 2, *SE* 165a 39.

[9] One has but to consider the explanation of *ethos* and *pathos* in *A* 2, 56a 5 ff., and the statement made about ἐν αὐτῷ τῷ λόγῳ in 56a 19—20. In this first book from *A* 4, 59a 30 onward when Aristotle discusses the material topics for the premises of enthymemes in the three genera of rhetoric we find that he is deriving them from the subject-matter under discussion, i. e. what is here called "pragma".

αὐτῷ τῷ λόγῳ) ἐνθύμημα as commentators do. I call it πρᾶγμα because Aristotle explains it in such a way (*A* 2, 56a 19—20) as to justify some such term, and because I discovered that in the *Rhetores Graeci*[10] Minucianus calls the three *pisteis* (πίστεων τρία εἴδη *A* 2, 56a 1): ἠθικαί, παθητικαί, λογικαὶ αἱ αὐταὶ καὶ πραγματικαί, and that Dionysius of Halicarnassus,[11] who appears to have discerned something of the character of the Aristotelian enthymeme, speaks of the three *pisteis* as πρᾶγμα, πάθος, ἠθος. The third *pistis*, then, derives from those aspects of the subject which are the logical, rational, elements in the subject which can be apprehended by reason.

The three *pisteis entechnoi, ethos, pathos, pragma,* can be used independently as a way of winning belief or conviction as far as the evidence of the text is concerned. This is done simply by presenting a series of ethical, emotional, or purely logical reasons for the acceptance of one's proposition. And in passages such as those at *A* 6, 63b 4; *A* 7, 65b 20; *A* 8, 66a 18; *B* 12, 88b 30; *B* 18, 91b 26 the word *pisteis* can be so interpreted. Such a presentation would still not constitute a formal way of proving or demonstrating as far as Aristotle is concerned in the *Rhetoric*. At the very most one would have an enumeration of ethical, emotional, or logical appeals to the audience. And while this independent use of the three *entechnic pisteis* can be accepted the argument for it within the context of the first two books is not strong.

For what we possess in *A* 4—*B* 17 where Aristotle considers these three *pisteis* is an account of particular topics in the area of *pragma* (*A* 4—14), *pathos* (*B* 2—11), *ethos* (*B* 12—17). These topics are meant to provide the means primarily for deductive argumentation by *enthymeme*, but also for inductive argumentation by *paradeigma* which are the only ways in which to demonstrate anything as we have seen. If Aristotle calls these particular sources for argumentation the *pisteis entechnoi* he tells us at the same time that as particular topics they are sources for the enthymeme which is one of the two *koinai pisteis*. As a final confirmation that these *pisteis entechnoi*, considered as particular topics, are viewed by Aristotle as sources for argumentation we have his statement at *Γ* 1, 03b 6—9: "There are three things in discourse which demand

---

[10] *Rhetores Graeci*, vol. IX, p. 601 (ed. Walz, Stuttgart 1832); see also vol. V, p. 506.

[11] *Lysias*, nos. 16 ff. (edd. Usener-Radermacher, Teubner 1965). In view of the general misunderstanding of the Aristotelian enthymeme among the subsequent technographers, possibly caused by the withdrawal of Aristotle's works, it is very instructive to see this understanding in Dionysius who was writing at a time shortly after Aristotle's works were quite probably accessible once again for study. Demetrius *(Peri Hermeneias)* frequently uses *pragma* as "subject-matter" (cf. 22. 11. 75). Volkmann, Die Rhetorik der Griechen und Römer, Leipzig 1885, p. 177 says that this use of πίστεις πραγματικαί goes back to Aristotle *A* 2, 56a 1—4; see also Süss, Ethos, Berlin 1910, pp. 126, 147 who speaks of this third pistis as πρᾶγμα, and has this comment (p. 147): ". . . was die Isokratcer πρᾶγμα nennen, Aristoteles aber die πίστις ἐν αὐτῷ τῷ λόγῳ . . ." Spengel in his commentary *(sub* 1356a 21) apparently identifies this third *pistis* with enthymeme, but his remarks on 1354b 18 would appear more to the point when he speaks of this *pistis* as "ex re ipsa".

systematic treatment, first the sources of proofs . . . we have spoken of the *pisteis* and from how many sources they come, namely, that they come from three sources, what kind they are, and why they are only three".

The first three instances of the use of *pistis* in the *Rhetoric* are at *A* 1, 54a 13—15, b 21; 55a 4. Aristotle here speaks of these *pisteis* as the substantial element in rhetoric as an art. At *A* 1, 54 b 21 they are called the *entechnic pisteis*. In each of the three instances these *pisteis* are connected in the text with enthymeme in such a way that one understands that control of these *entechnic pisteis* makes one master of the enthymeme, e. g. *A* 1, 54b 22: ὅθεν ἄν τις γένοιτο ἐνθυμηματικός "whereby one becomes master of the enthymeme". Further, enthymeme incorporates *pistis* (*A* 1, 54a 15). In each instance the word ἔντεχνος is used. In Aristotle the word is only used here and at *A* 2, 55b 35—37 and *SE* 172a 34—36. In each citation the word appears in a context which implies a *technique for reasoned statement*, a method for logical presentation. Thus we are told at *A* 1, 55a 4 that the *entechnic methodos* is one that involves these *pisteis* (περὶ τὰς πίστεις; and the *pisteis* here are apparently those of *A* 1, 54b 21: the *entechnic*). This passage together with A 1, 54a 13—15, b 21 and the entire development of *A* 4—*B* 17 suggests that these *pisteis entechnoi* are distinct from but related to enthymeme, that they are used by enthymeme.

Other instances of *pistis* in the sense of the source material suitable to effect conviction or belief are: *A* 2, 56a 1 (and *pisteis* is understood at 2—3), 13, 21; *A* 15, 75a 22, 77b 12; *Γ* 1, 03b 7, 9. I find questionable the use at *A* 6, 63b 4; *A* 7, 65b 20; *A* 8, 66a 18; *B* 12, 88b 30; *B* 18, 91b 26; *Γ* 16, 16b 34 (cf. above p. 60).

There is an obvious necessity to recognize difference in Aristotle's use of *pistis* throughout the *Rhetoric*. Vater, for example, realized this when he distinguished the *entechnic pisteis* between those used in a *sensus latior* as *pisteis* ("quae arte comparantur rationes faciendae fidei", e. g. *A* 2, 55b 35 ff.) and a *sensus angustior* ("quae solius oratoriae sunt propriae", e. g. *A* 1, 54b 21)[12]. But Vater did not see, nor for that matter did anyone else, that there is still difficulty unless we clearly differentiate between *pistis* as source material (ἦθος, πάθος, πρᾶγμα) and *pistis* as a methodological technique, or a means for organizing demonstrative argument. The ostensible result of such a discrimination is that we are faced with a distinct break with the traditional exegesis of the text. While this does cause one to proceed with caution, still the discovery of a more meaningful and intelligent coherence in Aristotle's exposition strengthens one's confidence.

[12] Vater, Animadversiones, op. cit., p. 13. The multiplicity of meaning present in πίστις, inescapable as it is, has never been discussed by students of the work and it was challenged by G. Wikramanayake, AJP 82, 1961, pp. 193—6; his objections were competently answered by J. Lienhard, AJP 87, 1966, pp. 446—454.

In the accepted interpretation Aristotle is attacking earlier technographers for their neglect of logical proof (*A* 1, 54a 13, 15; b 21), namely, the use of the enthymeme. Consequently when Aristotle identifies the three kinds of *pisteis* at *A* 2, 55b 35 ff. his remarks on the logical character of the third *pistis* (*A* 2, 56a 3—4) are immediately taken to refer to the enthymeme. Thus we find that the *pisteis* are interpreted as three independent modes of rhetorical demonstration: non-logical (or quasi-logical) demonstration by the use of *ethos* and *pathos*, and logical demonstration by means of the *enthymeme*, the syllogism of rhetoric. The consequence, however, of this exegesis is a series of insoluble difficulties in Aristotle's opening chapters — a place where one would not ordinarily expect an author to falter. The exegesis labors under the following problems:

1. It assumes a univocal and very limited meaning for *pistis* which is certainly not possible as we have already seen.

2. It ignores the fact that *paradeigma* is the correlative of enthymeme as a method for demonstration[13]. The fact of such an obvious correlation made by Aristotle forces one to ask the meaning of the statement found at *A* 2, 56a 1 ff.: πίστεων τρία εἴδη. Obviously if we argue that the third *pistis* is enthymeme then we must acknowledge that there are not three *pisteis* but four: ἦθος, πάθος, ἐνθύμημα, παράδειγμα. It is difficult to believe that Aristotle did not see this.

3. It is equally difficult, and no one fails to see this difficulty, to understand how Aristotle could slip into such open contradiction in his introductory chapters, and that, too, without the slightest perturbation on his part. Obviously, if rhetoric concentrates its effort on logical demonstration, or demonstration by the enthymeme which is *pistis par excellence*, Aristotle's extensive treatment in the *Rhetoric* of *ethos* and *pathos* is meaningless. Not only have we no grounds whatsoever for accepting his critique as in any way different from that of his predecessors, but there is no reason why it can't be as readily dismissed as Aristotle's own dismissal of his predecessors' work on the psychology of the person as an improper extension of the rhetorical endeavor: ἔξω τοῦ πράγματος (*A* 1, 54a 15 ff.).

4. There is another rather substantial difficulty which arises as Aristotle develops the theory of the enthymeme and discusses the sources from which statement by way of the rhetorical syllogism can be derived. He calls these sources the εἰκότα, σημεῖα, and τεκμήρια. He will also speak of special topics as sources for enthymeme. And yet all of these sources for the premises of an enthymeme are in turn derived from *ethos*, *pathos* and what I have called *pragma*. Obviously in this kind of analysis on the part of Aristotle the enthymeme, as a logical instrument, is set apart from its sources: *ethos*,

---

[13] This is stated a number of times in the *Rhetoric;* see especially *B* 20, 93a 23; also *A* 2, 56b 6 ff.; *A* 9, 68a 29 ff.; *B* 18, 92a 1 ff.; *B* 20, 94a 9 ff.; *Γ* 17, 18a 1 ff.; it also appears in *An. Post.* 71a 9—11.

pathos, pragma. If no distinction is made between *pistis* as source material, and *pistis* as a means of reasoning, Aristotle is forced into a rather strongly illogical and confused statement when he enlarges his initial comments on enthymeme.

If we follow with more care the text which Aristotle has given us we do arrive at a far more intelligent statement on the nature of rhetoric which is not only more consonant with the rest of the work but makes it perfectly easy to understand why Aristotle insists upon the centrality of the enthymeme for a valid understanding of the art of rhetoric. For we begin to realize that, in the last analysis, the enthymeme is the capstone whereby the *logos* is artistically structured in discourse.

In justice to Aristotle's endeavor, and in the light of the work of Isocrates, as well as a statement like that of the *Phaedrus*, we must locate the task which a theorist on the art of rhetoric faced. To begin with, in any confrontation of two minds on the truth or falsehood of an open subject, which is to say a subject which is contingent and subject to change, a common ground for intelligent discourse must be found. Meaningful discourse on any subject open to further deliberation or consideration must begin on ground acceptable to the persons engaged in discourse. This personalistic process is present and can easily be discerned in any Platonic dialogue. And as soon as we say "persons" we must accept the fact that the person as an integral entity enters into reasoned discussion. As a totality of intellect, will, and emotions, he approaches and attempts to resolve the problematic thesis placed before him. As Aristotle says at *A* 2, 56a 21 ff.: "Since the sources of conviction come through these three it is clear that mastery of these sources must be acquired by the person who can reason, has the ability to discern character, the virtues, and thirdly the emotions, that is to say the nature, the quality, and source of each emotion and how it is produced . . ."

There would seem to be no question that it is this which Aristotle has in mind when he speaks of the ὑπάρχοντα πιθανά which are to be found in any subject (*A* 1, 55b 10—11). The *endechomena pithana* (*A* 2, 55b 25—26), those potentially acceptable and convincing aspects of the subject, are the elements in the subject which are meaningful to this person or group of persons. They are different for a different person or group as any number of comments of Aristotle indicate. These constitutive elements of the subject of reasoned and persuasive discourse are Aristotle's *entechnic pisteis: ethos, pathos, pragma.* As *pisteis* they are understood as source material and are a part of the entechnic method, *A* 1, 55a 4: ἡ μὲν ἔντεχνος μέθοδος περὶ τὰς πίστεις ἐστίν; this is the method proper to rhetoric, by which word Aristotle means: human discourse subject to both art and reason. For both ideas lie behind his use of ἔντεχνος and μέθοδος. From *A* 1, 54a 1—11 we should expect that a τέχνη is a guide for action that is reasoned, reasonable, and capable of explanation.

Techne enables one to examine the causes of correct action (*A* 1, 54a 10—11); and as he says at *A* 2, 55b 37 ff. the *entechnic pisteis* are those which are derived as the result of a systematic method. Aristotle elaborates the meaning further by insisting that as reasoned activity the *dynamis* of rhetoric is the developed ability, or insight, which scans the whole subject-matter and selects with care the *endechomena pithana* which will carry meaning to the auditor (*A* 2, 55b 25 ff. and *A* 2, 56b 28 ff.). This methodology can be taught, and so eventually he himself will discuss in the *Rhetoric* the various *entechnic pisteis*. Furthermore, once the *entechnic pisteis* for the particular subject-matter have been chosen, they should be given form and organized effectively in a demonstrative process which will either be deductive or inductive: enthymematic or paradeigmatic. Thus the three *entechnic pisteis* which possess a potential probative force are integrated by means of the two *pisteis* which are the logical instruments: enthymeme and *paradeigma*.

Thus the various ways in which Aristotle has employed *pistis* come together in the final act of rhetorical demonstration or *apodeixis*. The substance for the demonstrative presentation is the source material drawn from *pragma, ethos, pathos (pistis* as source material); this is put into a form of deductive or inductive reasoning *(pistis* as a methodological instrument) which creates conviction, or acceptance in the mind of the auditor *(pistis* as a state of mind). The first two steps represent Aristotle's *entechnos methodos* (*A* 1, 55a 4), the last is the object and goal of the methodology.

In introducing the inferential process of deduction and induction, namely, the *enthymeme* and *paradeigma*, Aristotle has brought into rhetoric his logical system of deductive and inductive reasoning which for him is absolutely necessary for all *apodeixis*[14]. As a logical instrument the enthymeme is the syllogism of rhetoric (*A* 2, 56b 5) which uses the material offered by the *entechnic pisteis* and marshals it into an effective form of demonstration. It is, in fact, Aristotle's introduction of the inferential methodology of his philosophical system into the field of rhetoric.

In the light of the preeminent role Aristotle assigns to the syllogism — and in the *Rhetoric* to the *enthymeme* in comparison with *paradeigma* — as the mode of demonstration it is not difficult to understand what he means when he speaks of the enthymeme as κυριώτατον τῶν πίστεων (*A* 1, 55a 7). His remark, however, that it is the σῶμα τῆς πίστεως (*A* 1, 54a 15) appears most natural and quite intelligible, since, as syllogism, it is quite manifestly the

---

[14] In the *Posterior Analytics* 71a 1—11 Aristotle begins an attempt to show that all learning and teaching arises from pre-existing knowledge as can be seen in a study of the theoretical sciences, or from a study of the argumentation used in all reasoning: syllogism and induction, both of which teach through that which is previously known. He continues by stating the parallel in rhetoric of enthymeme and example to syllogism and example: in the same way rhetoricians persuade, either through examples which is induction, or through enthymemes which is syllogism.

container, that which incorporates, or embodies, the *pisteis entechnoi* imposing form upon them so that they may be used most efficaciously in rhetorical demonstration. It does not appear incorrect to say that in the field of demonstrating the probable, which is, by and large, the demonstration of rhetoric, the enthymeme parallels the role of *apodeixis* in the area of metaphysics, just as the practical syllogism plays a similar role in his ethics.

By way of conclusion if we compare Aristotle's analysis with the little we know of the heterogeneous and mechanical contemporary analyses of the art[15] we find a remarkable synthesis of the method of rhetorical discourse in Aristotle. In his treatise we find that fundamentally:

1) there are two methods of demonstrating or proving: *enthymeme* (deduction), *paradeigma* (induction).

2) there are two major sources for the two methods:

   a) particular topics — these will provide the individual *eikota*, *semeia*, *tekmeria* in each of the three major areas which primarily give rise to belief: *pragma*, *ethos*, *pathos*. These last can be used independently but they are meant to be used by the *enthymeme* from Aristotle's statements — and presumably by *paradeigma*.

   b) general topics — inferential forms to be used by enthymeme from what Aristotle says in the *Rhetoric*. But it is clear that the inductive process can use them by citing examples that prove the general principle each general *topos* asserts.

Independently of all that has been said thus far a careful reading of the *Rhetoric* would confirm the view that the enthymeme is central to Aristotle's exposition of the nature of rhetoric. Unfortunately the development of rhetorical study after Aristotle in the direction of petty detail and technique turned the study back toward the character of some of the pre-Platonic discussion such as is suggested in collections like SPENGEL's Technon Synagoge or RADERMACHER's Artium Scriptores. The consequence of this development was that rhetorical treatises became handbooks of "good" speaking and writing whose character is rather well described by Cicero: "*scripsit artem rhetoricam Cleanthes, Chrysippus etiam, sed sic ut siquis obmutescere cupierit nihil aliud legere debeat*" (*de Fin.* 4.7). A reading of SPENGEL's commentary on the *Rhetoric* reveals a fairly constant failure on the part of later technographers to understand Aristotle's work. As a consequence whatever assistance which might have been expected from post-Aristotelian rhetorical study toward an understanding of the enthymeme is non-existent. Any at-

---

[15] *Phaedrus* 266 d—e speaks of *prooimion, diegesis, martyriai, eikota, pistosis, epipistosis*, and Aristotle *Γ* 13, 14b 14 ff. of *diegesis, epidiegesis, prodiegesis, elenchos, epexelenchos;* cf. also RADERMACHER, Artium Scriptores, Wien 1951, pp. 34—35 (B. II. 23), p. 133 (B. XXII. 9), pp. 209, 213, 214—215 (C. 21, 32, 36).

tempt to determine its meaning must be made primarily from Aristotle's statements, and of these Ross represents a not uncommon viewpoint: "The enthymeme is discussed in many passages of the *Rhetoric*, and it is impossible to extract from them a completely consistent theory of its nature". (Aristotle's Prior and Posterior Analytics, Oxford 1949, p. 499). Oddly enough there has not been any formal study of the Aristotelian enthymeme aside from the related studies of J. Mc BURNEY, The Place of the Enthymeme in Rhetorical Theory (diss. U. of Michigan, no date), and FR. SOLMSEN, Die Entwicklung der aristotelischen Logik und Rhetorik, Berlin 1929. Each of them is helpful but limited in its contribution to a full understanding of the role of the Aristotelian enthymeme in rhetoric.

The very first observation which could be made with respect to Ross' comment is that both the word ἐνθύμημα and the meaning which it carries in the *Rhetoric* is novel. And if we are to discover what Aristotle intended by the word we must do so primarily in his own writings. It is still true, however, that the antecedent history of the word and its denotation, insofar as they can be traced, gives some slight evidence for a meaning which makes Aristotle's specification of the word and the concept as we find it in the *Rhetoric* more understandable. This is what could be expected insofar as Aristotle usually worked within the historical context of ideas and was quite conscious of their development. At the same time there can be no doubt that the enthymeme for Aristotle clearly represents the introduction of his newly discovered theory of inference by means of the syllogism into the field of rhetorical study. As a matter of fact this new and formal mode of reasoning seems to have been instantly successful and rather quickly adopted by his contemporaries. At least this would seem to be a safe deduction from a comment on Eubulides, a contemporary of Aristotle and the reputed instructor of Demosthenes. We are told by Diogenes Laertius (II. 108, Oxford 1964, ed. H. LONG) that Eubulides quarreled with and criticized Aristotle. Yet we read in Philodemus (ed. SUDHAUS, Teubner 1892) (I. 84. 31 ff.), that Eubulides was contemptuous of speeches that did not possess syllogisms.

The provocative question still remains, however, as to why Aristotle chose the word ἐνθύμημα for the syllogism of rhetoric. In the light of *Topics* 162a 15 ff.: "a philosopheme is an apodeictic syllogism, an epicheireme a dialectical syllogism, a sophisma an eristic syllogism, an aporeme a dialectical syllogism which concludes to a contradiction" one would expect that the word is more than a mere name for rhetorical syllogism. Indeed, if an epicheireme is an inference "from probabilities" *(Topics* 100a 30), one might rightly expect that when Aristotle calls rhetorical inference which argues "from probabilities" an enthymeme he has some further purpose in mind. Insofar as the usual quality of words ending in -μα is to designate the result of the action involved this would seem to imply that something more than simple logical inference is at issue in the use of ἐνθύμημα, as it is also in φιλοσόφημα, ἐπιχείρημα, etc.

In view of the fact, as has been said, that Aristotle worked within the tradition of his predecessors[16] one could expect the pre-Aristotelian literature to throw some light on the meaning of the word. Yet the common interpretation of ἐνθύμημα in pre-Aristotelian literature is "thought", an act of the mind, as VOLKMANN (Die Rhetorik der Griechen und Römer, Leipzig 1885, p. 192) observes, interpreting it by ἐννόημα. This, of course, reveals no quality peculiar to rhetorical syllogism which could not be found in any other kind of syllogism. Furthermore such a correlation between enthymeme and "thought" would on the face of it be rather strange. In a language which has recognized from its earliest literary remains a distinction between θυμός and νοῦς an identity between ἐνθύμημα and ἐννόημα might be justifiably suspect. It is a common axiom on the part of students of the language to attribute a certain precision and care to the Greeks in their use of words. And the evidence for such care is present in the distinction between ἐνθυμέομαι — ἐννοέομαι; ἐνθύμημα — ἐννόημα; ἐνθυμηματικός — ἐννοηματικός. To have something ἐν θυμῷ is not simply to "have a thought". The use of the word θυμός in the literature as the principle of feeling and thought does not permit such a precisive identity with "thought" as has been made. ἐνθύμιος for example = taken to heart, and ἐνθύμιον ποιεῖσθαί τι = ἐνθυμεῖσθαι: to take to heart, have a scruple about *(Thuc. 7. 50)*. WILAMOWITZ has recognized this in two different places[17], yet he is not too certain of the meaning of ἐνθύμημα. In the *Menander* (81) he tells us that originally the idea of *enthymios* was in *enthymema* but leaves it unclear as to whether this meaning is applicable to the use of the word in rhetoric. In the *Herakles* (186) he would derive the rhetorical term from the verb form and limit it to the meaning: ὅτι ἐν θυμῷ ἐστιν. Still a few lines later he must admit that the verb can be used in the broader sense such as is found in the Thucydides citation above, a meaning which he himself accepts for *enthymios*.

Since it is quite clear by now that in Aristotle ἐνθύμημα is not simply logical demonstration by syllogism the effort to discover whether something more than "thought" or "reason" resides in the pre-Aristotelian usage merits consideration. For it may point both to the reason why Aristotle used this

---

[16] For the *Rhetoric* a casual reading of either Spengel's *Synagoge Technon*, Stuttgart 1828, RADERMACHER's Artium Scriptores, Wien 1951, or SPENGEL's commentary on the *Rhetoric* (Lipsiae 1867) will give clear confirmation of this. As SPENGEL notes in the *Synagoge*, p. 173: "philosophus ille suas sententias saepe non minus quam Plato priorum . . . rationibus apfacit."

[17] WILAMOWITZ, Herakles II, Berlin 1895, p. 162; Menander: Das Schiedsgericht, Berlin 1925, p. 81; as he suggests *enthymios* had a specific meaning for fifth century Athenians: "was religionem habet, was gewissensscrupel macht".

term for the syllogism of rhetoric and what he may have had in mind by the rhetorical syllogism.

A survey of the general literature yields relatively little on the use of the noun, ἐνθύμημα, as well as the adjective and verb form[18]. There are two authors who use ἐνθύμημα more frequently: Xenophon and Isocrates. Of the latter WILAMOWITZ remarks somewhat assuredly: "Der rhetorische Terminus ist von Isokrates geprägt; von Aristoteles aufgenommen" (Menander, 81). Xenophon employs the word in several works: *Cynegeticus* 13. 9. 3; *Hellenica* 4. 5. 4; 5. 4. 51; *Oeconomicus* 20. 24; *Anabasis* 3. 5. 12; 6. 1. 21. In all of these instances the denotation "thought" certainly seems acceptable to the text, and it is so interpreted. But it would certainly be an over-simplification of the text to say that this is always the exclusive denotation of the word[19]. In Isocrates' use of the noun the same conclusion would have to be drawn. ἐνθύμημα is used in *Panathenaicus* 233a; *Evagoras* 190e, 191a; *Against the Sophists* 294d; *Antidosis* 319d. All of these passages are usually translated by some form of "thought", e. g. E. S. FORSTER on *Evagoras* 190e (Isocrates Cyprian Orations, Oxford 1912) "'those ideas which concern the actual facts'. ἐνθύμημα is here used in its literal sense; later in Aristotelian logic it has the meaning of 'a syllogism drawn from probable premises'"[20]. It is, of course, the literal sense which is at issue. For example one might ask what kind of "thoughts" a phrase like ἐνθυμήμασιν ὀγκωδεστέροις could possibly be *(Antid.* 319d)? Again how is it possible to interpret, as is done, *Ag. Soph.* 294d as "thoughts" e. g. "to adorn with striking thoughts"? It is difficult to understand the use of the verb καταποικίλλω in this manner; unfortunately Isocrates uses the word only here. He does, however, use ποικιλία and in each instance it refers to the use of rhetorical devices and varieties of style, and this is a meaning far more in keeping with the image imbedded in the

---

[18] The source for the following is always the *index verborum*, if it exists, combined with whatever other resources that offered themselves. *Homer:* no noun; *enthymios* is used. *Hesiod:* no form. *Herodotus:* *enthymios* once, and with meaning "scruple". *Thucydides:* *enthymios, enthymia* in sense of "religio"; verb; and *enthymesis* once. *Aristophanes:* verb appears four times; scholiast on *Nubes* 317 interprets γνώμην by ἐνθυμήματα even though νοῦν occurs in the same line. *Aeschylus:* verb appears once and Italie interprets as "curare, aegre ferre". *Sophocles:* *enthymios* twice; noun twice: *OC* 292, 1199 both obviously not susceptible to the simple translation "thought" as Wilamowitz recognizes for 1199 (Menander, op. cit., p. 186). *Euripides:* *enthymios* twice; *enthymesis* in *frg.* 246. *Pindar:* no form of verb, adjective, noun. *Plato:* verb appears. *Lysias:* verb form frequently.

[19] I will cite only the *Anabasis* as an example. The first citation will tolerate "thought", "idea", "notion". The second will not do so at all. Within the immediate context there are four verbs for thinking, including διανοέομαι; the ἐνθυμήματα in the text are the result of his hopes, thoughts, and desires which is clearly shown by the adjective τοιαῦτα which in turn makes ἐνθυμήματα the sum of the preceding actions. This passage is followed by the verb ἐνθυμέομαι, which, in the context, means an act that results from reason, feelings, the whole person, as the sentence shows.

[20] More recently R. FLACELIÈRE has given slight leeway (Isocrate: Cinq Discours, Paris 1961, p. 89) interpreting enthymeme as: "(de θυμός): réflexion, pensée, idée".

root word[21]. Furthermore a study of each of the passages cited above for his use of enthymeme reveals clearly that Isocrates is talking about style and the techniques and variety of style. Consequently we would have to conclude that when he uses enthymeme he may well be speaking not about "thought", but a figure of thought, that is, thought developed and expressed in a certain way. There is no evidence to demonstrate that he is talking simply of "thought". As a matter of fact when he wants to say "thought" he uses the more likely word διάνοια in the very passage of the *Evagoras* (191a) where he has just used ἐνθύμημα.

Turning from the general works of literature to the pre-Socratics and the technographers, the evidence for ἐνθύμημα is restricted. Among the pre-Socratics the only mention of the word occurs in a fragment about Nausiphanes the probable preceptor of Epicurus[22]. The importance of the Nausiphanes citation is that it makes a distinctly Aristotelian statement by correlating *enthymeme* with syllogism, and *paradeigma* (example) with induction. The text itself (DIELS-KRANZ, Die Fragmente der Vors. II, p. 249, 38 f.) indicates that syllogism is apparently understood in the technical sense given to it by Aristotle. This is inescapable from the parallelism of the four terms. Nausiphanes (b. ca. 360) was certainly a contemporary of Aristotle, and if the citation antedates Aristotle it would obviously be significantly important. While VON ARNIM believes that Aristotle is dependent upon Nausiphanes the point is disputed by SUSEMIHL and VON FRITZ[23]. In actual fact until evidence is on hand that Aristotle is not the author of the technical meaning of συλλογισμός as the instrument for deductive reasoning the presumption must be that Nausiphanes depends on Aristotle for this correlation of syllogism-enthymeme. Most assuredly there is no assistance from the fragments of Nausiphanes which we possess in securing even the possibility of such an authorship for him; and there is absolutely no evidence in any other author prior to Aristotle which makes such a correlation of *enthymeme* with syllogism, and *paradeigma* with induction.

When we turn to the remains of the pre-Aristotelian technical writing on rhetoric we find the word ἐνθύμημα used by only two of the technographers. From the evidence there is no question that the first of the two, Alcidamas, whose writing is known to Aristotle[24] did not think of ἐνθύμημα as

[21] For example cf. M. L. W. LAISTNER on Philip, 27 in Isocrates: De Pace and Philippus, New York 1927.

[22] Unfortunately most of the information on the teaching of Nausiphanes comes through Philodemus from a polemic written against the rhetorical doctrine of Nausiphanes by the Epicurean Metrodorus of Lampsacus.

[23] H. VON ARNIM, Dio von Prusa, Berlin 1898, p. 59; F. SUSEMIHL, Aphorismen zu Demokritos, Philologus 60, 1901, pp. 190—1; K. VON FRITZ, RE XVI, 1935 p. 2026 argues against VON ARNIM that the dependance of Nausiphanes on Aristotle is possible.

[24] Aristotle refers to his works on four occasions in the *Rhetoric: A* 13, 73b 18, *B* 23, 97a 12

συλλογισμός. If we couple this with the fact that the other technographer, Anaximenes, does not understand enthymeme as a syllogism the likelihood that Nausiphanes pre-dates Aristotle in this matter becomes weaker still. While it is questioned that Alcidamas wrote a *techne*, the work which concerns us is his περὶ σοφιστῶν[25]. The work is not technographical in character, and there is consequently nothing like a definition of the word ἐνθύμημα which actually appears thirteen times in the speech (nos. 3, 4, 18 (bis), 19 (bis), 20 (bis), 24 (bis), 25 (bis), 33). It is used as a term which is accepted and understood; it is never explained. As a student of Gorgias and, in turn, the putative teacher of Aeschines, Alcidamas was a contemporary of Isocrates (Tzetzes, *Chiliades* 11. 670; 746), and like Isocrates he called his art: rhetoric-philosophy *(Peri Soph.* no. 2). A reading of this work on the Sophists does encourage the view that Alcidamas belongs to the tradition which is usually accepted for the Sophists, namely, that of an eminently practical and somewhat mechanical, rather than theoretical, understanding of the art of rhetoric. The justification of this ascription to all the Sophists without discrimination can be questioned (cf. Introduction). In all probability, however, it does represent one phase of rhetorical study, and it can be seen at greater length and in more detail in the *Rhetoric to Alexander*. The burden of Alcidamas' essay is an attack on written speeches and logography in general, and in reading it one receives the impression that it is an attack upon Isocrates and his theory of carefully prepared discourse[26]. Cicero sums up rather well Alcidamas' concern for facility in speaking even at times to the neglect of what is

(Messeniacus); *B* 23, 98b 10—19; *Γ*3, 06a 1—b19. The citations indicate an intimate knowledge of the speeches of Alcidamas; on which see Brzoska on Alcidamas in RE I, 1894, p. 1534. Blass, Die attische Beredsamkeit II², Leipzig 1872, p. 351 correctly observes that Aristotle preferred Isocrates to Alcidamas. After Aristotle the first notice of Alcidamas is in Demetrius περὶ ἑρμηνείας 12, and Dionysius of Halicarnassus *de Isae.* 19, neither of which contributes in any way to the problem here.

[25] The text used here is that of Radermacher, Artium Scriptores, Wien 1951, pp. 135—141. This work of Alcidamas is generally accepted as genuine; his *Palamedes* is questioned. Vahlen, Der Rhetor Alkidamas (Sb. d. Wiener Ak. 1863); Brzoska, RE I, 1894, pp. 1533—9; Blass, op. cit. pp. 345—64; Baiter-Sauppe, Oratores Attici, Turici 1839—43, pp. 154—69; Spengel, Synagoge, Stuttgart 1828, pp. 172—180; H. Raeder, Alkidamas und Platon als Gegner des Isokrates, RhM 63, 1908, pp. 495—511; K. Hubík, Alkidamas oder Isokrates, WS 22, 1901, pp. 234—251; L. Robin, Phèdre, Paris 1947, p. clxv. Dionysius of Halicarnassus in *Ep. ad Amm.* I. no. 722 attributes to Alcidamas a *techne* antedating Aristotle. The only strong evidence for this *techne* is a definition of rhetoric attributed to him in *Rhetores Graeci* (ed. C. Walz, Stuttgart 1833), VII. 1. 8. 18—24. This same citation would indicate that Alcidamas did have a school of followers (οἱ περὶ τὸν Ἀλκιδάμαντα) which Blass (op. cit., p. 351) denies.

[26] Raeder, op. cit., p. 498, Hubík, op. cit., p. 240, Spengel, Synagoge, p. 174. For what it is worth Hubík, Raeder, Brzoska assume that this work of Alcidamas is a reply to Isocrates' *Against the Sophists*. Such an exchange might have occurred for there does appear to be a reference to our work in the *Panegyricus* 11; and *Philippus* 25—27, *Epist.* I. 2—3 could well be rejoinders to statements in this work.

said (e. g. *Peri Soph*. no. 20): *"rhetor antiquus in primis nobilis . . . cui rationes . . . defuerunt, ubertas orationis non defuit"* (*Tusc. disp.* 1. 48. 116; in its own way this is reminiscent of a comment made about Anaximenes: "a spate of words, a trickle of sense" (Stobaeus, *Florilegium* 3. 36. 20)). From his own apologia (nos. 29—34), however, as well as his insight into what can be called the primary structural elements of rhetorical discourse (subject-matter, *taxis*, and *lexis*, v. no. 33) it would be wrong to dismiss Alcidamas as a careless or haphazard rhetorician. His obvious concern with discourse and the definition of rhetoric attributed to him which is rather Aristotelian[27] in tone indicates his concern with rhetoric as a discipline. We read in the *Rhetores Graeci* (ed. WALZ, Stuttgart, 1833), 7. 1. 8. 18—24 that "the followers of Alcidamas" define rhetoric in this way: "rhetoric . . . is *dialogike*, and *dialogike* is thus defined: δύναμις τοῦ ὄντος πιθανοῦ". Obviously if Alcidamas wrote a *techne* and discussed enthymeme Aristotle might very well have incorporated his ideas.

We can only work, however, with the text of the *Peri Sophiston*, and the effort to interpret ἐνθύμημα here faces precisely the same problem found in the the other pre-Aristotelian literature. Enthymeme, as it occurs in the work, does not mean syllogism[28]. Further it cannot mean "thought" without any qualification, a simple act of the mind, although BLASS who is the only one to consider the word inclines to this meaning which he interprets as "Auffindung der Gedanken". Alcidamas has a variety of word forms for the act of thought: φρονέω (nos. 1, 2, 6, 10, etc.), οἴομαι (nos. 2, 14, 20), νομίζω (nos. 2, 5), διανοέω (no. 24) to mention a few. He also recognizes noun forms of διάνοια (nos. 16, 24, 28, 32) and cognates such as ἀγχίνοια (no. 16), πρόνοια (nos. 23, 33). In itself this recognition on the part of Alcidamas of terms for the act of thinking does not exclude ἐνθύμημα from denoting simply and exclusively "thought". Yet doubt does begin to arise when we find him (no. 16) calling the activity of the mind in written composition διάνοια, and making a clear distinction (no. 24) between ἐνθύμημα and διάνοια. The latter is used together with its verb form to express the action of the mind. Finally he describes the activity of the mind in extemporaneous discourse by διάνοια. The evidence from each instance of his use of the word ἐνθύμημα suggests that Alcidamas is using it, as Isocrates does, to denote something like a figure of thought — but not simply for thought itself. There is no indication that this figure of thought is antithesis, or opposition, or contrast.

---

[27] Cf. *Rhetoric*, A 2, 55b 25—6; see also SPENGEL, Synagoge, p. 173, BLASS, op. cit., p.348 n. 1.

[28] Aristotle does say (*B* 23, 97a 7—12, *B* 23, 98b 10—19) that he finds certain general topics which he himself uses as a source for inference by enthymeme in the *Messeniacus* of Alcidamas. But there is nothing more unusual in this than in BLASS (op. cit., p. 355) finding deduction and induction in the *Peri Sophiston*. All are very natural modes of reasoning and one would and could expect to find them prior to their formalization by Aristotle in the *Organon*.

While it is something more than a mere act of the mind, there is no clear evidence that it means "thought" as the act of the whole person: mind, will, emotions, feelings. ἐνθύμημα is something more than notional apprehension (an act of the intellect only), but we have no certain indication that it is real apprehension: an act whereby the mind grasps something as a reality known to the whole man, an object of experience, the process which he describes so well when speaking of discourse as ἔμψυχος, discourse which is living and real (no. 28).

There is little or no point in introducing Theodectes in an effort to discover the meaning of enthymeme prior to Aristotle[29]. While we have evidence for a treatise (or treatises) from his hand the only access we would have to its content would be by way of reconstruction almost exclusively from Aristotle's *Rhetoric*. Aside from the usually tenuous character of such undertakings its futility in the present instance is more than evident. Indeed the other pre-Aristotelian technographer, Anaximenes, presents many problems of his own[30]. But we do possess a *techne* with which to work, the so-called *Rhetoric to Alexander*, a title acquired from the prefatory epistle which is considered a late forgery. Until the time of Victorius this work was attributed to Aristotle but it is now accepted as very probably the *techne* of Anaximenes a pupil of Diogenes the Cynic and Zoilus the rhetor[31]. Since we have this treatise on rhetoric and the word enthymeme appears in it there is need to locate this work with reference to Aristotle. The evidence points rather sharply toward

---

[29] SOLMSEN, Drei Rekonstruktionen zur antiken Rhetorik und Poetik, Hermes 67, 1932, pp. 133—54 and RE X, 1934, pp. 1722—34 discusses the problem of Theodectes; as P. GOHLKE observes, we know nothing of his so-called treatise and the one reference to it in the *Rhetoric* Γ 9, 10b 3 fits cc. 27—29 of the *Rhetoric to Alexander* perfectly: Die Entstehung der aristotelischen Ethik, Politik, Rhetorik, Wien 1944, p. 114.

[30] P. WENDLAND, Anaximenes von Lampsakos, Berlin 1905; H. USENER, Quaestiones Anaximeneae, Göttingen no date; A. IPFELKOFER, Die Rhetorik des Anaximenes, Würzburg 1889; E. M. COPE, An Introduction to Aristotle's Rhetoric, London 1867; C. ROBERT, Anaximenes, RE I, 1894, pp. 2086 ff.; M. FUHRMANN, Anaximenis Ars Rhetorica, Lipsiae 1966, whose text I follow in the citations.

[31] Dionysius of Halicarnassus, ad *Amm.* 2, de *Isae*. 19 mentions a *techne*, and from Philodemus *Rhetorica II*, ed. SUDHAUS, p. 254. 21 ff. and Quintilian 3. 4. 9, we learn that he was apparently concerned with rhetorical education in order to turn out orators in the field of judicial and deliberative oratory. IPFELKOFER, op. cit., p. 8 ff. gives a history of the scholarship on this problem, as does USENER, op. cit., p. 1 ff. Among the many who would agree with Victorius the following can be mentioned: IPFELKOFER, USENER, SPENGEL, WENDLAND, ROBERT, WESTERMANN, BLASS. Recently V. BUCHHEIT, Untersuchungen zur Theorie des Genos epideiktikon von Gorgias bis Aristoteles, Munich 1960, challenged this ascription, and G. GRUBE, A Greek Critic: Demetrius on Style, Toronto 1961, pp. 156—63 questions the attribution to Anaximenes arguing exclusively from Quintilian; but he does accept the fourth century date. Fuhrmann comments (p. xl) on recent challenges of Quintilian: "equidem hanc nimiam diligentiam non probo; nam si Rhetoricam ad Alexandrum paulo post annum 340 a. Chr. n. a sophista quodam scriptam esse constat, utrum Anaximeni an aequali alicui attribuamus quid refert?"

a period prior to Aristotle's *Rhetoric*. This is so independently of whether or not we accept the author as Anaximenes whose *floruit* on the evidence of Diodorus (15. 76. 4) is 366 B. C. making him a contemporary of Plato, Isocrates and Aristotle. Insofar as the reasons for dismissing Anaximenes as author are not compelling there seems to be no reason not to speak of him as the author. The last datable event in the treatise is the Corinthian expedition to assist Syracuse under Timoleon ca. 343/2 (c. 8, 1429b 18 ff.). Taken together with Diodorus this would give us an approximate date for Anaximenes of 380—320 and place the treatise possibly about 340. This coincides fairly closely with the date generally accepted[32].

The substantial material of the treatise would certainly favor a period of time prior to Aristotle's work in the *Rhetoric*, for in matters of critical importance there is no indication of any awareness of Aristotle's work. This is difficult to accept[33], for certain things, whether Anaximenes wished to acknowledge them or not, such as a bow toward a definition of rhetoric, or a discussion of $\mathring{\eta}\theta o\varsigma$, would seem inevitable in a post-Aristotelian work. Yet neither appears, and their absence is incomprehensible. On the other hand there are a striking number of similarities between the two treatises[34]. There

---

[32] BLASS, op. cit., p. 391 and notes 2, 3; ROBERT, op. cit., p. 2090; USENER, op. cit., p. 23.

[33] A reading of the treatise without recourse to the discussion of the problem in the secondary sources definitely impresses one with the affinity of the material in general to the pre-Aristotelian technical writing. The work does reveal unity of concept and composition which argues to a single author. And yet the general division of rhetoric into three kinds with seven species is a cumbersome systematization which one could call post-Aristotelian with only great lenience. It is clear that in the treatment of *eikos* and all matters connected with logic, as COPE remarks (Introd., p. 421), the author demonstrates an ignorance of what Aristotle has said; and this can also be stated for his discussion of *tekmerion*. All of the technographers after Aristotle took up Aristotle's theory on *tekmerion* (v. SPENGEL's commentary at 1357b 6 and RADERMACHER, Artium Scriptores, p. 215); our author ignores it. It is again quite difficult to explain how this *techne*, emphasizing as it does the elementary idea of persuasion at any cost, could come after Aristotle's *Rhetoric* without even the slightest discussion of the firm Aristotelian position on this point. The more one involves oneself with the problem the more inclined one is to agree with IPFELKOFER, op. cit., p. 13 that the only way one can explain the *Rhetoric to Alexander* is that it is written "ohne alle Kenntnis der aristotelischen *Rhetorik*" and indeed prior to it; see also WENDLAND, op. cit., p. 27: "In dem Texte des Lehrbuches ... ist ... unsere aristotelische *Rhetorik* nirgends benutzt"; ROBERT, op. cit., p. 2093; SPENGEL, Die Rhetorica (des Anaximenes) ad Alexandrum kein Machwerk der spätesten Zeit, Philologus 18, 1862, pp. 604—646. Isocrates has been proposed, and also rejected, as the influence on this work. Whether he is or not is immaterial to this discussion save in the matter of the four-fold division of a speech which is Isocratean in character. For here again it is difficult to understand how anyone writing after Aristotle could disregard Aristotle's ridicule of such divisions in *Γ* 13, 14a 31 ff. FUHRMANN (pp. xl—xli) speaks of the relationship to Aristotle.

[34] Even though it is difficult after reading the *Rhetoric to Alexander* to accept it as post-Aristotelian one can discern reasons for the arguments about its relation to Aristotle's work. Despite rather firm convictions on the the matter I must admit that to find in the work the presence, on occasion, of divisions, definitions, and specifications of terms such as one is accustomed to meet them in Aristotle is a cause for wonder, e. g. c. 1, 1421b 7—1423a 12. I do not know that this fact can be

has been an effort to explain these by Aristotle's and Anaximenes' use of a common source: our unknown Theodectes. A more likely explanation would be Aristotle's use and development of the work of Anaximenes. This last point might very well be confirmed by the statements of each man on enthymeme. For it is certainly possible to understand Aristotle on enthymeme with Anaximenes as a reference work. Anaximenes' statements on the enthymeme, after Aristotle's work in the *Rhetoric*, are quite beyond comprehension.

In Anaximenes we first meet ἐνθύμημα (c. 7, 1428a, 16 ff.) as a species of what is called by the general name πίστις. As such it is one of seven types of *pistis* among which are *eikota, paradeigmata, gnomai, semeia* and *elenchoi*. About the only parallel one could devise between this statement and Aristotle is that Anaximenes' *pistis* is in concept similar to what Aristotle calls *pistis entechnos*. This statement is followed by a definition of each of these species and finally at c. 10, 1430a 23 ff. we reach a definition of enthymeme: "Enthymemes are oppositions not merely in language and action but in all other things as well. You will acquire many of them by inquiry, as was noted under the investigatory branch of rhetoric, and by examining whether the speech is anywhere in opposition to itself or the actions in opposition to justice, the law, the expedient, the honorable, the possible, the facile, the probable, the character of the speaker, or the character of the circumstances."

Perhaps the most pointed comment on this definition, in respect to what is being said in this chapter, is the most recent observation of GRUBE (A Greek Critic: Demetrius on Style, Toronto 1961, p. 160): "at 1430a 24 the word is defined as contradiction . . . The meaning contradiction is quite unique". Grube is of the opinion that the word as found elsewhere in the treatise, e. g.

explained with WENDLAND (who rejects later interpolation of the text with Aristotelian material) by saying that Aristotle in re-working an earlier *Rhetoric* of his own used the *techne* of Theodectes which had also been used by Anaximenes. Aside from the fact that such an explanation raises a further problem of an earlier form of the present *Rhetoric*, and so an enterprise of higher criticism still unsatisfying in its results, it is quite possible to explain the similarities by Aristotle's use of Anaximenes in which he took what was acceptable and rejected that with which he could not agree. Certainly the matters common to each are striking. Anaximenes (c. 2, 1423a 13 ff.), like Aristotle, considers the object of deliberative oratory: at c. 1, 1421b 15 ff. he discusses the various τέλη of rhetorical discourse but without the much more sophisticated analysis of Aristotle. Anaximenes' two kinds of *pisteis* (c. 7, 1428a 16 ff.) roughly parallel Aristotle's *pisteis entechnoi* and *pisteis atechnoi*, and his discussion of *semeion* (c. 12, 1430b 30 ff.) is quite similar to Aristotle's definition. It is also of interest to note that, while Anaximenes (c. 15, 1431b 23—6) speaks of using enthymemes as ἐπίλογοι to witnesses, Aristotle uses the same word when he recommends that *paradeigmata* be so used with enthymemes (*B* 20, 94a 11). The discussion of *gnome* (c. 14, 1431a 35 ff.) in Anaximenes and in Aristotle also bears comparison. These are some of the more obvious instances of a relationship between the two. Insofar as these relations represent technical matters of rhetoric present for the most part in precisely this way in none of the earlier writing it seems quite probable that if there is a relationship between the two it is Aristotle re-working Anaximenes.

cc. 22, 32, 1434a 36, 1438b 35 "seems to have the Aristotelian meaning" by which GRUBE understands "a rhetorical syllogism". It does not seem possible to derive "rhetorical syllogism" from either of these passages. Indeed in all that Anaximenes has to say about enthymeme[35] in the rest of the work there is nothing which would substantially change the definition given above, and it is certainly not the Aristotelian understanding of the enthymeme[36]. We can, as has been done above, interpret the definition of Anaximenes in a less restrictive way than GRUBE, and in a way to which the Greek word readily submits, namely as opposition, not contradiction. This still leaves enthymeme in Anaximenes as a species of opposition which is found in language or reality either naturally or, as we see at 14, 1431a 34—5, artificially, that is to say, subject to the speaker's ingenuity in devising it. If we were to seek an exact parallel to this in Aristotle we find it in the enthymeme which he derives from the general topic of opposites (B 23, 97a 7 ff.). Interestingly enough this is the first general topic for enthymemes given by Aristotle which might indicate that he finds this quality of opposition of some importance for the enthymeme. It should also be noted that in this same passage Aristotle remarks that Alcidamas uses this formal topic from opposites in his *Messeniacus*. This might also indicate that Anaximenes' usage is not particularly unique for the rhetoricians. The fact remains, however, that the technical meaning given to enthymeme by Anaximenes is substantially different from Aristotle's[37]. Obviously this creates a rather intolerable difficulty if Anaximenes is writing after the time of Aristotle's *Rhetoric*. On the other hand a number of intriguing parallelisms become understandable if we accept the possibility that Aristotle introduced his new methodology of reasoned inference by syllogism into the rhetorical *pragmateia* with the work of Anaximenes in mind. Many of the statements which the two authors make yield to this possibility. The reverse process permits of no other reasonable explanation save the questionable common source already mentioned.

One of the very first qualities we find in the enthymeme of Anaximenes is that it should be expressed with brevity (c. 10, 1430a 36—8): "compactly and

---

[35] ἐνθύμημα is found in Anaximenes in the following places: cc. 7, 1428a 21; 10, 1430a 23—39; 14, 1431a 28—39; 15, 1431b 26; 18, 1432b 27, 1433a 26; 20, 1434a 4 (verb form); 22, 1434a 35; 32, 1438b 34 (or, ἐπενθυμήματα), 1439a 6 (ἐνθυμηματώδεις), 20, 34, 1440a 23; 35, 1441a 20, 40, b11; 36, 1442b 39, 1443a 3, b42.

[36] SPENGEL, *Anaximenis Ars Rhetorica*, Leipzig 1847, p. 162: "Aristoteli ἐνθύμημα genus probationis est ῥητορικὸς συλλογισμός quaevis sententia cui ratio addita est, *Rhet.* I. 2; II. 21—2, Anaximeni, ut Isocrati aliisque oratoribus, species, sententia cui qualiscumque ἐναντίωσις inest". In actual fact there is little in Anaximenes' definition of enthymeme to distinguish it from his definition of *tekmerion* (c. 9), aside from the greater extension of enthymeme, a fact which he recognizes himself in c. 14.

[37] And yet in the one place where Anaximenes uses the verb form (c. 20, 1434a 4) he does so with a meaning found throughout the literature.

in as few words as possible". In Aristotle's whole discussion of enthymeme brevity is such a significant matter that his comments have been traditionally interpreted to mean that the enthymeme was an abbreviated syllogism[38]. Related to this idea of brevity in the enthymeme are Anaximenes' comments on *asteion legein* and the enthymeme. Aristotle also joins the two (*Γ* 10, 10b 20 ff.), and for both Aristotle and Anaximenes the dominant idea in *asteion legein* is brevity[39]. This matter of brevity and antithesis (ἐναντίωσις) in the enthymeme of Anaximenes is important and we shall return to it presently. For it appears possible that Aristotle is not simply using Anaximenes but with the introduction of his theory of reasoned argumentation into the field of rhetoric is developing ideas of Anaximenes into a more ordered presentation of his own centered around his inferential methodology. There are a number of things which encourage this line of thought. At c. 7, 1428a 16 ff. Anaximenes speaks of two kinds of *pistis*. Although he does not specify them as *entechnic* and *atechnic*, as Aristotle does at *A* 2, 55b 35 f., his explanation makes it eminently clear that the same distinction is at work. Anaximenes places among the *pisteis entechnoi: eikota, tekmeria, semeia, enthymemata, paradeigmata*, and says that these *pisteis* are derived from words, persons, and circumstances, or the reality itself (c. 7, 1428a 16—23). Aristotle, as we know, also speaks of the *entechnic* proofs, by which he means those which the speaker devises, and he derives them from persons and the circumstances or the reality itself (*A* 2, 56a 1—20; and see above pp. 60 ff.). Very early in his treatise, however, Aristotle declares that the only way in which we can reasonably demonstrate anything is by deduction (*enthymeme* in rhetoric) and induction (*paradeigma* in rhetoric) and these become for him the *pisteis par excellence* of rhetoric: the *koinai pisteis*. This he calls the entechnic methodology of rhetorical demonstration (*A* 1, 55a 4). Aristotle then proceeds further. For him *eikota* and *semeia* are not correlates of enthymeme as a form of *pistis* but rather are sources for reasoning by enthymeme, the rhetorical syllogism (*An. Pr.* 70a 10). Aristotle would also agree in general with Anaximenes (c. 14, 1431a

---

[38] Aristotle's phrase at *Γ* 18, 19a 19: τὰ ἐνθυμήματα ὅτι μάλιστα συστρέφειν δεῖ can be compared with Anaximenes on enthymeme 10, 1430a 36—8: δεῖ δὲ τούτων ἕκαστα συνάγειν ὡς εἰς βραχύτατα καὶ φράζειν ὅτι μάλιστα ἐν ὀλίγοις τοῖς ὀνόμασι; see also 18, 1432b 25—7, 1433a 25—26.

[39] For Aristotle see either Cope, Commentary III, p. 107 n. 1, or Süss, Ethos, Berlin 1910, p. 176, and of course the text. For Anaximenes see 15, 1431b 25—6: "unless you wish to express an enthymeme briefly for the sake of *asteion*" and 22, 1434a 34—7. This last is quite interesting. Not only does it offer by implication a suggestion similar to Aristotle, namely, that a good enthymeme is such that, when enunciated in part, the hearers grasp the rest of the meaning (*B* 23, 00b 30—4; *Γ* 10, 10b 20—8), but it urges explicitly that only half the enthymeme be spoken so that the hearers may complete it (with which cf. *A* 2, 57a 16—21). The passage also implies (1434a 38—40) that one should not use enthymemes one after the other; on this point see Aristotle *Γ* 17, 18a 6. Rather than the use of a common source (Wendland) these passages suggest that Aristotle in developing his own theory is modifying and incorporating Anaximenes.

39—42)[40] that the enthymeme is the source of probable knowledge. He is not, however, satisfied with this. Rather we find in Aristotle a radical reorganization of the ideas. All of Anaximenes' *pisteis* produce only opinion with one exception: certain kinds of *semeia* which effect certain knowledge (c. 14, 1431a 42: καὶ σαφῶς εἰδέναι). In Aristotle, on the other hand, we find a very clear division of *semeion* (*A* 2, 57b 1 ff.) into *tekmerion* the source of certain knowledge, and *semeion anonymon* the source of probable knowledge. Insofar as *semeia* in Aristotle are not correlates of enthymeme as a type of proof, but rather are sources for reasoning by the rhetorical syllogism, Aristotle has simplified the process and made possible inference by enthymeme which will give both probable and certain knowledge.

Another area in which this radical re-formation can be seen is the relationship between enthymeme and maxim *(gnome)*. Anaximenes stresses the close connection between the two. Aristotle also emphasizes it[41] particularly in *B* 20, 93a 25—26 where he calls maxim a part of enthymeme. Once again we find in Aristotle an advanced and more developed analysis of matter seminally present in Anaximenes. With Anaximenes Aristotle distinguishes enthymeme from maxim but like Anaximenes he perceives a close relation between the two and brings them together stating that: enthymemes are to all extents and purposes syllogisms concerned with human actions as maxims are concerned with human actions, consequently the conclusions or the premises of enthymemes are *gnomai* with the syllogistic form omitted (*B* 21, 94a 25—9). Where Anaximenes speaks of enthymeme (c. 32, 1438b 30 ff.; c. 36, 1442b 33 ff.) as a means of confirming (βεβαίωσις) your proof Aristotle places the full weight of rhetorical demonstration in the enthymeme itself at the very beginning of his treatise. For Anaximenes the enthymeme is a kind of mechanical device external to and shoring up demonstration, as can readily be seen in comments on its use in cc. 32, 36 above, or again in c. 35 on encomiastic oratory. Aristotle has made the enthymeme the integrative force in rhetorical demonstration, but in doing this he stresses in the enthymeme the very qualities which underlie all of Anaximenes' statements about it. The characteristic prominent in the enthymeme of Anaximenes is its ability to express the substance of an argument in a concise and emphatic manner precisely because it brings the issue into sharp focus by contrast. The enthymeme, as Anaximenes understands it in the treatise, is grounded in the idea

---

[40] From the text enthymeme is clearly included in the phrase τῶν προειρημένων ἁπάντων and so it, like the others, only effects opinion.

[41] Anaximenes first distinguishes between enthymeme and *gnome* (c. 14, 1431a 35—8), and in every subsequent mention of enthymeme in his text (cf. note 35) he joins it with *gnome*. This could well be compared with Aristotle *B* 21, 94a 22—b 12; in particular the definition of *gnome* in c. 11, 1430b 1—b 29 should be compared with Aristotle *B* 21, 94b 7—12 where one can discern the kind of analysis which is going on in Aristotle with respect to the matter found in Anaximenes.

of contrast and opposition. USENER (Quaestiones Aniximeneae, op. cit., p. 37 f.) underlines this fact rather emphatically, for he finds the enthymeme of Anaximenes totally foreign to both the theoretical and practical ideas of Greek rhetoric. Usener would locate it, if anywhere, in Greek eristic. Yet it is precisely in this idea of contrast that there is a likely relation between the more developed enthymeme theory of Aristotle and the enthymeme of Anaximenes. The theory of learning, if we can call it such, continually at work in the Aristotelian enthymeme is a form of contrast and relation between two things: known-unknown; more known-less known[42]. He expresses this rather pointedly at *B* 24, 01a 4—6. Convinced as he was that "opposites become better known when set side by side" (*Γ* 17, 18b 4) he tells us at *B* 24, 01a 4—6 that a condensed and antithetic form of expression belongs to the enthymeme: χώρα ἐστὶν ἐνθυμήματος (6). This aspect of contrast and opposition in the enthymeme is discussed in more detail in c. 3 of this study. The point of interest at the moment is that once again Aristotle could easily be thought of as developing in his enthymeme theory the material he found in the *Rhetoric to Alexander* — if not doing so in actual fact.

Consequently, despite certain inadequacies, the evidence on hand as to the meaning and the use of ἐνθύμημα both in Greek literature and in the rhetorical writing prior to Aristotle encourages one to think that Aristotle worked in rhetoric as he always did, namely, within the historical tradition. While it is quite easy to say that he simply adopted a term of no particular significance there are no reasonable grounds on which to do so. Why, or how, he came to select the word ἐνθύμημα is not known; but we do know that his general approach to a problem was to work from out of the tradition, and, as we have seen, we find the word in the tradition. We find further that in the general literature and the technographers it is used in ways which suggest similarities to Aristotle's enthymeme. We discover that it signifies something that is more than a simple act of the mind, an act grounded only in reason. Its usage appears to implicate an act of the whole person, his emotions and feelings as well as his intellect. When it becomes a technical term of rhetoric, such as it appears in Anaximenes, we find it described as a form of brief, pointed opposition, echoes of which we again come upon in Aristotle's comments on his own enthymeme. A study of Aristotle's enthymeme as used in the *Rhetoric* reveals that it cannot be equated completely with syllogism interpreted as the rational demonstration of the subject. Aside from other difficulties with such an interpretation it does seem that if Aristotle wanted to understand the syllogism of rhetoric in this way he could easily have called it a syllogism without further qualification. There was no need to say that the

---

[42] J. M. LE BLOND, Logique et Méthode chez Aristote, Paris 1939, pp. 21—4, in his analysis of the methodology of the *Topics* finds it radicated in opposing viewpoints of a problem.

syllogism of rhetoric has a particular name: the enthymeme (*A* 1, 55a 6), that it is a kind of syllogism (συλλογισμός τις, a 8), observations which imply in themselves the differences he himself suggests at *A* 1, 55a 8—14. The evidence from the text suggests that the enthymeme is not a demonstration by reason alone. Aristotle makes it clear in the *Rhetoric* that in the effort to effect judgment and decision whose consequences involve the one judging, and further to do this in the area of the probable and contingent, one must seek out as sources to convince not only the rational explanation of the subject *(pragma)* but also the emotive elements in the subject *(ethos* and *pathos)*. If this is so, then his significant contribution to the art of rhetoric, a contribution which truly made it the art of discourse grounded in reason, namely, the introduction of the theory of deductive and inductive argumentation, should reflect the sources of conviction and belief. The deductive process cannot be the simple scientific syllogism, the syllogism of pure reason. Not only does the modality of the subject-matter in rhetoric prevent this, but the very object intended by rhetorical argumentation, i. e. personal conviction which will motivate personal action, does not permit it. Such a goal calls for assent on the part of the whole person: intellect, will, emotions; and, ideally, these should find their way into any demonstrative process be it by deduction or induction. And so it is proposed here that, since the word ἐνθύμημα carried with it in the tradition a sense of form and denoted something more than an act of mere reason, Aristotle used the word which best suggested what he had in mind by the rhetorical syllogism.

Chapter III

THE ENTHYMEME AS THE METHOD OF
RHETORICAL ARGUMENTATION

Aristotle, then, gives us two logical modes of demonstration which organize the material of discourse, enthymeme and example. They are the correlatives of syllogism and induction which in his philosophical treatises is the methodology whereby we move toward further knowledge of the world of reality. In the *Rhetoric* he calls them (*B* 20, 93a 23) the κοιναὶ πίστεις for all rhetorical discourse and they so dominate his analysis that both discourse and speakers may be qualified as either παραδειγματώδεις or ἐνθυμηματικοί (*A* 2, 56b 1—27) and some kinds of discourse are more suited to one type of reasoning, some to another[1]. The grounds for this distinction reside in the nature of deductive and inductive inference as Aristotle says at *A* 2, 56b 11—18, a passage unnecessarily confused by the commentators[2].

To reason deductively is to reason from the general rather than from the particular which is induction. Obviously deduction requires from the auditor a larger intellectual grasp of a problem, more sophisticated skill, attention and critical discernment. This point is made quite well in *Problemata* 18.3 (a work not by Aristotle but clearly representative of the Aristotelian tradition): 'men learn with less effort from examples for they learn individual facts; enthymemes on the other hand are a demonstration from universals which we know less well than particulars'. The statement is an accurate echo of Aristotle for he says fairly much the same at *A* 2, 57b 27—30 and *A* 2, 56b 14—18. It is also the reason why he observes at *Topics* 105a 16—19 that induction ("example" in the *Rhetoric)* is more persuasive, and clear, and experientially more known, although syllogistic reasoning is more forcible and effective[3]. Again he remarks at *Topics* 157a 18—20 that induction should be

---

[1] At *A* 9, 68a 29 ff. we learn that examples are best for deliberative rhetoric (restated at *B* 20, 94a 6 f. with the reason given: the future is like the past), enthymemes for judicial, since the past lends itself to demonstrative proof and to the examination of causes. This statement at *A* 9, 68a is repeated in substance at *Γ* 17, 18a 1—5. Aristotle does not stress this point and if one is tempted to push the distinction too far his comment at *Metaphysics* 995a 6—12 should be considered. Spengel observes (Commentary s. 1356b 21—2) that Demosthenes is enthymematic, Cicero paradeigmatic in character.

[2] See Spengel, Commentary at 1356b 10.

[3] See *An. Pr.* 68 b32—37, and Alexander on *Top.* 105a 10 who has an intelligent observation on induction and syllogism in which he notes that the quality of induction is suasiveness *(pithanon)* but that of syllogism coercive in its demand for assent *(anagkaion)*.

used for those less skilled in reasoning but syllogism for the more dialectically skilled mind[4]. Induction is clearly more appropriate for the ordinary person since it permits more ready comprehension and understanding.

In spite of these difficulties found in deductive inference it occupies a prominent position for Aristotle in rhetorical discourse. This is clear from the fact that the enthymeme is the center of his analysis of rhetoric. He insists that the enthymeme is a syllogism and frequently makes this identification in the *Rhetoric: A* 2, 56a 22, b 5; *A* 2, 57a 23; *B* 21, 94a 26; *B* 22, 95b 22; *B* 23, 00b 27 ff.; *B* 25, 02a 29 ff. He underlines the identification further when, in explaining what the enthymeme is, he repeats the formula used to define syllogism in the *Prior Analytics* (24b 18—26) and the *Topics* (100a 25 ff.; 165a 1 f.)[5]. In the light of his statements on the syllogism in the *Prior Analytics*

---

[4] See also *Top.*164a 12—14; *Prob.*18. 3 and the commentary of SEPTALIUS to this last (In Aristotelis Problemata Commentaria, Lyons 1632): "et sicut inductio maiorem in se verisimilitudinem continet, et planior, faciliorque est . . . ita syllogismus maiorem probandi vim in se habet et ad contradicendum est efficacior". He then adds the comment that in the first book of the *Rhetoric* examples are to be used with the ordinary person but enthymemes with the learned. This is a distinction which Aristotle could not have made in the *Rhetoric* but it does underlie some of his thinking on the enthymeme and is one of the reasons why the shortened form of the enthymeme, while not of its essence, is still of primary importance. Aristotle was conscious of the greater demonstrative and suasive power of the enthymeme when compared with example.

[5] As is generally known there has been question of the meaning of "syllogism" in the *Topics*. It is used in a technical sense as understood above and also in a broad sense of "reasoning". The difference in usage has since MAIER's time (Syllogistik des Aristoteles II. 2, p. 78) been one of the grounds for distinguishing between an earlier *Topics* (usually books 2—7. 2) and a later *Topics* (1. 7. 3—5, 8, 9). It is also acknowledged that the earlier *Topics* has small additions from the later *Topics*. There is some added testimony for this early-later format from other evidence gathered by GOHLKE and HUBY (see P. HUBY, 'The Date of Aristotle's *Topics* and its Treatment of the Theory Ideas', *CQ* N. S. 11—12, 1961—62, pp. 72—80 for further reference). BRUNSCHWIG in his recent edition of the *Topics* (Aristote Topiques I—IV, Paris, 1967) while he does say that there is no relation between "syllogism" in the *Topics* and the *Prior Analytics* (p. xxx: "on en chercherait en vain, dans les *Topiques*, la structure charactéristique . . .") does admit (p. xxxi) its presence as understood here in the text. Yet he cannot accept (p. xxxi, note 1) any correlation between the two passages in the *Analytics* (24b) and *Topics* (100a). On the other hand A. MANSION (Symposium Aristotelicum, Paris 1961, pp. 66—67) has argued effectively that at 100a 25 ff., 164b 27—165a 2 syllogism is to be understood in its technical sense (". . . il est difficile de croire que le même raisonnement appelé *syllogismos* dans les *Topiques* y ait été conçu comme un raisonnement dont la forme spécifique n'avait pas encore aux yeux de son auteur celle d'un syllogisme véritable, du fait que, à ce moment, Aristote n'avait pas encore élaboré dans son esprit cette forme fondamentale du raisonnement désignée finalement par le terme: συλλογισμός"). LE BLOND (Logique et méthode chez Aristote, Paris 1939) would also argue (p. 30) that in the later section of the *Topics* such as 100a 27 the word is used in its technical sense. In the light of the evidence there can be no question that "syllogism" can be used in the *Topics* in its technical sense. Consequently owing to the lack of evidence for the date of the final revision of the *Topics* there is no problem in assuming that the constant cross-references to the *Topics* in our *Rhetoric* are to the revised edition particularly in view of the fact that throughout the *Rhetoric* "syllogism" is only understood in a technical sense.

there is no problem here. At 25b 26—31[6] he observed that the syllogism has a wider extension and includes more than strict scientific demonstration. It is, so to speak, a genus for other species of deductive reasoning and as far as the structure is concerned in his definition at 24b 18—26 a syllogism is the same whether it occurs in formally scientific, in dialectical or rhetorical argumentation. This is the whole point of his comment in the *Topics* 162a 15 ff.: "a philosophema is an apodeictic syllogism, an epicheirema a dialectical syllogism, a sophisma an eristic syllogism, an aporema a dialectical syllogism which concludes to a contradiction". Had he continued with an addition which we can make from *Rhetoric A* 2, 56b 4—5 in precisely the same language "the *enthymema* is a rhetorical syllogism" (ἐνθύμημα μὲν ῥητορικὸν συλλογισμόν) we would have here a fairly complete statement of his use of syllogism. It is, of course, quite possible that the enthymeme is not mentioned because he had not yet brought his theory of the syllogism into the field of rhetoric. In any event his analysis of the enthymeme as a form of syllogistic inference clearly locates it with the other kinds of syllogism mentioned in the *Topics* passage.

Before considering more closely the structure, or form, of the enthymeme and the modality of the kind of statement it makes let us glance briefly at some of the implications for Aristotle's theory of rhetorical discourse which follow upon the fact that the enthymeme is the syllogism of rhetoric. In building his theory of rhetoric around the syllogism despite the problems involved in deductive inference Aristotle stresses the fact that rhetorical discourse is discourse directed toward knowing, toward truth not trickery. To one acquainted with Aristotle it should be evident that syllogism and induction are inextricably connected with the demonstration of truth. From the analogy drawn between "enthymeme-example" as the rhetorical forms of "deduction-induction" Aristotle directs rhetoric toward the demonstration of the true. Indeed the view of the *Rhetoric* as a collection of sharp techniques, a sophist's *vademecum*, is not only false but irreconcilable with the whole tenor of the work and such explicit statements as *A* 1, 54b 10; *A* 1, 55a 17—8, 21—3, 31—3, 37—b 7; *B* 24, 02a 23—8 and the entire discussion of apparent enthymemes *B* 24, 00b 35—01a 28. In so emphasizing the role of discursive reasoning Aristotle rejects decisively the Platonic criticism of rhetoric in the *Gorgias* 465d—466a, a rejection made more specific by his repetition of certain key words of Plato. Rhetoric is no longer a "part of flattery" (μόριον κολακείας 466a) but a "part of dialectic" (μόριόν τι τῆς διαλεκτικῆς *A* 2, 56a 31); it is the "counterpart of dialectic" (ἀντίστροφος τῇ διαλεκτικῇ *A* 1, 54a 1) not the "counterpart of cookery" (ἀντίστροφος

---

[6] Thus a statement like Cope's on *A* 2, 56a 22 (Commentary I, p. 33) should be read with care: "συλλογίσασθαι improperly applied here, as ἀπόδειξις above, I 11. p. 19 to *rhetorical* reasoning". *An. Post.* 71b 23—25 again admits the possibility of syllogism without *apodeixis*.

ὀψοποιίας 465d)[7]. If rhetoric is so clearly related to dialectic, a discipline whereby we are enabled to examine inferentially generally accepted opinions on any problem whatsoever (*Topics* 100a 18—20)[8], then it is the rhetorical syllogism which moves the rhetorical process into the domain of reasoned activity, or the kind of rhetoric Plato accepted later in the *Phaedrus*. It is also the rhetorical syllogism which relates *Rhetoric*, *Topics* and *Analytics*. For example at *A* 1, 55a 8—14 Aristotle notes that the individual who knows the sources and the methodology of the syllogism would be naturally equipped to develop enthymemes. He makes one restriction however: this individual must know the subject-matter of enthymemes and the specific difference between an enthymeme and the scientific syllogism[9]. From this we might conclude that in its structural form the enthymeme is like all syllogism but that in the character of the statement made it will be different from the scientific syllogism. Insofar as the primary concern of rhetoric is discourse in the area of the probable it would appear that the modality of all of its statements would be probable and that it would be like the dialectical syllogism in this respect. There is, however, reason to believe that Aristotle has not so restricted the enthymeme but has given it the right to use certain as well as probable statement (cf. *infra*, pp. 91—92). This means that discourse in rhetoric can reach beyond probable knowledge. From Aristotle's statements one can conclude that in the modality of its premises the rhetorical syllogism is usually like the dialectical syllogism but sometimes like the scientific syllogism (*apodeixis* in its strict meaning). The enthymeme appears to be a form

---

[7] At *A* 2, 56a 27 f. Aristotle's use of ὑποδύεται is another echo of Plato. At 464 c—d speaking of the way spurious arts insinuate themselves into the genuine arts which minister to the mind and body Plato charges rhetoric, a mere *eidolon* of *dikaiosyne*, with the attempt to usurp the place of *dikaiosyne* which (with *nomothetike*) constitutes the genuine art of πολιτική. Aristotle takes up the word and remarks that rhetoric "slips into the guise of πολιτική", as do those who lay claim to it, for two reasons: a) the close relation of rhetoric to "the science of ethics which may be rightly called politics", and, b) the misunderstanding [of this relationship] by the practitioners of the art, or their pretentiousness, or other human failings. Without pressing the matter further Aristotle's assertion in his opening lines (*A* 1, 54a 9—11) that rhetoric is an art since it submits to reason is in direct opposition to Plato's claim that rhetoric is no art since it does not submit to reason (465a).

[8] W. D. Ross, Aristotle's Prior and Posterior Analytics, Oxford 1949, p. 484 speaks somewhat to the point: "The object of dialectic and rhetoric alike is to produce *conviction* . . . Many of their arguments are quite regular syllogistic ones, formally just like those used in demonstration. But many others are in forms that are likely to produce conviction, but can be logically justified only if they can be reduced to syllogistic form; . . . The distinction between dialectical and rhetorical arguments is logically unimportant. They are of the same logical type . . ."

[9] WAITZ, Aristotelis Organon, Leipzig 1844, commenting on *Posterior Analytics* 82b 35: "Unde fit ut λογικόν idem fere sit quod διαλεκτικόν . . . id quod non ad ipsam veritatem pertinet, sed ad disserendi artem qua sententiam sive veram sive falsam defendimus". When he comes to our passage in the *Rhetoric* he continues: "quamquam 1355a 13 . . . quum λογικὸς συλλογισμός et hic et in iis quae proxime sequuntur opponatur rhetorico syllogismo (ἐνθυμήματι), veram demonstrationem significare videatur".

of inference which may partake of both the nature of the dialectical and the scientific syllogism.

Let us turn now to what Aristotle has to say about the form of the enthymeme. From his statements there is nothing to indicate that he did not consider the enthymeme to be an ordinary syllogism of three statements. Thus in structure its power like that of any syllogism resides in its ability to sum up the implications and scope of an argument in a fairly precise, condensed, and reasoned inference of two premises and a conclusion. While this position of Aristotle on the form seems clear enough the enthymeme from the earliest times has been defined as a truncated syllogism in form, a syllogism with a suppressed premise or an omitted conclusion[10]. The debate on specifying enthymeme by its structural form as an abbreviated syllogism has been continuous and is still common. Yet in 1729 FACCIOLATI (following PACIUS) wrote: "Nego enthymema esse syllogismum mutilum . . . Nego, inquam, et pernego enthymema enunciatione una et conclusione constare, quamvis ita in scholis omnibus finiatur et a nobis ipsis finitum sit aliquando . . ." In support of Facciolati the very most that can be said is that the statements of Aristotle would favor an abbreviated form but do not make such a form an essential part of the enthymeme in contradistinction to the ordinary form of the syllogism[11].

The two passages where Aristotle seems to justify those who define the enthymeme as an abbreviated syllogism do not permit one to draw such an

---

[10] Planudes, for example, *Rhetores Graeci,* ed. WALZ, Stuttgart 1832, vol. 5, pp. 403. 10—404. 2, makes a distinction between dialectical syllogism and enthymeme which he claims is that of Alexander. The gist of it is that the dialectical syllogism uses all three propositions while the enthymeme need not state all the premises or may omit the conclusion. Anonymus *(Commentaria in Aristotelem Graeca,* Berlin 1882—1909, vol. 21, p. 2. 26—27; p. 130. 22 ff.) understands the enthymeme to omit a premise. Alexander in his commentary on the *Topics* 100a25 *(Commentaria,* vol. 2 part 2, p. 9. 13—21) speaks of the enthymeme as a shortened syllogism, as does Philoponus on *An. Post.* 71a 1 *(Commentaria,* vol. 13, p. 6. 2—3). The same is true of Minucianus *(Rhetores Graeci,* ed. SPENGEL, Teubner 1894, vol. 1, p. 343. 4—11) who gives a definition accepted by VOLKMANN (Die Rhetorik[2], p. 192). See also W. KROLL in Das Epicheirema, Sb. d. Ak. d. Wissenschaften in Wien, 216 (1936—37), p. 2; H. MAIER, Die Syllogistik II. 1, p. 476, COPE in his Commentary and An Introduction to Aristotle's Rhetoric (with the exception of his passing comment on p. 103 of An Introduction).

[11] Thus the distinction on form is hardly as insignificant as Ross would make it: "purely superficial characteristic" (Aristotle's Prior and Posterior Analytics, p. 500) or MADDEN in "The Enthymeme", The Philosophical Review 51, 1952, pp. 375—376. Nor again is it as essential as MAIER (Die Syllogistik, p. 476), COPE (Commentary II, pp. 209, 221—222) and others would consider it. As shall be seen later a study of the sources of the enthymeme *(eikota* and *semeia),* of its inferential forms *(koinoi topoi)* favors an abbreviated form. For example, *eikota* are general probabilities in which frequently the minor premise may be assumed; *semeia* permit either a major or minor premise to be omitted, e. g. *A* 2, 57a 19—21; and the *koinoi topoi* offer a form of inference which is usually a relation: if x then y, a form in which either a premise or a conclusion may be assumed depending upon the evidential immediacy of the topic used.

absolute conclusion. The first is at *A* 2, 57a 16—17 and it is followed by an example which is meant presumably to be a syllogism without a major premise. The text and context are more than clear and all that can be drawn from them is that the enthymeme should not be a long inferential process and often may permit the ellipsis of a premise. The second passage *B* 22, 95b 24—26, although it is interpreted by COPE to mean an abbreviated form, is not at all that explicit in its statement. The key word is πάντα, but this is explained by Aristotle at lines 26, 30—32 and it means quite simply (a possibility even COPE must admit) that one should not introduce all kinds of unnecessary argumentation.

We cannot say, then, that the enthymeme is by definition an abbreviated syllogism and yet all of Aristotle's remarks on it are rather well summarized at *Γ* 18, 19a 18—19: "enthymemes should be condensed as much as possible". There is a definite predilection for enthymeme as a brief, direct and compact inference, and possibly in an abbreviated form. The reason for this attitude of Aristotle is determined by the factor which always plays a key role in his analysis of rhetoric: the audience. Here specifically it is his concern about the ability of the auditors to acquire the knowledge and understanding introduced by the deductive process. Aristotle states this fairly early at *A* 2, 57a 3—4, 11. At *B* 23, 00b 30—34 we learn that the best enthymemes are those which, while substantial in content, are nevertheless apparent to the audience when first enunciated, or shortly thereafter. Aristotle is concerned that the audience acquire knowledge, but knowledge which he qualifies as μάθησις ταχεῖα: a quick, comprehensive grasp of the problem (*Γ* 10, 10b 10—12, 20—21, 25—26; *B* 23, 00b 31—34; *A* 2, 57a 21). It is essential that understanding come across to those engaged in discourse quickly and effectively; as he says at 10b 20—21: "of necessity a style and enthymemes which possess elegance (ἀστεῖα) are those that give us μάθησις ταχεῖα". He makes this point more explicit at 10b 27—36 where he says that such a rapid insight is achieved in three ways: 1) by enthymeme with respect to thought, 2) by antithesis with respect to style, and, 3) in language by metaphor. The point at issue here for Aristotle is the most effective way to convey to an other this quick, comprehensive insight, and he centers his attention on the three components which mediate it, namely, thought, language, style. From what he says we may suppose that enthymeme does it by the way in which it organizes the thought, since clearly style does it by the way in which the idea is emphasized by sentence structure, and in language it is the structure of analogy in metaphor which obtains the same result.

Each contributes to μάθησις ταχεῖα, and one cannot help but note that their underlying logic is a movement from idea to idea, or statement to statement, e. g. "this" and so "that", or, "if this is so" then "that is so". Indeed somewhat earlier Aristotle joined the enthymeme quite closely with the antithetic style saying quite simply that this style is the *locus* for enthymematic statement (χώρα ἐστὶν ἐνθυμήματος B 24, 01a 4—6). The particular logic of the antithetic style for effective communication of thought is revealed at B23, 00b 28—29: "when two things are set beside one another they are more clear to the hearer". Antithesis is based on a relationship between two concepts or propositions whereby we move directly, concisely, and with new knowledge from the known concept or proposition to the less known. The movement is quite similar to that which takes place when a syllogism is shortened.

These statements of Aristotle which favor a shortened syllogistic structure for the sake of the auditors indicate his desire that the language of discourse speak to the hearers in an immediate and direct way even when the syllogism is used. The introduction of his major mode of demonstration into rhetorical theory could work against such immediacy. For deduction develops usually from the area of more general principles, of concepts in themselves, or of the more universal ideas entailed by the subject itself. Such discourse can easily lose itself in theoretical analysis and lose rapport with those not sufficiently skilled to follow a line of deductive reasoning, or to perceive its relevance. In suggesting a modification of the form Aristotle apparently wishes to retain the strength which deductive demonstration contributes to discourse as a reasoned activity, and at the same time to make this power more accessible to a general audience. We have an example of how effective this can be in the *First Olynthiac*. Demosthenes works from the major premise that "freedom involves self-sacrifice and personal responsibility" (2—6) — a secure general principle which would command assent, but whose development would carry little weight in the situation. Thus this major premise is never formally articulated. Demosthenes develops the minor which is more immediate and obvious: "our freedom is here and now at issue" (2), and the conclusion: "we must make sacrifices and assume our responsibilities". The power of the argument is patent: the immediate concern about the danger and how to cope with it is raised to a level which grounds the whole motive for action in a principle acceptable to most, if not all, men.

In many ways this permissible modification of the syllogistic form on Aristotle's part appears to be caused by a desire to make the constraining force inherent in deductive inference as immediate for an ordinary audience as the appeal of induction[12]. This would appear to be the point of his comment at B

---

[12] In actual fact a study of the character of induction, or example, as it is presented in the *Rhetoric*, reveals a structure of inference analogous to that of the abbreviated syllogism. Even when we admit that inductive example is not quite the same as ordinary induction (*A* 2, 57b 26—30; *B* 20, 93a 26—27), yet if both kinds of induction are to work successfully a mental process similar to that met in the enthymeme in its abbreviated form is called for. Example makes its induction from particular to particular, or inference by resemblance. However in such inference the mind always assumes as its ground the general proposition which is being inferred about one particular by means

22, 95b 22—25 where he remarks that he has previously discussed three facts about the enthymeme: that it is a syllogism; how it is a syllogism; and in what way it differs from a dialectical syllogism[13]. He explains this last point immediately with the comment that those who use the enthymeme "must not draw the conclusion from an extended series of inferences (πόρρωθεν) nor include all relevant material". If we ask where he has engaged in such a discussion the only likely passage is A 2, 56a 35—57a 21. In this section he notes, among other things, that the enthymeme is used with an audience "which is not able to comprehend in all its detail an argument built of many stages nor able to reason through an extended series of inferences" (A 2, 57a 3—4). There is an obvious relation between these two passages in the demand for conciseness in the rhetorical syllogism. As a further point Aristotle seems to contrast the syllogistic process in rhetoric and dialectic. The point of the contrast is that dialectic employs a series of interrelated syllogisms which develop an argument to a conclusion. The rhetorical syllogism must capture the evidence forcefully enough to stand alone. When Aristotle writes as he does at A 2, 57a 7—10 he can only be describing the dialectical syllogism: "it is possible to construct syllogisms and draw conclusions from evidence that is itself the result of syllogisms or from evidence not demonstrated by syllogism but in need of syllogistic proof since it is not probable." The dialectical syllogism as seen in the *Rhetoric* permits an extended inferential

---

of another particular. On "example" cf. *An. Pr.* 69a 13—16; Alexander on the *Topics (Commentaria*, vol. 2 pt. 2, pp. 85. 28—87. 14); Zeno in *Stoicorum Veterum Fragmenta* (ed. VON ARNIM) vol. I. 83.

[13] The kind of reasoning called for in the *Topics* is concerned with detailed investigation. As E. WEIL says quite well (La place de la logique dans la pensée aristotélicienne, Rev. de Met. et Morale 56, 1951, p. 295): investigation by the method of the topics is to subject the terms of a proposition, of philosophical theses, or of a particular *scientia* to the demanding investigation of substance, genus, species, accident etc. Or as BRUNSCHWIG (Aristote, Topiques p. xxix) indicates: method in the *Topics* is "d'élaborer une argumentation tendant à établir la proposition contradictoire de celle que soutient le répondant". Without question this is usually closely articulated argumentation developed through a series of steps. We may correctly assume that when Aristotle revised the *Topics* and introduced to it the methodology of syllogistic reasoning he intended topical inquiry to use the syllogism where possible. Owing to the nature of topical inquiry this would necessitate a series of inferences developed one from another. This is an assumption but the grounds for it are strong: a) in the *Rhetoric* syllogism is used only in its technical sense, b) consequently when Aristotle speaks of a difference between rhetorical and dialectical syllogism there is certainly no reason to conclude that the difference resides in the meaning of "syllogism", c) particularly is this so when his statements suggest quite strongly that the difference lies in the length of the inferential process. In a well reasoned statement WEIL (La place de la logique . . . p. 286 note) argues that the *Analytics* never replaced the *Topics* as a methodology for Aristotle as the very fact of the revision of the *Topics* with the introduction of the syllogism would confirm. He further comments (p. 302) that the true dialectician proceeds to his examination of a problem according to the rules of the syllogistic methodology ("le vrai dialecticien est celui qui procède à l'examen selon les règles de la technique syllogistique").

process leading to a conclusion. A moment's reflection on the nature of dialectical argument would recall that it is a detailed and analytic inquiry which
advances gradually from a set of initial hypotheses or statements through detailed reasoning to a tentative conclusion. In contrast to this the enthymeme
confines its demonstrative or probative statement to a concise and direct
form, and one which may be shortened. Indeed this difference would seem to
be more properly the point of the well-known distinction of Zeno between
dialectic (the closed fist) and rhetoric (the open hand): *"Zeno ... manu de-
monstrare solebat quid inter has artes interesset, nam cum compresserat digitos
pugnumque fecerat, dialecticam aiebat eiusmodi esse ; cum autem diduxerat et manum
dilataverat, palmae illius similem eloquentiam esse dicebat."* (Cicero, *Orat.* 32. 113).

Let us now consider the kind of statement permitted by the rhetorical syllogism. The syllogism as inference will differ with the character of its propositions or premises. If their modality is apodeictic they assert necessary relations, if problematic they affirm contingent or possible relationship. Obviously the character of knowledge achieved in the conclusion will differ. As
has been said rhetoric for Aristotle concerns itself mostly with problematic
statements and probable knowledge. Its object is to secure a position as far as
that can be done which will enable one to engage in intelligent, reasonable
and human action, or to confirm a position taken as rational and acceptable,
or simply to speculate on the acceptability or non-acceptability of a proposal.
These are all legitimate objects for discussion in the area of conditioned and
consequently probable human situations. In view of this contingency of the
subject-matter of rhetorical discourse (A 2, 57a 14—15) we might accept that
the enthymeme would be confined to problematic modal propositions and
would reason to probable conclusions.

There are, however, some observations of Aristotle which demand attention insofar as they extend the character of inference by enthymeme and consequently the nature of rhetorical discourse. Neither the observations nor
their consequences are formally developed by Aristotle. He assumes that
they are known from his other works (e. g. his comment at *A* 2, 57a 29 ff.).
At the same time they widen the horizon of rhetorical discourse and locate
his study of rhetoric in the context of the *Phaedrus*. They extend the *vis loquen-
di* of rhetoric to forms of discourse which could certainly include philosophical discourse and they indicate that for Aristotle rhetoric is the art of the *logos*
in all avenues of discourse (a more detailed discussion of the reason for this
is taken up in c. 4 following). They imply that for Aristotle, as for Plato, "the
art of rhetoric, viewed in its totality, would be a kind of *psychagogia* (i. e. in-
fluencing the whole person) by the use of language" *(Phaedrus* 261a 7—b 2)
in every area of concern to men, even that of philosophical discussion. This
interpretation is dictated by Aristotle's introduction of apodeictic modal
propositions into rhetorical discourse. With this material which Aristotle

calls *anagkaia* and *tekmerion* (*A* 2, 57a 22—b 25) rhetoric is moved from the realm of probable statement and knowledge to knowledge which Aristotle specifically designates more strictly as philosophical knowledge: the knowledge that a thing cannot be other than it is *(An. Post.* 88b 30—32; 71b 10—12). Of course for Aristotle philosophic knowledge in its full sense is not simply knowledge (as we have it here) of the unconditioned. It is knowledge both of the fact and of its cause as well. The kind of necessity we have in the *anagkaia* of rhetoric will permit one to conclude only to knowledge of the fact in the conclusion, not to the reasoned fact. To this extent the rhetorical syllogism which infers from *anagkaia* differs from the scientific syllogism or strict *apodeixis* as seen, for example, in the *Posterior Analytics* 71b 9—24. Rhetorical inference while called *apodeixis* (e. g. *A* 1, 55a 5—7; *B* 25, 03a 10—15) does not carry with it the same demonstrative force of scientific *apodeixis*. And yet one cannot overlook the fact that by this necessary subject-matter Aristotle has drawn rhetoric within the orbit of what is more properly philosophic discourse. This fact was recognized by Stephanus in his commentary on *A* 2, 57a 22 ff. where he speaks of this as another instance of what he calls "the communion of philosophy and rhetoric" *(Commentaria Graeca* vol. 21, p. 263. 5—10). Aristotle gives rhetoric the right to certain as well as probable knowledge, a right claimed at least by Isocrates in his theory of rhetoric and often exercised by Plato in his dialogues. This extension of rhetoric beyond the area of the contingent and the probable with which it is generally identified should not be surprising. Aside from the fact that there is the initial correlation between rhetoric and dialectic (the methodology of inquiry) there are throughout the *Rhetoric* a number of cross-references to what Aristotle calls his work on dialectic, analytics, ethics. He gives the justification for such reference fairly early at *A* 1, 55a 14—18 where he remarks that the reality (τὸ ἀληθές) which is ordinarily the concern of philosophical speculation is the legitimate object of rhetorical discourse just as the faculty (the intellect) which directs itself upon this object is the same in each discipline. Later at *A* 4, 59b 8—12 he states: "Indeed what we have had occasion to declare previously is true: that rhetoric is composed of the science *(episteme)* of analytics, of the science of politics relative to ethics, and is partly like to dialectic and sophistic"[14].

---

[14] The word "analytics" causes concern to the commentators here. Yet the manuscript tradition is for the word and there is no conceivable reason at this particular place in the text for any copier or editor to insert such a word. In most cases where the word is cited the references are to forms of reasoning or the formal logic of the *Prior Analytics*. When there is discussion, however, of the apodeictic modality of propositions the reference would be to the material logic of the *Posterior Analytics*. The discussion of *anagkaia* and *tekmeria* involves sources for propositions which are properly the subject of the *Posterior Analytics*. While commentators refer citations such as *A* 2, 57a 29 and *B* 25, 03a 12 to the *Prior Analytics* the matter is open to question. For there is no absolute way, when "analytics" is used, to know whether Aristotle meant the *Prior* or the *Posterior Analyt-*

The instrumentality of the enthymeme as the major form of rhetorical inference in Aristotle's theory of rhetoric underscores the transcendence of rhetoric as a *techne*. Aristotle speaks of this transcendence early in the treatise (*A* 1, 55b 8—9; *A* 2, 55b 31—34, 56a 30—33) in calling rhetoric a *dynamis* which stands apart from the *dynamis* of the specific disciplines. When this power is located we discover that it resides ultimately in the artistically effective control of language as it is used to speak to the other. This is intrinsic to rhetoric. As the instrument of rhetorical argumentation the enthymeme possesses a similar universality by reason of its form. By reason of the matter which it may legitimately organize into inference it is free to use the varied sources of knowledge wherein man speaks to man. This is simply to say that while we must acknowledge that the formal and primary denotation of rhetoric and rhetorical argumentation is discourse directed toward effecting judgment on open questions we cannot think that this primary objective confines its effort exclusively to the area of practical reasoning as opposed to speculative reasoning, or to the area of the problematic as opposed to the certain — at least this appears to be the firm implication of statements such as those at *A* 1, 55b 8—9; *A* 2, 55b 25—26; 31—33[15]. Where judgment is the final objective, even judgment directed toward action, every facet of human knowledge which makes judgment possible is legitimate material for discourse. This can, and frequently will, mean certain as well as probable knowledge. When Aristotle in his analysis of rhetoric brought syllogistic reasoning into the realm of ordinary human discourse he utilized a vehicle which by its general character in his work assumes an effort at reasoning, and

---

ics. Usually when Aristotle wanted to make such a distinction he spoke of the *Prior* as "on the syllogism", "in the first" (cf. Waitz, Organon, p. 336, Ross, Aristotle's Prior and Posterior Analytics, p. 1). Without entering into the question there is the same problem with citations of the word "dialectics". It is not possible to assert that these are references only to the *Topics*. There are clear cases where the *Prior Analytics* must be understood, e. g. *A* 1, 55a 9 (certainly the *Topics* does not study the syllogism and it has nothing to do with strictly demonstrative syllogisms at *A* 1, 55a 13); *A* 2, 56a 36 (where Dionysius Halicarnassus *(Ep. ad Amm.* I. 730 ff.) citing this passage of the *Rhetoric* almost verbatim reads "analytics" for the text reading "dialectics"; for the text and context "analytics" makes much more sense); *B* 22, 96b 25—26 (where the reference can be both to the *Prior Analytics* 66b 4 ff. and the *Sophistici Elenchi* 168b 27 ff.). In general it could be said that Aristotle's correlation of rhetoric with dialectic, analytics, and ethics is not at all discordant with the statement made by "good *logos*" in the *Phaedrus* at 260d: "and I will make a boast: without me the man who knows truth will not master the art of persuading".

[15] Isocrates in the *Antidosis* 256 speaks of rhetoric as the faculty "whereby we struggle with subjects open to dispute and examine matters which are unknown to us". Intelligent decision requires understanding first and the Aristotelian approach to rhetoric is that of a methodology to reach understanding. The challenge implicit in Aristotle's analysis of rhetoric is to the person, for the person must resolve through decision the inner tension generated by the problematic. Rhetorical discourse is simply the method to place before him the means for making the decision as intelligently as possible.

consequently assumes an effort at rational discourse as opposed to sophistry. Furthermore in the manner in which he developed the methodology of the enthymeme in the *Rhetoric* he presented us with a more substantial answer to the problems raised by those who had discussed rhetoric. For the methodology of the enthymeme involves the range of human knowledge at man's disposal for intelligent discussion as well as the whole complex of human psychology.

It is interesting to note that in the study of the *Rhetoric* there is rarely any discussion of what Aristotle calls the apparent enthymeme (*B* 24) and the refutative enthymeme (*B* 25). The reticence is surprising since they represent another aspect of the enthymeme and an understanding of them would seem necessary to a full comprehension of enthymeme and enthymematic reasoning. In the present context they are particularly relevant and instructive for they confirm the three points just mentioned in the discussion of the enthymeme as the instrument of deductive reasoning: 1) the fact that rhetoric is concerned with truth, 2) the structural form of the enthymeme, and, 3) the character of its subject-matter. For Aristotle's critique in these chapters of the apparent and refutative enthymeme assumes that it is an ordinary syllogism of three propositions in which the premises correctly enunciate reality as it can be known in what is generally a conditioned human situation. Aristotle gives the larger part of his attention to the apparent enthymeme, and it is well to understand the intent of his discussion.

We can locate this fairly well if we recall his comment (*A* 1, 55a 29—33) that rhetoric must be able to contend with false argumentation, or his words in the *Sophistici Elenchi* (165a 24—27): "To employ a single point of comparison: it is the task of the one who has knowledge to speak the truth with respect to each subject in which he is learned and to be able to expose the individual who uses false reasoning."

Assuredly Aristotle's concern with false reasoning is not with deception as a constructive element in the art of rhetoric. On the contrary its purpose is to defend the *logos* against misleading and incorrect argument. His discussion of the apparent enthymeme allows no doubt that Aristotle viewed the rhetorical syllogism as inference that is valid and genuine both in its formal structure and material content. For the ground on which his critique of the apparent enthymeme rests is that it is false inference either in form or content. Thus it is clear that rhetorical discourse directs itself, within the limits usually imposed upon it, to the exposition of the true. What is wrong with the apparent enthymeme is that somewhere it is involved with a misrepresentation of reality as it is, and as it can be known. Aristotle's sense of the inadequacy of the fact that there is no name for the false *rhetor* and false rhetoric (*A* 1, 55b 17—21) is sharply pointed here. His argument in his presentation of the apparent enthymeme implies that there is a false rhetoric and that it is grounded in fallacious argumentation, in the failure or the refusal to present the truth as it can be known in a given situation[16].

From all that Aristotle has said of inference by syllogism in the *Analytics* apparent enthymeme which leads to error will be false inference either formally or materially or both. This is to say that an apparent enthymeme will be deficient either in its form as a syllogism in one of the three figures of syllogism, or in the content of the statements it makes in its premises. One cannot argue that what makes an enthymeme "apparent" is that it only yields probable knowledge. The major burden of rhetorical argumentation, as Aristotle recognizes, consists in reasoning to probable conclusions from sources which give probable statements. The very same situation exists in the *Sophistici Elenchi* whose relation to the rest of the *Topics* is often considered parallel to the relation of our chapter 24 on apparent enthymeme to the rest of the *Rhetoric*[17]. No one obviously would deny that the basis of the dialectical syllogism is to reason from probabilities to probable conclusions. Consequently when Aristotle discourses on apparent dialectical syllogisms in the *Sophistici Elenchi* he certainly does not find their falsity in the fact that they infer the probable. The only foundation for their "apparent" syllogistic character would be that either they are not proper syllogisms, or do not reason from the truly probable. In the light of everything he has said in the *Rhetoric* up to chapter 24 the same should be true for the apparent enthymeme. If chapter 24 makes any contribution to our understanding it should reveal that apparent enthymemes fail either in correct syllogistic form, or in reasoning from the apparently (but not truly) probable, or in both. In each instance the apparent enthymeme does not validly demonstrate even probable knowledge but merely gives the appearance of demonstrating: φαίνεσθαι δεικνύναι (*A* 2, 56a 36).

It has been said that Aristotle would not consider formal fallacy since it would be so transparent. Yet when we turn to the *Topics* (100b 23—101a 4) we find him distinguishing inference which is false in two ways: (a) inference which is formally false: an *apparent syllogism* from probable or apparently probable premises (from 101a 3—4 an "apparent syllogism" is not a syllo-

---

[16] Aristotle faced the same problem in the *Topics*. The technique of the sophist and the dialectician can no more be separated than that of the sophist (false rhetor) and the rhetorician: the technique in each instance is the same. Because of the introduction of eristic into legitimate dialectics in the *Topics* scholars have drawn the same conclusion that they have made with regard to the *Rhetoric*, i. e. that both methodologies are studies in sophistical argumentation. This reveals a failure to comprehend the character of both disciplines as *technai* and to understand that both the true dialectician and rhetorician, from Aristotle's statements, want (a) as their starting point, propositions truly held by men, and, (b) as their goal, the acquisition of truth in a given problem. Neither methodology is a game. The *Topics* offer a method to move discursively toward the true, *Rhetoric* a method for the effective communication of the true as it can be apprehended.

[17] In the light of *A* 2, 56a 34—b 2 the parallelism spoken of would seem well founded.

gism since it appears to reason but does not reason), and, (b) the syllogism which is materially false: a syllogism from apparent but not true probabilities. This distinction is just as clearly made at 165b 7—8.

In terms of this distinction, then, an apparent enthymeme is not an enthymeme which concludes to probable knowledge, but rather an enthymeme which is defective to the extent that it will not conclude to a statement of any kind, not even probable, save one which is false. When we turn to the *Rhetoric* (*B* 24) and study the sources from which the apparent enthymeme is derived we find that the nine topics given as the sources confirm this distinction insofar as they are sources which occasion either formal or material fallacy[18]. These topics present sources which cause either invalid form or fallacy in the statement of the premises[19]. In the *Sophistici Elenchi* (165b 23 ff.) these two general classes of false reasoning are called *in dictione* and *extra dictionem*[20]. While Aristotle explicitly mentions only one of them *(in dictione)* in the *Rhetoric* a comparison of our passage in the *Rhetoric* with that of the *Sophistici Elenchi* indicates that he is speaking about both. A glance at the topics in the *Rhetoric* shows that topics V, VI, VII effect a false statement in one of the premises and therefore an inference which is materially false. The other topics are connected with form: topics Ib, II, VIII, IX give an inference which is formally invalid while topics Ia and III yield no inference at all.

One of the sources for apparent enthymeme, topic IV fallacy of *semeion*, has been omitted and the reason for this should be obvious. The whole burden of the *Rhetoric* to this point is that one of the sources for valid enthymeme is *semeion*. A ready but somewhat superficial solution to this apparent contradiction would be to suggest that Aristotle is speaking here at *B* 24, 01b 9 ff. of those *semeia* which are the *semeia anonyma*: non-necessary signs. The use of the word ἀσυλλόγιστον at b10, 13 might seem to strengthen this suggestion when we recall the use of the same word at *A* 2, 57b 14 and 24 in reference to these same *semeia anonyma*. Since Aristotle never challenges the *tekmerion*, or necessary sign, we could then argue that these *semeia anonyma* which are contingent and non-necessary will never give certain knowledge

---

[18] The numbering is that of ROEMER's text. In view of all that has been said it is difficult to understand how MAIER's statement (Die Syllogistik II. 2, p. 493, also note 1) that the *rhetor* may legitimately use the apparent enthymeme can be right.

[19] In this respect the topics for the apparent enthymeme are quite similar to the particular and general topics for the valid enthymeme; we discover that they offer sources for the content of the premises or for the form of syllogistic inference.

[20] WAITZ (Organon), sees the distinction and expresses it this way: "Vitia quae in redarguendo admittuntur aut in dictione sunt . . . aut non in dictione . . . Alterum vitium positum est in prava verborum interpretatione (Wortverdrehung), alterum in falsa argumentatione (Schlußfehler)." The difficulty with this interpretation, however, is that it seems rather clear that what he calls *in dictione* fallacy is really the fallacy that attacks valid form (Schlußfehler), while his *non in dictione* fallacy is one that attacks the character of the statement in the premises.

and can only be used as the source of probable knowledge. In this respect one might consider them false and misleading. The only difficulty with this interpretation should be fairly obvious from what has been said: the task of rhetoric by and large is grounded for Aristotle in reasoning to probable conclusions. He has no problem about the validity of the probable as one of the sources of knowledge. Therefore he cannot be discarding non-necessary signs here as sources of valid enthymemes because of their reasoning to probable knowledge[21]. If he is calling enthymemes derived from *semeia anonyma* apparent enthymemes (and as he says at *B* 24, 00b 37 "apparent" means not an enthymeme but only with the appearance of being an enthymeme) we have the same kind of nonsensical statement which is wrongly urged against his presumably contradictory statements in the first chapter of Book *A* on *pathos* and *ethos*. The problem is further complicated by the fact that these comments at *B* 24, 01b 9 ff. are not passing observations. He makes similar statements on *semeia anonyma* in the *Prior Analytics* 70a 3 ff. and the *Sophistici Elenchi* 167b 8 f.

What, then, can Aristotle mean by these comments on sign at *A* 2, 57b 10—25; *B* 24, 01b 9—15; *B* 25, 03a 3—6; *An. Pr.* 70a 3—38; *SE* 167b 8—11? While a number of these passages speak of *semeia* without specification there is no need, as has been said, to complicate the problem since Aristotle accepts the validity of inference by necessary sign which he calls *tekmerion*. The passages question the validity of inference by non-necessary sign, the *semeion anonymon*. Aristotle gives the inescapable impression that any inferences from *semeia anonyma* are invalid and so false. He bases their falseness on the fact that the *semeia anonyma* can only be used in the second or third figure syllogism and used only in a way which gives a formally invalid inference[22]. His examples make this clear, e. g. *A* 2, 57b 19 ff. for the second figure (Everyone with fever breathes rapidly, This man breathes rapidly, This man is with fever); *A* 2, 57b 11 ff. for the third figure (Socrates is wise, Socrates is just, The wise are just). Obviously sign enthymemes developed in this way will be formally invalid. In his second figure example Aristotle vio-

---

[21] In a passage at *Sophistici Elenchi* 167b 8—11 Aristotle states that in rhetoric signs involve the fallacy of consequent. WAITZ (Organon), in a note s. 167b 8, appears to accept this and to see the opposition in b 8—13 between rhetoric (which seeks verisimilitude) and analytics (which seeks truth). One cannot conclude from Aristotle's statement here that reasoning from sign is *in se* fallacious. To conclude correctly to the probable (even to verisimilitude), as rhetoric frequently does, is not the same as concluding to what is false.

[22] In this respect it is noted again that Aristotle's critique in all passages assumes that the enthymeme is like the syllogism in structure, i. e. two premises and a conclusion. W. HAMILTON (Lectures on Metaphysics and Logic, Boston 1867) is still to the point (p. 276): "I shall therefore . . . show that . . . the restriction of the enthymeme to a syllogism of one suppressed premise cannot be competently maintained". He goes on to argue (pp. 276—281) correctly that neither the *Organon* nor the *Rhetoric* gives any textual support for this common understanding of the enthymeme.

lates a basic law of his syllogism (a distributed middle term), and in his third figure example he concludes to a statement not warranted by the premises. Indeed if Aristotle had drawn the correct conclusion in the third figure: Some wise men are just, the *semeion* argument is not only valid but helpful for it does enable us to establish a proposition that can be of assistance in developing a thesis.

Here, then, is the difficulty. Aristotle in his statements on *semeia anonyma* appears to say that enthymemes drawn from them will be necessarily invalid formally. If this is so then enthymemes from *semeia anonyma* would be "apparent enthymemes" and we do have a substantial contradiction.

In opposition to this we must acknowledge the following. Aristotle tells us in the *Rhetoric* that sign — without any qualifications — is a source for enthymematic reasoning (*A* 2, 57a 30—33); and we have no reason to think that the reasoning is any less valid than that from *eikos* also mentioned here as a source. Almost by way of confirming this he uses a *semeion anonymon* in a valid inference in the *Prior Analytics*, 70a 25 ff. This sign has the same intrinsic value as that used invalidly at 70a 20 ff. The difference is simply that at 70a 25 ff. he uses *semeion* in the first figure syllogism and makes a formally valid inference. If this is so *semeia anonyma* enthymemes do not of themselves necessarily implicate formally invalid inference. Stephanus in his discussion of sign argument (*Commentaria Graeca* vol. 21, pp. 264 ff.) would agree. Writing on Aristotle's statements on sign at *A* 1, 57b 1 ff. he maintains that the *semeia* will yield a valid inference if they are formally and materially valid. By way of confirmation he notes that commentators take the *semeion anonymon* enthymeme on quick-breathing (which Aristotle has placed in the second figure and in a formally invalid inference) and give it valid form by placing it in the first figure. When we turn to Aristotle's remarks on fallacy in sign arguments at our passage in the *Rhetoric B* 24, 01b 12—15 there is further difficulty. His example does not illustrate formal fallacy which is apparently the point of all his strictures against *semeia anonyma* enthymemes. The example he gives on Dionysius is in fact involved in a material not a formal fallacy. The major is a false statement. It is only "apparently" probable, not truly probable, that "every bad man is a thief". There is no ground for thinking that "badness" is in any way a sign which leads to the predicate "thief". This sign argument is materially false and this was recognized by the commentator Anonymus (*Commentaria Graeca* vol. 21, p. 151) who says quite correctly that there is no syllogism here "because the major premise is false", even though the inference is in valid form. This evidence that *semeion* does not of itself involve invalid inference is strengthened by two other statements of Aristotle in the *Prior Analytics*. At 70a 6—7 he explains *semeion* as "that which by its nature tends to be a demonstrative premise that is either necessary or generally accepted". Now a πρότασις ἀποδεικτική as ordinarily used by

Aristotle even with the qualification here of ἔνδοξος means one that establishes a solidly firm relation between subject and predicate. And as BONITZ says of the phrase βούλεται εἶναι (which accordingly I have translated: "by its nature tends to be") "significatur quo quid per naturam suam tendit". Shortly later at 70a 37—38 Aristotle remarks "in all *semeia* truth is present". Both the text and context of the chapter make it clear that the kind of truth he has in mind here is truth which results from inference by syllogism. To interpret the phrase in a restrictive sense, e. g. "there is truth in *semeia*" is gratuitous, if indeed meaningful.

It certainly does not appear, then, that enthymemes from *semeia anonyma* are of themselves invalid. The most extreme judgment which Aristotle's statements would warrant would be that *semeia anonyma* enthymemes *may not* be, by the very fact that they are *semeia anonyma*, intrinsically valid for probable argumentation. But we certainly cannot say what his comments here (*B* 24, 01b 9—15) and in the other passages seem to imply, namely, that such enthymemes *are intrinsically invalid* for probable argumentation. Aristotle's analysis of sign inference in the *Rhetoric*, *Analytics* and *Sophistici Elenchi* appears to labor under the same kind of incompleteness of statement which Ross notes in some detail (pp. 491—495 of his commentary on the *Analytics)* for the analysis of counter-argumentation in chapter 26 of the *Analytics* which immediately precedes our c. 27 on sign-inference. As a further indication of this possible incompleteness and uncertainty we may point to the somewhat confusing comments in the *Sophistici Elenchi* and our passage in the *Rhetoric* specifically *B* 24, 01b 9—15 and 20—30. The *Rhetoric* mentions the fallacy from sign and the fallacy from consequents as two distinct and separate fallacies with their own examples. In the *Sophistici Elenchi* there is no mention of fallacy from sign; fallacy from consequents is discussed. We are told further that fallacy from sign is the same as the fallacy from consequents, e. g. "in the *Rhetoric* demonstrations from sign are from consequents" (167b 8—11). Then to make the problem more confusing the example used to illustrate sign fallacy (167b 10—11) is the example used in the *Rhetoric* to illustrate the fallacy from consequents.

We would have to admit, however, when we turn to the statement on the apparent enthymeme in the *Rhetoric* that the results for the nature of the enthymeme far outweigh the inadequacies of the explanation of fallacy from sign. In the criticism of the enthymeme which is only apparent and not a true enthymeme we acquire a firm and clear illustration of the form and character of enthymematic reasoning. Many aspects of the enthymeme, which up to this point in his treatise has been presented positively, are confirmed by his critique of the apparent enthymeme. We are also put in possession once again of Aristotle's conviction that the object of rhetorical discourse is truth, a theme he sounded in the opening chapter, *A* 1, 55a 19—b 24.

His brief study of refutation (*B* 25, 02a 29—b 13) restates both of these ideas. It concentrates almost exclusively upon the enthymeme and deductive reasoning (in which he assumes at all times a syllogism of two premises and a conclusion). The study, however, also incorporates the other mode of demonstration, induction. The statement on refutation is fairly simple and explicit. When of necessity we go behind some of the comments in an effort to understand them more fully we must turn to the *Prior Analytics* and the *Sophistici Elenchi*. Once again we discover an unclearness which characterized his words on the apparent enthymeme from *semeion*.

Refutation is called λύσις in the *Rhetoric* and it is described in the *Sophistici Elenchi* 176b 29—30 as "the exposure of false reasoning" (see also *Topics* 160b 33—35). We are told in the *Rhetoric* that it works either by counter-syllogism or by a specific objection against one of the premises or the conclusion. At once it is clear that the methodology of demonstration (deduction-induction) comes into play in refutation. For we refute either by counter-inference or by instancing one or more facts contrary to a statement made. The first method is the refutative enthymeme. It is clearly not some special "kind" of enthymeme. Aristotle tells us (*B* 25, 02a 32—33) that it argues from the same *topoi* as the demonstrative enthymeme, and at *B* 22, 96b 23—28 we learn that it bears the same relation to the demonstrative enthymeme as *elenchos* does to the dialectical syllogism[23]. Indeed he calls the refutative enthymeme the elenchic enthymeme (*B* 22, 96b 25) and it is more than clear from his comments (*B* 22, 96b 26—28) that what he said of *elenchos* and syllogism in the *Sophistici Elenchi* (164b 27—165a 3) is strictly referable to the deictic and elenchic enthymeme. As *elenchos* and the dialectical syllogism are both syllogisms, one destructive, the other constructive, so are the elenchic and deictic enthymemes both enthymemes. Any difference between them resides solely in the fact that the elenchic enthymeme (just as *elenchos* itself) is inference directed to disprove the conclusion reached by the deictic enthymeme it is refuting. Indeed this explanation is precisely that which Aristotle himself gives in a more explicit manner at *B* 26, 03a 25—31. At *Γ* 17, 18b 2—6 ff., the one other place in which he speaks of the refutative enthymeme, he repeats once again that the refutative enthymeme does not differ essentially from the demonstrative enthymeme. In calling our attention to

---

[23] Cope (Commentary II p. 332) experiences some difficulty in reconciling *B* 22, 96b 23—28 with our passage at *B* 25, 02a 31 ff. However, εἴδη δύο at *B* 22, 96b 24 means no more than "kind" in a very broad use of the word such as we find it at *B* 20, 93a 28, *B* 20, 94a 18 when used of example and *B* 21, 94b 26 of maxim. Indeed our statement here at *B* 25, 02a 32—33 is most probably repeated at *B* 26, 03a 30 where αὐτοῖς contrary to the common interpretation of "arguments", "instruments" more likely stands for "the same topics". For in actual fact *topoi* is the subject around which the various problems posed in this c. 26 are resolved. The clause (*B* 26, 03a 30) should probably be translated: "for both (deictic and elenchic) enthymemes use the same topics".

the fact that refutative and demonstrative enthymemes use the same topics and that these topical sources are usually probabilities Aristotle throws light on an earlier passage often criticized, e.g. *A* 1, 55a 29—36. He readily acknowledges (*B* 25, 02a 33—35) that, since the sources for enthymeme are probabilities, opposing probabilities are often possible. Thus there is ample opportunity for anyone to make use of a refutative enthymeme which can infer a conclusion negating the conclusion of a demonstrative enthymeme. Of more significance, however, is the fact that *A* 1, 55a 29—36 now becomes rather obvious, although most opponents of his *Rhetoric* still succeed in misreading it. There, in what has been taken as an admission of the sophistry intrinsic to the rhetorical *techne* Aristotle said that rhetoric by its very nature can demonstrate opposites — not that it should as he attempts to make clear shortly later at *A* 1, 55b 10—24 since this is not its purpose. As can now be seen the general character of its subject-matter, the contingent and probable, rather readily lends itself to such action. To determine the character of rhetoric or anything else, however, from the misuse to which it is open is its own kind of sophistry as Socrates once remarked.

Refutative enthymeme is one kind of λύσις. The second type Aristotle calls *enstasis*. While a relatively coherent explanation of *enstasis* can be obtained from the *Rhetoric* it is not very satisfying and if we move out of the *Rhetoric* into the *Analytics*, the *Topics* and the *Sophistici Elenchi* where he also discusses the subject the picture becomes more confused. The cause of the problem is fairly simple: Aristotle has apparently given a perfectly valid double method of refutation: 1) a form of deduction in counter-syllogism (counter-enthymeme in rhetoric), and, 2) what can be called a form of induction in *enstasis*. When, however, we examine his statements on *enstasis* more closely the distinction disappears. Some refutation by *enstasis* appears to be syllogistic in character. In the *Rhetoric enstasis*, or objection as it may be called, is clearly denied a deductive character (*B* 25, 02a 31—32; *B* 26, 03a 31—32), and it appears to be what Aristotle had in mind by using the word itself: i. e. to block an opponent's way by denying one of his premises. We are told that it is not an enthymeme but rather a probable proposition which makes clear either that the opponent has made a false statement in one of the premises (ψεῦδός τι εἴληφεν), or that his reasoning is invalid (οὐ συλλελόγισται) (*B* 26, 03a 32—33). This explanation corresponds remarkably well with the definition of *enstasis* given in the *Analytics* at 69a 37: "an *enstasis* is a premise opposite to another premise". It also fits quite well the distinction between counter-enthymeme and objection that is assumed at *Γ* 17, 18b 5—22 and in the *Topics* 160a 39—b 13.

Turning from this to the four topics for *enstasis* which Aristotle names and illustrates (*B* 25, 02a 35—b13) one could still accept the propositional character of *enstasis* as an inductive instance against the statement in one of the premises or the conclusion of the demonstrative enthymeme — a process shown rather well at *Topics* 157a 34—157b 33. A more careful study, however, does cause problems. Despite the clear statement on *enstasis* in the *Analytics* passage just cited there is no question that Aristotle's explanation in what follows upon it is made in terms of his figures of the syllogism and clearly assumes that *enstasis* is syllogistic in character. "The kind of ἔνστασις dealt with in the present chapter [our passage, 69a 37 ff.] turns out to be a perfectly normal syllogism[24]." The propositional character of *enstasis* disappears and its distinctness from counter-syllogism is certainly clouded. This confusion is not removed by the passage in the *Topics* 160a 35—161a 15, in the *Sophistici Elenchi* 176b 29—177a 8, nor, in actual fact, in the *Rhetoric*. Superficially, as was said above, one could accept the *Rhetoric* passage as keeping the distinction between counter-syllogism and *enstasis* and COPE (Commentary, and Introduction) as well as SPENGEL (Commentary) so accept it. The fact is, however, that if we understand the first topical source (as it is usually interpreted) to mean "from the enthymematic statement itself", then one of the two examples which Aristotle gives of this kind of *enstasis* is in reality counter-enthymeme. Its value as refutation is otherwise not discernible. Aristotle says (*B* 25, 02a 37—b 4): "By the phrase 'from itself' I mean, for example, if the enthymeme should intend to demonstrate that love is good, *enstasis* can assume two forms: for one may assert as a general proposition that all privation (want) is evil, or, as a particular statement that Caunian love would not be used as a commonplace if there were not indeed evil loves". It is quite easy to understand how the specific instance of incestuous love seriously challenges the unqualified statement that "love is good". It does not appear, however, that there is any effective refutation to this statement in the counter-proposition "all privation is evil" unless this is developed as an enthymeme directed specifically against the enthymeme developed from "love is good". This kind of statement "all privation is evil", while it may convey meaning to members of the Academy and need no proof, is used as an example here of a kind of refutation, and it makes no sense as an isolated proposition in the example given. It does take on meaning as a stage in a counter-inference. In other words this kind of *enstasis* appears to be the kind of *enstasis* described in the *Analytics* (69a 37—b 37; Ross, Commentary, says that it "agrees exactly") which is in fact counter-syllogism.

Thus the distinction established between *enstasis* and counter-inference is undermined in this first topic for refutation by *enstasis*, just as it is in *Analytics* 69a 37—b 37. On the other hand it is interesting to note that the

---

[24] Ross, Aristotle's Prior and Posterior Analytics, p. 495; on pp. 491—494 he explains the difficulty well. E. POSTE, Aristotle on Fallacies, London 1866, pp. 144—147, 192—202 is also to the point.

distinction is preserved in the other three topics. These three topics for *en-stasis* refutation correlate exactly in name and order of presentation with the other types of *enstasis* at the end of the *Analytics* passage. There Aristotle only mentions the types in order to say that they should be given further consideration (69b 38—70a 2). He does not enter upon such a consideration but it is found in the *Rhetoric* for each of the topics. Topic I, on the other hand, is the kind of refutation which is discussed in the *Analytics* where we find that it is not only called *enstasis*, but in reality is a form of counter-syllogism.

There is, then, in Aristotle's account of refutation (λύσις), as in his account of fallacy from *semeion anonymon*, a degree of ambiguity and uncertainty. However, that which does emerge from his discussion of refutation is of more importance. This is the clear evidence that for Aristotle the methodology of deductive and inductive inference is the root of all rhetorical argumentation, even refutation. At the very beginning of his study Aristotle indicated that his study of rhetoric was grounded in the idea that the *logos* was a peculiar property of man and consequently something which merited study and structure (*A* 1, 55a 38—b 2). His structure was announced quite early when he stated that rhetoric could be submitted to method (*A* 1, 54a 4—8) and that the methodology would revolve about the *pisteis* (*A* 1, 54a 13). Eventually this methodology assumed its dominant form in the process of deduction and induction, with the deductive process of the enthymeme receiving the larger part of his attention. His analysis of rhetoric developed around this central core: enthymeme and example incorporate the *entechnic* method and enable one to give form to the sources in the effort to communicate knowledge and conviction. Everything proper to the art in the first two books pivots on this axis and when we arrive at the conclusion of the second book and the defense of the *logos* we discover that the deductive and inductive process is still at work.

CHAPTER IV

THE SOURCES OF RHETORICAL ARGUMENTATION
BY ENTHYMEME

Once the general form of the enthymeme as the syllogism of rhetoric is determined the next question which arises is the kind of subject-matter which is used by the rhetorical syllogisms in the development of an argument. For the quality, or the modality, of the subject-matter used in the premises will control the kind of knowledge attained in the conclusion. Aristotle states that the sources for argument by enthymeme are the *eikota* (probabilities) and *semeia* (*A* 2, 57a 32—3) and then proceeds to specify *semeia* into non-necessary signs *(semeia anonyma)* and necessary signs *(tekmeria)* (*A* 2, 57b 3—5). Somewhat later (*B* 25, 02b 13—25) he appears to introduce another source: example. In as far as this appears to be in direct opposition to his statement that the two instruments of rhetorical demonstration are enthymeme for deduction and example for induction this remark at *B* 25 should be clarified before we move on to a discussion of the *eikota* and *semeia*. A substantial question is raised by this statement of Aristotle at *B* 25, 02b 13—14: does *paradeigma* disappear as an independent and coordinate method of rhetorical demonstration; if not, what is the possible meaning of Aristotle's statement? Ross in his commentary on the *Prior and Posterior Analytics* (pp. 499—500) offers a solution which is not adequate to the statements in the *Rhetoric*[1].

In reply, then, to the question posed: *paradeigma* does not cease to be a coordinate instrument with enthymeme for rhetorical demonstration; it remains one of the two *koinai pisteis*. The point which Aristotle is making is a rather simple one[2]. Example may be a source of enthymeme insofar as example (or examples, *B* 25, 02b 17) can give you a probable universal principle or truth from which you may then reason by the use of enthymeme to a particular conclusion. Example gives the universal by that "flash of insight by which we pass from knowledge of a particular fact to direct knowledge of

---

[1] Ross is speaking of the *Rhetoric* passage; aside from the fact that he does not explain how *paradeigma* can be a source for the enthymeme, his comment on "types of enthymeme" could be confusing. It appears more correct to speak of ἐνθύμημα as the type just as φιλοσόφημα etc. (*T.* 162a 15 ff.) might be called types of syllogism. Any difference in enthymemes would then be found in the modality of the premises, an explanation which Ross would admit.

[2] This is not to minimize the problem which SPENGEL sees (commentary s. 1402b 13) although I do not know what justification he has for his statement: "Nunc et παράδειγμα in numero enthymematum referre licet." COPE seems somewhat confused in his paraphrase as far as I understand him by διὰ παραδείγματος. If he means to correlate it with διὰ τεκμηρίου (b19) and διὰ σημείων (b21) which he interprets correctly his English translation does not reveal it.

the corresponding principle[3]." It is an operation of the mind in which the mind transcends sense experience, even one instance of it, and perceives the universal inherent in the terms and their necessary connection. In actual fact a moment's reflection will show that in using an example some transition to the universal has already been made by the mind if the mind is to discern any likeness or relevance of the example in the first place. Thus in our passage example is nothing but the ground for educing a general proposition or principle. This proposition is then employed independently as a premise in the enthymeme. As a source of enthymeme example is no more a "part of" enthymeme than induction is a "part of" syllogism in such a statement as *An. Post.* 81a 40—b9[4]: "demonstration is from universals, induction from particulars; but it is impossible to perceive universals without induction."

Returning, then, to the sources originally given by Aristotle, the *eikota* and *semeia*, the first task is to discover what difference, if any, exists between them. From the *Rhetoric* there is no doubt that in Aristotle's mind there is a difference in both concepts. And he expresses this with a brief and pointed comment in *An. Pr.* 70a 2—3: "*eikos* and *semeion* are not the same thing." The precise nature of the difference is not perhaps as sharp as one could wish, yet it is not as elusive as HAVET makes it: "Tout le second chapitre du premier livre est très-pénible à déchiffrer. Le distinction de l 'εἶκος, du σημεῖον, du τεκμήριον, n' est pas plus nette que celle du syllogisme et de l' enthymème. Je ne pourrais le faire bien voir qu' en le traduisant; mais à quoi bon traduire des choses aussi peu satisfaisantes[5]." Those who attempt a distinction between the two sources develop their distinction on the kind of knowledge obtained when these sources are used in the rhetorical syllogism. Thus for some[6] an enthymeme built upon *eikota* will give what is called the "ratio essendi" of the fact stated in the conclusion, that is to say the explanation why this conclusion actually is. The premises, in other words contain the reasons for the fact stated in the conclusion. A *semeion*-enthymeme, on the other hand, presents the "ratio cognoscendi" of the fact stated in the conclusion, namely, the grounds on which one can acknowledge that the conclusion ex-

---

[3] Ross, op. cit., p. 50; a good illustration of my statement is in Anonymus commenting on *B* 25, 03a 5 *(Commentaria Graeca*, vol. 21, p. 155. 29 ff.) in which he takes an example of Aristotle and shows how a syllogism may be formed from the example. I would not agree with VATER, Animadversiones, p. 17, and I find his objection answered at *Prior Analytics* 68b 38. SOLMSEN, Die Entwicklung, p. 23, n. 4 would agree on the process.

[4] See also *Nicomachean Ethics* 1139b 27—28; Ross, op. cit., commentary on *Prior Analytics* 68b 27—28. MARX' inability to see this enables him to interpret *B* 25, 02b 14 ff. as a reversion to Isocratean teaching and so further proof of confusion in the editing of the *Rhetoric* ("Aristoteles' Rhetorik", p. 323).   [5] E. HAVET, op. cit., p. 57.

[6] J. H. McBURNEY in "The Place of the Enthymeme in Rhetorical Theory", Speech Monographs 3, 1936, pp. 49—74; E. MADDEN, The Enthymeme: Crossroads of Logic, Rhetoric, and Metaphysics, The Philosophical Review 51, 1952, pp. 368—376.

ists without, however, being able to explain the reason why the conclusion as stated is valid. One could question the distinction on the ground that an *eikos*-enthymeme might very well give the "ratio cognoscendi" of the fact for there does not appear to be anything intrinsic to the logic of the *eikos*-enthymeme which would justify the absoluteness of the distinction. But the most immediate difficulty with this explanation is that one would wish to know what difference exists between non-necessary *semeion*-enthymemes and necessary *semeion*-enthymemes. Ross in his commentary on the *Prior Analytics*[7] gives his attention to all three sources and distinguishes them in this way: 1) enthymemes from non-necessary signs are syllogistically invalid, 2) those from *eikota* argue merely from probability, 3) enthymemes from necessary *semeia* are syllogistically valid but may not give "the reason for the fact stated in the conclusion but only a symptom from which it can be inferred." There are difficulties with this proposal. The statement about non-necessary sign enthymemes is open to question as we have already seen in the discussion of the apparent enthymeme. Moreover from the nature of non-necessary signs valid syllogistic inference from them is clearly as much an inference from probability as inference from *eikota*. As far as necessary signs are concerned one cannot dispute the statement that they will only permit an inference that is absolutely secure on the fact reached in the conclusion, but not the reasoned fact. If Aristotle, however, does differentiate between these three sources for rhetorical reasoning he must see some distinction in the kind of argumentation they allow. Further study of *eikos*, *semeion anonymon* and *tekmerion* leads one to conclude that the difference resides in the certitude with which one can affirm one's conclusions from each source. As a general guide it can be said that enthymemes developed from *eikota* and *semeia anonyma* represent the kind of reasoning which can be found in Aristotelian dialectics, while those from *tekmeria* present more the character of scientific reasoning as found in his *Analytics*. Once again we have the rhetorical *pragmateia* bringing together the field of probable and certain knowledge. From all that has been said thus far this should not be unexpected[8].

---

[7] Op. cit., pp. 499– 500; see also S. SIMONSON, A Definitive Note on the Enthymeme, AJP 66, 1945, p. 303.

[8] C. RITTER, Platon II, Munich 1923, p. 40 f. with certain qualifications of his opening phrases has pointed the thrust of Aristotelian rhetoric in his comments on the *Phaedrus*: "Nun ist es unmöglich, die Masse wissenschaftlich zu belehren und zur vollen Erkenntnis der Wahrheit zu führen; wissenschaftliche Gründe sind ihr nicht faßbar und so ist sie nur durch einen Schein der Wahrheit, die 'Wahrscheinlichkeit' bestimmbar. Eben darum kann sich die Philosophie nicht mit der Masse abgeben und hat neben ihr die Rhetorik einen wichtigen Platz. Sie soll die wissenschaftlichen Beweise, die sich gleichsam an einen abstrakten Verstand wenden, in der Weise umformen, daß sie auf die Anlagen, Stimmungen, zufälligen Erfahrungen des einzelnen, an die sich anknüpfen läßt, Rücksicht nimmt. Sie wäre dann eine Technik des erziehenden Unterrichts. Und gründen muß sie sich nicht bloß im allgemeinen auf Psychologie, sondern auf psychologische

In the *Rhetoric* (*A* 2, 57a 34—b 1) Aristotle defines *eikos* in this way: "that which generally happens, not 'generally' in any unlimited sense of the word; rather its extension includes all reality which can be other than it is, and in this area its relationship to that reality to which it is an *eikos* is like that of any universal to a particular." Expressed more directly we have this: with reference to any reality that has a number of possibilities an *eikos* is that possibility which usually happens. An example of such an *eikos* would be the statement that "parents love their children".

There are one or two things to be noted here. *Eikos* is not that which simply happens. In this sense it would apply without any qualification to sheer chance among other things, or to anything possible, for example to that aspect of the possible spoken of in *An. Pr.* 32b 10—11: the indeterminate[9]. Such an understanding of *eikos* leads to the absurdity criticized in *B* 24, 02a 8—16: the improbable is probable, because many improbable things happen. If the enthymeme as a syllogism is reasoned inference then its sources must be reasonable and rational. *Eikos* in the sense of the "indeterminate" is neither; and, if anything, it would be a source for sophistic reasoning as is indicated at *B* 24, 02a 16 ff. In the *Rhetoric eikos*, or the probable, possesses a note of stability and permanence. This stability is described well when Aristotle makes *eikos* a kind of universal with respect to individual probabilities (*A* 2, 57b 1). While this stability is not inherently necessary yet it is not subjective and extrinsic. It is intrinsic and objective since it is grounded in reality. This relative intrinsic necessity is aptly described in the *Nicomachean Ethics* 1112a 18—b 11. There Aristotle speaking of deliberation (which is, of course, the occasion of rhetorical discourse, e. g. *A* 2, 56b 37 ff.) tells us that deliberation involves things which follow certain general rules, things calculable with probability. Further at *Metaphysics* 1027a 20—21 he states that with respect to such a stabilized contingent (τὸ ὡς ἐπὶ τὸ πολύ) there can be knowledge: e. g. all *episteme* is of that which is always (τοῦ ἀεί) or of that which is for the most part (τοῦ ὡς ἐπὶ τὸ πολύ). In the *Prior Analytics* (32b 20 ff.) this is car-

---

Beobachtung der Individuen. So muß sie sich der Philosophie unterordnen und von ihr sich die Richtung und die allgemeinen Grundsätze vorschreiben lassen, die wichtiger sind als jene Einzelregeln rhetorischer Lehrbücher." Aside from the fact that Aristotle through the introduction of the syllogism into rhetoric has surely given the grounds for such a union of analytical and dialectical reasoning in the rhetorical *pragmateia*, it is time to recognize that far from being separate and unrelated methodologies the *Topics* and the *Analytics* are disciplines that are both necessary to each other and complement each other. This is well demonstrated by WEIL (La place de la logique . . . RMM 56, 1951, 283—315) who makes the rather telling point that if the *Analytics* replaced the *Topics* Theophrastus was clearly unaware of this move on the part of his teacher.

[9] At *An. Pr.* 32b 5—10 Aristotle puts forward an explanation of ἐνδέχεσθαι which aptly describes the situation in which *eikos* is legitimate: "that which generally happens but falls short of necessity . . . or in general what belongs to a thing naturally." COPE in his Introduction, p. 163 interprets the *Rhetoric* passage on *eikos* differently and in a way difficult to justify from the Greek text.

ried further and we learn that this kind of stable contingent can be used in a demonstrative syllogism.

In the *Rhetoric*, then, there is a clear emphasis placed upon *eikos* as something which is permanent and stable. The reason for the emphasis becomes manifest when one considers other Aristotelian statements such as those mentioned above: namely, that *eikos* offers ground for reasonable inference and can be known (cf. *EN* and *Met.* passages above). As such it can lead to further knowledge, and thus the rhetorical enthymeme which uses *eikos* as a source is a way to a knowledge which is both reasonable and wholly acceptable to the mind. In Aristotle that which is ὡς ἐπὶ τὸ πολύ leads one to seek both the universal and the cause which are the ultimate foundation of *episteme*. *Eikos* represents the kind of reality mentioned by Aristotle when speaking of the different kinds of knowledge in the *Posterior Analytics*. There are, we are told, things in the order of reality which "are true, and yet capable of being other than they are" (88b 32—33). These are the object of *doxa*, one of the states of mind which can know the true. *Doxa* can know the real and the true, not with scientific knowledge since it originates with that which is contingent, but nonetheless with knowledge since it is concerned with that which is and which possesses a certain stability[10]. The possibility of such knowledge is readily accepted in the *Prior Analytics* (70a 4 ff.): "that which men *know* (ἴσασιν) happens or does not happen, is, or is not, for the most part in this way, — that is an *eikos*." Aristotle illustrates this with an example of such an *eikos*: our knowledge that those who are resentful hate.

Since knowledge is possible with regard to this *eikos* we obtain through it the means whereby we may move to other knowledge in the same order. That is to say that we can have in *eikos* the basis of suasive and probable demonstration. As he says *(An. Post.* 87b 22 ff.): "every syllogism works through propositions which are either necessary, or, for the most part true; if necessary, the conclusion is necessary; if for the most part true, such, then,

---

[10] Ordinarily "knowledge" is a correct translation of ἐπιστήμη and it means a knowledge of the *ousia* which is knowledge that is certain, absolute, and of the universal. However the word "knowledge" is an analogous one for Aristotle and *episteme* as defined above would be the primary analogate. He also recognized other kinds of knowledge one of which is *doxa*, and admitted different degrees of knowing as the treatises on ethics, the topics, and rhetoric itself reveal. In Aristotle one knows the concrete reality of things but not with exactitude since the real can be incomplete or imperfect, or, as we have been saying, "for the most part so". This knowing is engaged with things that can be other than they are and thus for him *eikos* is a perfectly legitimate starting point of knowledge. Just as the word *episteme* is used analogously by Aristotle so, too, is *apodeixis*. Ordinarily it means strict scientific demonstration of which he speaks in the *Metaphysics*. In our own treatise the noun or adjective is frequently used in an analogous sense: *A* 1, 55a 5—7; *A* 2, 56a 3—4 with which compare *A* 8, 66a 8—10; *A* 2, 58a 1; *B* 20, 94a 9—10; *B* 22, 96a 34—b 11; *B* 24, 01b 7 ff. where there is an interesting nexus implied between enthymeme and *apodeixis*; *Γ* 17, 17b 21 ff.; *Γ* 17, 18a 5, 39—40.

is the conclusion." The enthymeme represents the latter kind of syllogism. As a matter of fact it is precisely in its use in such a demonstrative process that the analysis of *eikos* is carried further in the *Rhetoric*. In *B* 25, 02b 21 ff. we are told that because of the non-necessity of *eikos*-enthymemes they are always open to objection, since the very nature of *eikos* occasions this. However, the only kind of objection which invalidates such argumentation is not an objection which shows the conclusion as *not-necessary*, but one which proves that it is *not probable*.

With the nature of *eikos* thus determined by Aristotle it appears that we have a rational basis for the whole domain of probable argumentation such as we possess it in rhetoric. For in *eikos* whose content expresses that which is generally (but not necessarily) the truth one possesses grounds for reasoned inference from any particular *eikos* to what is quite probably (but not necessarily) the fact in any given situation. In *eikos* we have, or may formulate, a *protasis endoxos*, as *eikos* is called in the *Prior Analytics* at 70a 3. Such premises are then used in the rhetorical syllogism. *Eikos* expresses a reasonable and stable aspect of the real order and as a source for the rhetorical syllogism we find that the rhetorical *pragmateia* is built upon sound, though probable, reasoning and that *pistis* is underpinned by the real order.

In his analysis of *eikos* Aristotle validates probable truth and reasoning from probable sources: there is another way to apprehend that which is. It is not the way of first philosophy which works through absolute, unconditioned, and necessary principles to certain knowledge and certain truth. This second way works through premises *(eikota)* which may be false. But insofar as these premises express that which is generally true it is legitimate to conclude to the probability that, all being equal, such and such is the fact in this concrete instance. An inference from *eikos* does not conclude to an unconditioned truth; but it does present an eminently reasonable guaranty that the conclusion represents the objective fact.

There appears to be an important point here. This Aristotelian explanation of *eikos* seems to move against such Platonic criticism as would reject the validity of rhetoric on the grounds that the only knowledge is knowledge of the absolute and the unconditioned (e. g. *Rep.* 510e — 511d). Any knowledge derived from the world of sense data was neither knowledge nor a knowledge of the real. For Plato sense data can be incentives to knowledge. Aristotle accepts the world of sense experience as the world of the real. Indeed he specifies *eikos*, as we have seen, by this reality and in this he is opposed to Plato. For Aristotle the fact that something generally happens this way, or is this way, is genuine ground for the mind to think that such is the actual fact. In brief there is a foundation in the world of reality *(v. Rhetoric B* 25, 02b 15: ἢ ὄντων ἢ δοκούντων) which validates the mind thinking and knowing as it does. Plato specifies *eikos* differently. It appears to be more subjective than objective as we find it in the *Phaedrus* 272c; 259e; 260. *Eikos* is that which the generality of men think, or may think, and as such it carries persuasive force to the mind[11]. Aristotle's *eikos* and the knowledge which comes from it is rooted in the real order and it is this existential aspect of it which makes it a legitimate source for further knowledge. This character of *eikos* is further underlined by Aristotle when he indicates the kind of *eikota* to be used in rhetorical discourse: they will be determined by the *eide*, i. e. the special topics of the subject under discussion (*B* 1, 77b 18 ff.) and they will be *eikota* which are precisely determined and clearly accepted by men (*B* 22, 95b 31 ff.). Both qualifications simply re-state the fact that the *eikos* is so substantially and obviously grounded in the real order that the majority of men accept it as a totally acceptable representation of the truth.

The second source for argumentation by enthymeme is Aristotle's *semeion*, sign. What can be discovered about it does bear out Aristotle's comment in the *Analytics* that *eikos* and *semeion* are not the same. Indeed without turning to the *Analytics* there seems to be no question about a difference in the first mention of *eikos* and *semeion* in the *Rhetoric* at *A* 2, 57a 30—33, specifically the phrase at 57a 33: "consequently each of these *(eikos* and *semeion)* corresponds exactly to each of the aforementioned [i. e. contingent reality and necessary reality]." In this phrase *eikos* is obviously referred to in: τὰ δὲ πλεῖστα ὡς ἐπὶ τὸ πολύ (31—2) and *semeion* in: τὰ μὲν ἀναγκαῖα (31). The nature of this difference becomes clearer with a study of the statements on *semeion* in the *Rhetoric* and the *Analytics*. In the *Rhetoric* there is a description and a division

---

[11] In 272d 8—e 1 Plato makes *eikos* and the persuasive equal. It may be that this concept of *eikos* is not Plato's but an earlier view, see 273a; DUFOUR, Aristote Rhétorique Tome 1er, Paris 1932, p. 10 interprets it as Plato's attack on the theory of probability of Tisias and Corax. It may also be that we have here a criticism of the social relativism of some of the Sophists who accepted the popular concepts of justice, courage, etc. These concepts, while suasive, are of little value toward understanding since they cannot be submitted to critical evaluation. An instance of *eikos* as simply "plausibility" can be seen at *Phaedo* 92d. Since the passages cited do not misrepresent Plato's views on *eikos* I do not intend to become more involved than this with the place of the probable in Plato's thought. Certainly Plato cannot accept an *episteme* of the non-exact (thus the problem of becoming always remains troublesome). Aristotle, however, does admit that the reality of things is given by the senses and that the objects so known can be incomplete and imperfect; consequently he acknowledged that concrete knowing (which comes through the senses and forms the major part of man's knowing) is occupied with that which can be otherwise, or the probable. As for the character of these *eikota* in the *Rhetoric* perhaps the following should be noted here: *Eikota* (and *semeia*) for Aristotle are drawn from the particular topics. Aristotle does not usually formulate these topics as *eikota;* an example, however, of how it is done is found in Thucydides I. 121. 2 ff.: here Aristotle's particular topics on war and peace for the deliberative speaker (*A* 4, 59b 33—60a 5) are used by the Corinthians as *eikota* that they will be successful. (On *semeia* we find Aristotle at *A* 9, 66b 23—67a 5 using as the σημεῖα τῆς ἀρετῆς: actions of a good man, actions of a just man, etc.) One further point: while Aristotle does not usually formulate the topics as *eikota* or *semeia* he states explicitly at *A* 3, 59a 8 that the *eikota* and *semeia* are the rhetorical *protaseis.*

of *semeion* but the *Prior Analytics* (70a 7—9) offers a descriptive definition of the term: "Whenever by the fact that one thing exists something else exists, or by the fact of its coming-to-be something else has come-to-be prior to it or consequent upon it, the first is a sign of the other's becoming or existing." What we have here is a very definite and firm relationship between two realities in the order of existence which leads from the knowledge of one to a knowledge of the other. From what Aristotle says sign is a relationship between two realities which has its foundation in the nature of these realities and exists objectively as soon as one of the realities exists[12]. The relationship between sign and signate leads the mind from the known to the unknown because of this one to one correspondence. Aristotle's signs in the *Rhetoric* and elsewhere are usually natural signs, entities which involve in their being the being of something else. There is a real relation which has its ground in the *esse* of the sign. It is the relationship of formal causality: present in the sign is the knowability of the signate, or we can say that the signate is in the sign in another mode of existence *(in alio esse)*.

Owing to this relationship *semeion* for Aristotle possesses a stronger demonstrative force than *eikos*. This can be seen clearly in his discussion of *semeion* in the *Prior Analytics* 70a 11—b 6 by means of the three syllogistic figures; for the figures of the syllogism (prescinding from their effective probative power which is not the point here) by the very way in which Aristotle has constructed them implicate an internal necessity, *an intrinsic relationship*, between premises and conclusion. Further in his introduction to this passage he remarks that the whole thrust of *semeion* is to be a demonstrative premise, that is, a proposition which leads to more than a probable conclusion: σημεῖον δὲ βούλεται εἶναι πρότασις ἀποδεικτική (70a 6—7). It does not completely achieve this goal in every instance because of the fact that there are different kinds of sign. This difference is specified in the *Analytics* passage by the qualifying phrase: ἢ ἀναγκαία ἢ ἔνδοξος which corresponds to the distinction in the *Rhetoric* A 2, 57b 3—5 between the necessary *semeion* called τεκμήριον and the non-necessary *semeion* called σημεῖον ἀνώνυμον. The *tekmerion* contains within itself an element of necessity in relation to the signate (the πρότασις ἀποδεικτικὴ ἀναγκαία of the *Analytics* passage), whereas the *semeion anonymon* indicates the signate only with probability (πρότασις

---

[12] An understanding of the relationship, particularly a non-necessary relation, which is present between sign and signate may be found in the *Sophistici Elenchi* 167b 1—8 where Aristotle speaks of the nature of consequent and signs. The citations under the so-called περὶ σημείων in V. Rose, Aristoteles Pseudepigraphus, Lipsiae 1913 pp. 243 ff. indicate that placing the ground of sign in the realities themselves was in the Aristotelian tradition; related to this is R. A. Markus' comment in "St. Augustine on Signs", Phronesis 2, 1957, p. 61. Trendelenburg, Elementa Logices Aristoteleae III, Berlin 1845, p. 106 has a definition of Aristotelian sign: "externum est indicium, quod si ita rei est proprium ut ex nulla alia re existere potuerit, necessarium est; si aliis aeque accidat, dubium."

ἀποδεικτικὴ ἔνδοξος). Thus it is that we find the *Analytics* passage differentiating between the probative force of each sign by way of the middle term in each of the first three figures of the syllogism[13]. The point of the presentation in the *Analytics* would seem to be that *semeion* by its very nature, as opposed to the nature of *eikos*, has within itself a strong demonstrative power. Sign argues almost immediately and directly to signate. Whether or not this potency to demonstrate the signate will be realized is determined by the fact that not all *semeion* is the same. *Tekmerion* and sign *enthymeme* built upon it is apodeictic in the more strict sense of the word with respect to its signate. Such an *enthymeme* infers a necessary conclusion and cannot be refuted even though the conclusion states only the fact and not the reasoned fact (the reasoned fact is the conclusion of the fully apodeictic syllogism in Aristotle, *An. Post.* 75a 31—34). *Semeion anonymon*, on the other hand, and any sign *enthymeme* constructed on it can only give a probable conclusion with respect to its signate, that is, a very strong likelihood grounded in the experience of reality.

In either case, however, it is clear that in fact and in concept the *semeion* is something other than *eikos*. Because of the inner structure of the *semeion* it leads of and by itself to the probable or necessary truth of the thing signified, and so possesses a peculiar force for the demonstration of this signate. Anaximenes[14] presents us with a fairly clear notion of what Aristotle appears to have intended by *semeion:* "A sign is one thing of something else, not any one thing of any other thing, nor everything of everything [else]. Rather a sign is that which usually comes to be prior to, or simultaneously with, or subsequent to the thing [of which it is a sign]. That which has come to be is a sign not only of that which has come to be but also of that which has not, just as that which has not come to be is a sign not only of that which is not but also of that which is. One class of signs effects belief, the other effects knowledge; the best sign, however, is that which causes knowledge."

When we turn to the two kinds of *semeion* there is a noticeable difference in the kind of knowledge they lead to. The non-necessary *semeion* carries with it a general but non-constant relationship between itself and its signate. In an

---

[13] The distinction we find in the *Rhetoric* between *semeia* is recognized in the *Analytics*. In 70b 1—6 *semeion* is identified with the middle term in the second and third figure syllogisms and this is the *semeion anonymon* of *Rhetoric A* 2, 57b 10—25. *Tekmerion*, on the other hand, is identified in the same passage with the middle term in the first figure syllogism and this is the *tekmerion* of *Rhetoric A* 2, 57b 3—10. On this question see Ross, op. cit., p. 501; MAIER, Die Syllogistik, p. 482, n. 2; WAITZ, Organon, p. 538; SOLMSEN, Die Entwicklung, p. 22, n. 3 believes that we have in the *Rhetoric* an identity of *tekmerion* with the first figure syllogism, a point about which Aristotle was still doubtful in the *Analytics*. COPE, Introduction, p. 163 has a strange remark: "the distinctive name τεκμήριον does not occur in the *Analytics*".

[14] See M. FUHRMANN, Anaximenis Ars Rhetorica, Lipsiae 1966, c. 12, 1430b 30—38.

effort to demonstrate this relationship in the *Analytics* (70a 3 ff.) by identifying the non-necessary sign with the middle term in the second and third figure syllogism Aristotle is able to develop both the idea of relation and the idea of non-necessary relation. He does this specifically by using non-necessary sign in the second and third figure syllogism in a way whereby the correct form is violated with the result that the conclusion is invalid and refutable, e. g. *Rhet. A* 2, 57b 10—14 (for third figure); b18—21 (for second figure); see also *B* 24, 01b 9—15, *B* 25, 03a 2—5, *An. Pr.* 70a 16—24, 30—37.

Obviously the *semeion anonymon* is not strictly apodeictic and will only give a probable conclusion which is a probable truth. This is also true of *eikos*. The difference should be somewhat clear by now. The *semeion* (whether necessary or not) as used by Aristotle is radicated in the nature of the subject in such a way that it establishes a *relationship* of the subject to something else. *Eikos* is a general probability, again grounded in reality as man experiences and knows it; but the *eikos* exists in and by itself *without any formal relation* to an other. If one were to stress the similarity of *semeion anonymon* and *eikos* as sources of probable argumentation this might be said: the *semeion anonymon* could provide the basis for a general probable proposition (an *eikos*), as can be seen at *B* 6, 84a 5—7: 'those who continually speak of their accomplishments are boastful'. Indeed at *B* 19, 92b 25 f. Aristotle apparently makes a *semeion anonymon* into an *eikos*. This kind of proposition based on a *semeion anonymon* reminds one of Anaximenes' type of sign which creates the most persuasive opinion (τὸ δόξαν πιθανωτάτην ἐργαζόμενον). By and large one could agree that "where the general principle implied is not irrefragable [i. e. a *semeion anonymon* is used] but true for the most part, it is hard to distinguish the συλλογισμὸς ἐκ σημείου from a συλλογισμὸς ἐξ εἰκότος" (H. JOSEPH, An Introduction to Logic, Oxford 1916, p. 350, n. 1). If one compares *B* 25, 02b 15—31, a statement on the character of argument from *semeion* and *eikos* with *A* 5, 61a 28 (the expression here is used a number of times in *A* 4—14, e. g. *A* 9, 66b 23—24, *A* 9, 67b 26—35) one can see that τιμή at 61a 28 can be used as a *semeion anonymon* argument to demonstrate "one who does good", or changed into an *eikos:* "those who do good are held in honor".

The necessary sign, or *tekmerion*, is of interest because of the dimension it gives to the subject-matter of rhetorical discourse, restricted as this subject-matter usually is to the field of probability. The necessary sign indicates a constant and unchanging relationship between sign and signate such that evidence for the sign guarantees the fact of the signate. This *tekmerion* implies unchanging entities in the sense in which Aristotle speaks of *anagkaion* in *Metaphysics* 1026b 27—30, a statement which expresses the contrast set forth in the *Rhetoric* at *A* 2, 57a 30—b 10. This *tekmerion-anagkaion* relationship is underlined further by the identification of the *tekmerion* with the middle term of the first figure syllogism; this figure is the usual locus of the strictly scientific syllogism which uses necessary subject-matter and concludes to *episteme*[15]. As Aristotle says in the *Analytics* (70b 2 f.): τὸ γὰρ τεκμήριον τὸ εἰδέναι ποιοῦν φασὶν εἶναι, which recalls Anaximenes' comment on sign: κάλλιστον δὲ τὸ εἰδέναι ποιοῦν. The *Analytics* passage is picked up at *Rhetoric A 2*, 57b 8 where we are told that with a *tekmerion* men assume that their conclusion is δεδειγμένον καὶ πεπαρασμένον which Anonymus explains by the words τετελειωμένον διὰ προτάσεων ἀκριβῶν καὶ ἀληθῶν, a rather accepted expression for scientific demonstration.

Tekmerion, then, introduces into the field of rhetorical discourse subject-matter which falls not under the probable but the certain and unconditioned. There should be no difficulty with this fact if rhetoric is understood as the art of the *logos*, of human discourse on human problems. If one is to discuss any problem rationally and reasonably — and from Aristotle's comments throughout the *Rhetoric* he expects this — there will be need to employ on occasion the special principles of that subject which in themselves are generally of an absolute and unchanging character. To speak intelligently on a problem which involves, for example, the nature of government, or law, or justice demands of necessity the introduction of certain *anagkaia*. There is no justification in the *Rhetoric* to force the discipline into a kind of case study as THROM seems to do (Die Thesis, Paderborn 1932, p. 12 ff.), or to decide that rhetorical argument is "persuasive rather than demonstrative" (G. LLOYD, *Polarity and Analogy*, Cambridge 1966, p. 406). There is no reason whatsoever that in the effort to achieve *pistis* with respect to the probability or improbability of an issue one may not entertain certain and necessary truth in the move toward the final objective. When Socrates, for example, in the *Phaedrus* desires to achieve the conviction *(pistis)* among his audience that the soul is immortal he argues among other things from knowledge that Plato would accept as certain and necessary truth: the theory of forms.

In noting the relationship between *tekmerion* and *anagkaion*, the *anagkaion* which for Aristotle leads to *episteme*, there is no intention of identifying *tekmerion* (πρότασις ἀποδεικτικὴ ἀναγκαία) with the πρότασις ἀποδεικτικὴ of the *Prior Analytics* 24a 22 ff. whose function is more fully described in the *Posterior Analytics* 71b 9 ff. as the instrument of strict scientific apodeixis: a demonstration of both the fact and the reasoned fact. None of the statements in our analysis here would lead to that conclusion. On the other hand *tekmerion* by reason of its necessary relation to its signate does possess the qualities requisite to give certain knowledge at least of the fact of the existence of the

---

[15] Aristotle's example of such a necessary sign, *A* 2, 57b 15—16 is almost identical with his example in *An. Pr.* 70a 13—16 which is, as he says, in the first figure and which he calls *tekmerion* at 70b 1—2. Further it is quite possible that *syllogismos* at *A* 2, 57b 5—6 is the first figure syllogism (see SOLMSEN, Die Entwicklung, p. 14, n. 1). The fact that the *tekmerion* is irrefutable, *A* 2, 57b 16—17, also points in the same direction, e. g. *An. Pr.* 70a 28—30.

other. Thus is it ordinarily used by Aristotle and thus it is analyzed here. The *tekmerion* is capable of demonstrating with certainty the *fact* in the conclusion (*ratio cognoscendi*), not with certainty the *reasoned fact (ratio essendi)*. From Aristotle's examples of *tekmerion* and his statements about *tekmerion* this is surely his intention.

In presenting to us the sources for reasoning by enthymeme Aristotle appears to have remained consistent to his analysis of the rhetorical *pragmateia* as something larger and more significant than the mere art of persuasion. For *eikos* and *semeion anonymon* representing contingent and probable reality possess the formality of the kind of inference we find in his *Dialectics*. The *tekmerion* as necessary and unconditioned possesses in part the character of scientific reasoning as it is met in the *Analytics*.

THE TOPICS

When Aristotle has presented us with the sources of the enthymeme, *eikota* and *semeia*, and told us that they are the premises of enthymematic reasoning (*A* 3, 59a 7—10) the question which immediately arises is where does the rhetor turn for the material which will provide him with such *eikota* and *semeia*. The answer is: the topics. Aristotle states clearly at *A* 2, 58a 10—35, and later at *Γ* 1, 03b 13—14 that the topics supply the material of enthymemes. If we inquire what Aristotle meant by the topics in the *Rhetoric* the answer is not as readily obvious. By way of a general and fairly safe answer we can say that the topics are sources, or *loci*, both particular and general, to which one must have recourse in constructing probable argumentation by enthymeme in an effort to effect *pistis*. The more, however, that one attempts to understand the meaning of these particular and general topics the more substantial are the difficulties met in the actual statements made by Aristotle in the text of the *Rhetoric*. And yet the effort to specify and discover the meaning of his comments opens the way to a reasonable understanding of the topics and the nature of the methodology of the Aristotelian topics. Certainly it is true that his observations on the *topoi* in the *Rhetoric* assume a coherent and consistent character. And the methodology outlined in the *Rhetoric* for the enthymeme seems quite capable of a legitimate extension to the methodology offered in the *Topics*.

By way of introduction it can be said that while the influence of the Aristotelian *topoi* has been extensive in our western tradition, particularly in literature, it does seem that their methodology has not been fully understood. A number of factors have contributed to this: the absence in Aristotle of a forthright and formal discussion of what he has in mind[16], the neglect of the methodology after Aristotle[17], a partially misdirected emphasis given to the method by Cicero, one of the first to concern himself with the topics[18], and the continuation of the Ciceronian interpretation by Quintilian with whom it passed into the Middle Ages and the stream of our western tradition.

The rather truncated form in which the topics have come to us has been rather unfortunate since there has been lost along the way the far richer method of discourse on the human problem which they provide. Seen as mere static, stock 'commonplaces,' stylized sources for discussion on all kinds of subject-matter they have lost the vital, dynamic character given to them by Aristotle, a character extremely fruitful for intelligent, mature discussion of the innumerable significant problems which face man. Indeed their genesis within an intellectual environment which included among other things discussions on φύσις and νόμος and related problems of the First Sophistic, on the nature of justice, goodness, virtue, reality, etc., of the Platonic dialogues, on education and political science of Isocrates' discourses, seems to give a clue to their nature.

In his understanding of τόπος, it would seem that Aristotle was attempting to validate a mode of intelligent discussion in the area of probable knowledge comparable (but not equal) to that enjoyed in the area of scientific knowledge (i. e. the certain knowledge of metaphysics) and, even more than that, to enlarge where possible the subject of scientific knowledge. And in this last sense the topical method would not only be a propaideutic for *scientia*[19] but also an assistant discipline.

Even though this idea of the *topoi* as a formal discipline and an integrated methodology concerned with both the form and the content of discussion in

---

[16] The Port-Royal logicians rejected the *Topics* as "des livres étrangement confus." Bocheński, La logique de Théophraste, Fribourg 1947, p. 122, claims that Aristotle never gave us the meaning of τόπος, while Solmsen, Die Entwicklung, p. 164 maintains that *B* 26, 03a 18—19 is Aristotle's only genuine statement on the essential character of the term.

[17] Theophrastus, of course, wrote on the topics, and apparently Straton continued the work (D. Laert. Straton 5. 3). Collections of τόποι for prooemia and epilogues apparently existed in the 4th century (RE suppl. VII (1940) p. 1066). For the general trend in rhetoric between Aristotle and Cicero see ibid. 1071—1089; and on the topics see Volkmann, Die Rhetorik der Griechen und Römer, Leipzig 1885, pp. 199 ff., 299 ff., 322 ff.

[18] He himself found Aristotle's work somewhat obscure *(Topica* 1); W. Wallies, Die griechischen Ausleger der aristotelischen Topik, Berlin 1891, p. 4, and E. Thionville, De la théorie des lieux communs, Paris 1855, p. 9 would agree with this, for they believe that Cicero's work in this field has nothing more in common with Aristotle's than its title. This is too severe, just as Viehweg, Topik und Jurisprudenz, Munich 1953, p. 10, is a bit too sanguine in his opinion that Cicero's work will help us to understand the Aristotelian topics. The diversity of Cicero's remarks, however, implies at times that he may have seen into the nature of Aristotle's topics; on this question see B. Riposati, Studi sui 'Topica' di Cicerone, Milan 1947; his bibliography, pp. 15—30, is a good one for a study of the general problem.   [19] *Top.* 101a 34 ff.

the field of probable knowledge was lost shortly after Aristotle, as it would seem, it is interesting to note that in one form or another the *topoi* have influenced our western tradition. Understood in a rather static sense as 'rhetorical invention' they have enjoyed a dominant, and one would have to say a frequently creative, role in the literature of the West. CURTIUS gives abundant evidence for this but he has missed, it appears, the vitality of their contribution. This quality was seen by R. TUVE in her study of one phase of English poetry[20]. She notes with insight that it was in the area of the topics that the faculty of the imagination was thought to be most active: "Thinking of the adjuncts of something has provided the pattern for innumerable short poems, and for innumerable longish images within poems . . ." And there is surely no need to comment upon the importance of the imaginative faculty or the pervasive presence of metaphor and image in all significant poetry. Vico had an idea similar to Miss TUVE's in mind when he wrote *De nostri temporis studiorum ratione*, but he was more concerned with the possible exclusion of the whole area of probable knowledge. Apparently he feared that the rejection of the topical method would encourage that attitude of mind which does not examine all the possible aspects of a problem. In our own day this neglect of 'problem thinking' (as opposed to 'system thinking') could well limit the quest for truth. No subject is fully exhausted until intelligent queries can no longer be raised. The critical examination of subject-matter was one phase of the topical method. Another aspect of the method as Aristotle worked it out was the inferential phase, i. e. how one may legitimately advance by deductive reasoning the material gathered by the *topoi*. And here we have the *topoi* as sources of inference. Relatively little has been done with these latter topics, but R. WEAVER[21] has developed from them a way of analysis whose application to prose literature could bring to light the currents of thought influential in various periods of our western tradition. In the course of a discerning study of the topical argumentation of Burke and Lincoln he remarks: "the reasoner reveals his philosophical position by the source of argument which appears most often in his major premise because the major premise tells us how he is thinking about the world"[22].

Aristotle in his topical methodology combined both of the elements just mentioned. His dominant concern in the topical method appears to be that of problem thinking, but thinking informed by intelligent procedure. It does seem that in the whole area of the problematic, the probable, and the contingent, it is his desire to enable one, as far as this is possible, to reason as intelligently, as accurately, and as precisely as one can do in the areas of certain, scientific knowledge. Such reasoning becomes possible when one is in a po-

---

[20] R. TUVE, Elizabethan and Metaphysical Imagery, Chicago 1947, c. XI, p. 3.
[21] R. WEAVER, The Ethics of Rhetoric, Chicago 1953, cc. 3, 4.   [22] Ibid., p. 55.

sition to examine the material of the problem with precision in order to determine it with all the accuracy permissible. After this one must be able to
develop and enlarge this material by discursive reasoning to further conclusions. The kind of formal reasoning used, since one is engaged with the contingent and the probable, will generally be that which relies upon forms and
principles of discursive reasoning which are usually considered to be, and are
accepted as self-evident principles. The topics in the language of the *Rhetoric*
and the explanation given there are the method devised to supply both the
content for the critical examination of the subject and general inferential
statements which would present legitimate forms for deductive reasoning.
For the moment and on the basis of what is found in the text let us call the
first the "particular topics", or the various aspects under which a given subject may be studied in order to arrive at a clearer understanding of it. The second type of topic can be called "general topics", or forms of inference in
which to develop this understanding to further conclusions.

In the *Rhetoric* Aristotle uses the topical methodology both as a logic of
invention and as a logic of inference. He presents us with a method which is
more properly dynamic (cf. *Top.* 100a) rather than static. In the second sense
we have a mere listing of likely materials readily usable in discussion, or, as
the *topoi* have been called, "opinion surveys"[23]. For Aristotle the *topoi* are the
methodology of Dialectics, the area of probable knowledge, just as in the
Analytics we are given a methodology for the area of certain knowledge,
scientia.

In view of the fact that any methodology concerned with language must
occupy itself with the form and content of statements (propositions, to use
Aristotle's word)[24], it is possible to see where misinterpretation has arisen.
Many commentators, from Cicero on[25], have fastened upon the content (the
particular topics) and then reduced the topics to the mere mechanics of invention, i. e. ways and means of developing and enlarging upon a theme. In
more recent studies[26], though not exclusively, the formal element has been
stressed. While this captures the axiomatic character of the general topics,

---

[23] K. BURKE, A Rhetoric of Motives, New York 1950, p. 56. On 57 f. he does see a difference
in the topics: there are the 'commonplaces' just mentioned, and then 'another kind of "topic"';
this other kind, from his description of it, is actually the general topic as presented in this chapter.

[24] For Aristotle the topics are the sources for the προτάσεις and, as *A* 2, 58a 10—35 and *B* 1,
77b 16—24 would indicate, this means sources for both their content and form.

[25] THIONVILLE, op. cit., c. vi, traces briefly the development from Cicero to Marmontel. R. NA-
DEAU gives some attention to this area in "Hermogenes on 'Stock Issues' in Deliberative Speaking," Speech Monographs 25. 1, 1958, pp. 59—66.

[26] SOLMSEN, op. cit., pp. 163—6; RIPOSATI, op. cit., pp. 21 ff.; E. HAMBRUCH, Logische
Regeln der platonischen Schule in der aristotelischen Topik, Berlin 1904, p. 31; THIONVILLE,
op. cit., pp. 30 ff.

it neglects entirely the non-axiomatic, non-propositional character of the
particular topics as they are found in the *Topics* and the *Rhetoric*.

In other words, the τόποι, which are the sources for intelligent discussion
and reasoning in dialectic and rhetoric (*A* 2, 58a 10—35; *B* 1, 77b 16—24),
are concerned with both the material and formal element in such discussion.
As sources for the content of discussion (the ordinary meaning of *loci communes*: persons, places, things, properties, accidents, etc., the περιστάσεις or
aspects of the subject pertinent to discussion) they ultimately provide the
material by means of which general or particular propositions are enunciated. As sources for the forms of reasoning in discussion (*A* 2, 58a 12—17)
they are axiomatic forms, or modes of inference, in which syllogistic (or
what is called 'enthymematic' in the *Rhetoric*) reasoning naturally expresses
itself. Neither aspect can be neglected. For, granted that the τόποι are concerned with propositions (a point obvious to one acquainted with the *Topics*
and the *Rhetoric*), it must not be forgotten that propositions consist of terms
which must be clearly defined and determined before they can be used in
meaningful discussion, or in intelligent, convincing, although probable,
inference. There must be a precise apprehension of the subject as far as is
possible, and there must be reasonable, inferential modes in which to develop the subject further. In the methodology of the topics Aristotle was apparently concerned with both ideas.

In what follows an attempt will be made to justify this distinction from the
Rhetoric. It is generally admitted[27] that we must go to the *Rhetoric* for a relatively clear explanation of the term τόπος and more than this, one can clearly
show from the *Rhetoric* a definite distinction in the τόποι and how Aristotle
has developed this idea of the τόποι.

The idea of τόποι, as far as one can decide historically, does not seem to
originate with Aristotle. On the other hand he does seem to have isolated
and formulated the technique or method which was at work in the collections
of τόποι which were probably on hand. His apparent purpose was to arrive at
the general method underlying discussion (T. 100a 18 f.; 102b 35—103a 5),
not to burden the mind with the kind of lists of specific subject-headings and
arguments for various occasions, which had probably been collected. And in
this is the genius of his topical method.

When we turn to the pre-Aristotelian τόπος to make a brief review of the
history of the idea, we find nothing quite similar to the meaning Aristotle
gives to the term[28]. The ordinary use of the word is primarily one of local de-

[27] VIEHWEG, op. cit., p. 9; SOLMSEN, op. cit., pp. 163—4; THIONVILLE, op. cit., pp. 30 f.; and
most recently J. BRUNSCHWIG in his edition Aristote Topiques I, Paris 1967.

[28] As SOLMSEN, op. cit., p. 156 remarks: the Aristotelian idea is something new; he discusses
the term in general 151—175; see also F. SCHUPP, Zur Geschichte der Beweistopik in der älteren
griechischen Gerichtsrede, Wiener Studien 45, 1926—7, pp. 17—28, 173—85.

signation and we find this common in Plato[29] and Isocrates; and in the latter it is very frequently conjoined with χώρα.

There are, however, four passages in Isocrates which are germane to one aspect of the Aristotelian idea of τόπος as the place to go for material concerning one's subject, or for a clarification of it — the Aristotelian ὑπάρχοντα[30]. In *Philip* 109 the τόπος is the ἀγαθὰ τῆς ψυχῆς, a topic peculiar (τόπος ἴδιος) to Heracles, and one, as Isocrates says, πολλῶν μὲν ἐπαίνων καὶ καλῶν πράξεων γέμοντα. These ἀγαθά (see also *Helen* 38) are τῇ ψυχῇ πρόσοντα, which is again an echo of the ὑπάρχοντα idea of Aristotle[31]. In *Panathenaicus* 111 we have τόπος as material for discussion, and the same use in *Helen* 4[32].

Demosthenes[33] gives further evidence that τόπος was used in his time and quite apparently with reference to the particular topics. RADERMACHER[34] gives rather substantial evidence that not only were such ἴδιοι τόποι known and used, but that writers frequently called them καιρούς rather than τόπους before Aristotle's time. These καιροί for the most part concerned themselves with determining the nature of, and examining in detail, not merely such words and ideas as the good, the useful, the right, the beautiful, the possible,[35] but also other ideas such as war, government, peace, etc.[36].

Such is the more direct evidence which is found on the pre-Aristotelian use of the word τόπος in a way that is at all similar to Aristotle's. Indirect evidence for the pre-Aristotelian existence of the idea in the manner in which Aristotle understood it is twofold: the testimony of Aristotle himself and lat-

---

[29] See Ast, Lexicon Platonicum *sub* τόπος; this is also true of all the pertinent references in Diels, Die Fragmente der Vorsokratiker[6], Berlin 1952, with the exception of the Cicero and Quintilian citations which will be seen later.

[30] See *Top.* 105b 12—18 for the idea, and 112a 24 ff. and *Rhet.* B 22, 96a 32—b 9 where Aristotle says that what he was trying to do in the *Topics* was to determine the ὑπάρχοντα.

[31] Solmsen, op. cit., p. 167 mentions these two references and he tries to connect the *Helen* citation with his idea of the Aristotelian τόπος as 'Formprinzip', or a propositional, axiomatic *topos*. This appears no more possible here than Thionville's attempt, op. cit., pp. 55—77 to formulate many of the τόποι in the *Topics* as propositional, axiomatic statements, a process of which he must say: "j'ai dû parfois interpréter, parfois changer la forme" (p. 63).

[32] In *Panathenaicus* 88 the use is ambiguous; it may mean the subject previously under discussion, but it more probably indicates the place in his speech at which he digressed.

[33] *In Aristogeiton* 76 (ed. Dindorf-Blass, Teubner 1888).

[34] L. Radermacher, Artium Scriptores, Vienna 1951, see the notes on pp. 48—9, 224.

[35] What later rhetoricians called the τελικὰ κεφάλαια, see Radermacher, op. cit., p. 226 note to 62.

[36] See the scholiast to Thucydides 3. 9. 1 (ed. Hude, Teubner 1927) where we find Thucydides doing this very thing for δημηγορία; or see Anaximenes c. 19 (ed. Fuhrmann) where various meanings of δίκαιον and ἄδικον are given. Syrianus examines συμφέρον in this manner and introduces the examination thus: ἐξετάσομεν δὲ τὸ συμφέρον διὰ τόπων ἑπτὰ (Radermacher, op. cit., p. 227). I mention Syrianus here since Radermacher in his note is of the opinion that the τόποι may be quite old.

er writers, and the fairly abundant evidence of Aristotle's τόποι at work in various pre-Aristotelian writers.

In the *Rhetoric* Aristotle cites on a number of occasions previous authors or technographers who have employed the particular *topos* of which he is speaking[37]. One conclusion that may be drawn from this is that the methodology of the topics as Aristotle understood it was being used, even if the term τόπος was not employed to identify it. And actually in the *Topics* 105b 11 ff. Aristotle suggests the listing of key ideas on life, on the good, a procedure which we have reason to believe was introduced by earlier rhetoricians. For Cicero[38] and Quintilian[39] mention Protagoras and Gorgias as those who were the first to present such 'communes locos'[40], while Doxopater[41] speaks of a tradition which has Corax devising τοὺς τῶν προοιμίων τόπους.

Were one, however, to question this commonly accepted tradition, it still remains true that the actual use of Aristotle's method of particular and general topics is convincing. Aside from Aristotle's illustrations of his topics by citations from earlier writers, the general topics have been exemplified from these earlier writers rather frequently by SPENGEL in his commentary[42] and by PALMER[43]. The particular topics have not been so fortunate, quite possibly because they were not considered τόποι[44]. Why this should be, is strange in view of the fact that the Aristotelian τόπος was certainly understood in the sense of 'particular topics' by Cicero, Quintilian and Plutarch[45] among others. Furthermore we find Gorgias continually using such particular topics in his *Palamedes*[46] and in 22 we find some of them mentioned: τὸν τόπον, τὸν χρόνον, πότε, ποῦ, πῶς. Aristotle himself when speaking of the particular topics connected with honor speaks of the importance

---

[37] E. g. *B* 23, 99a 15—7, 00a 4—5, 00b 15—7; *B* 24, 02a 17; and see RADERMACHER, op. cit., p. 221 note to 48.

[38] *Brutus* 12. 46. 8 (ed. G. FRIEDRICH, Teubner 1893).

[39] *Institutiones Oratoriae* 3. 1. 12 (ed. L. RADERMACHER — V. BUCHHEIT, Teubner 1959).

[40] SOLMSEN, op. cit., pp. 167—8 discusses the Cicero text.

[41] RADERMACHER, op. cit., p. 34.

[42] E. g. ad 1398a 30 ff. and see note of RADERMACHER, op. cit., pp. 57 and 223 note to 52; and comment of SOLMSEN, op. cit., p. 166.

[43] G. PALMER, The ΤΟΠΟΙ of Aristotle's *Rhetoric* as Exemplified in the Orators (Diss. Univ. of Chicago 1934).

[44] MARX, Aristoteles' Rhetorik, BSG 52, 1900, p. 281 ff. does not consider the εἴδη (i. e. ἴδιοι τόποι) to be topics, he speaks of enthymemes from *topoi* and *idiai protaseis;* SOLMSEN does not admit *eide* either, op. cit., pp. 17, 34 ff., 165 and note 3.

[45] *Quaest. conviv.* 616 c—d (ed. BERNARDAKIS); Plutarch remarks that to appreciate the social position of dinner guests who differ in so many ways — ἡλικίᾳ, δυνάμει, χρείᾳ, οἰκειότητι — one would need τοὺς 'Αριστοτέλους τόπους. These are particular topics. We also find such particular topics in the scholiast on the *Staseis* of Hermogenes *(Rhetores Graeci*, ed. WALZ, vol. IV. 352. 5 ff.); the scholiast calls them τόποι and finds them used in a work by Lysias.

[46] RADERMACHER, op. cit., pp. 59 ff.

of τὸ ποῦ and τὸ πότε, or as he calls them, *A* 5, 61a 33 f.: οἱ τόποι καὶ οἱ καιροί (cf. *A* 9, 68a 12—13: τὰ ἐκ τῶν χρόνων καὶ τῶν καιρῶν). We also get both of these in the *Phaedrus* 272a with a slightly different reference. In the *Meno* we find the particular topics for ἀρετή[47]. And this same process can be seen at work in Prodicus' efforts at definition, or the specification of a term, e. g. pleasure[48]. Further citation does not seem necessary, for, as RADERMACHER says (and he is speaking of what have thus far been called here 'particular topics'): "Non potest esse dubium quin de sedibus argumentorum, quae τελικὰ κεφάλαια vocantur, velut de iusto, utili, honesto, pulchro, possibili in scholis sophistarum iam ante Aristotelem sit disputatum"[49].

It would seem, then, that the idea of both particular topics and general topics, or topics to supply one with the material for propositions, as well as topics to supply one with ways of putting this material in a form of inference, was operative prior to Aristotle. Further it does appear that collections of τόποι were made which were concerned for the most part with material and with lines of argument specific to a definite, limited problem or case[50]. These would be the materials and the arguments to be used when a similar problem arose. The process as can be seen is rather static and similar to the study of case law. Aristotle's contribution was to derive and describe the method at work[51], and he may have kept the name τόποι for the method since it describes the process: these are the places from which originate both the material and the formal elements in all dialectical and rhetorical discussion.

A moment's thought brings before one very distinctly the realization that if you are going to discuss a subject with another in an intelligently informed, but not necessarily scientific, way (e. g. *A* 2, 55b 27—34, *A* 2, 58a 23—26, *A* 4, 59b 5—15) you must know what you are talking about and to whom you are talking. This is certainly one of the purposes of rhetorical study and Aristotle leaves no doubt throughout his work that this is his objective. Indeed he expresses himself quite explicitly on the matter of being informed on the subject at *B* 22, 96a 4 ff. (which is a re-statement of *A* 4, 59b 33—37): "Well, then, first of all we must understand that it is necessary to

---

[47] RADERMACHER, op. cit., p. 49 number 27 with note.

[48] Ibid. pp. 68 f., numbers 7—11 with notes.

[49] Ibid. p. 226 note to 62.

[50] NAVARRE, Essai sur la Rhétorique grecque, Paris 1900, speaks of collections of τόποι that were made, pp. 60 ff., 124 ff., 166—74.

[51] As NAVARRE, ibid., p. 166, says in comparing the treatment of ἤθη in the *Rhetoric* and in the Παρασκευαί attributed to Lysias: "l'ouvrage de Lysias n'était pas un traité théorique, mais un recueil de modèles (τόποι γεγυμνασμένοι)." As far as can be judged (see Navarre, pp. 166—174) these collected *topoi* appear to be concerned with stock offense and defense tactics for typical situations, not for an intelligent discussion of the problem, which was what Aristotle had in mind: *Top.* 101a 25 ff., *Rhet. A* 1, 54a 11 ff. In the *SE* 183b 36 ff. Aristotle himself criticizes the formulaic quality of these collections.

have control of either all or some of the facts of the subject (τὰ τούτῳ ὑπάρχοντα) about which one must speak or reason — whether it be by political reasoning or by any other kind; for without control of any of the facts you could draw no conclusions. My meaning is this: how, for example, could we advise the Athenians as to whether they should engage in war if we have no idea of the nature of their power — whether a naval or land force, or both, and its size, and then the character of their revenues . . ." In other places, as we have seen, he states just as clearly the need of being informed about one's audience and one's relation to the audience (i. e. *ethos* and *pathos*); see, for example, the end of the present passage, *B* 22, 96b 31—34.

An art of rhetoric must, among other things, tell you how to come upon this information. For Aristotle the sources for such information are the *topoi*. But when we look at the text of the *Rhetoric* we begin to realize that Aristotle has something more in mind by *topoi* than mere sources for information about the subject and the audience. The topics also present one with the ways in which to use the information. In an analysis of rhetoric built primarily upon the enthymeme and thus upon his theory of deductive reasoning Aristotle gives in the topics sources for propositional statements and sources for the use of these statements in inferential forms. The *Rhetoric* introduces a distinction among *topoi* and further gives a clue to the nature of the methodology which Aristotle has in mind. A similar division does not exist in the *Topics* but it appears to be operative there. This last point might well be argued, and while the recent work of DE PATER on the *Topics* does not apparently accept the explanation of this distinction as it will be presented here the author must accept the fact of the distinction between particular (εἴδη) and general (κοινοί) topics[52]. Our objective here is not the methodology of Aristotle's *Topics* but the methodology of the *Rhetoric*. I am still inclined to believe that the function of the topics in the *Rhetoric* can also be found at work in the *Topics*, as I will attempt to indicate briefly at the end of this chapter. On the other hand if one accepts DE PATER's very competent analysis as valid for the *Topics* it must still be acknowledged that it does not work for the *Rhetoric*. There can be no question that Aristotle in the *Rhetoric* bases rhetorical argumentation by syllogism on the topics as sources, and distinguishes these topics into particular topics and general topics. If we question the text on the character of these sources the only answer we find in the *Rhetoric* is quite

---

[52] W. S. DE PATER, Les Topiques d'Aristote et la Dialectique platonicienne, Fribourg 1965, pp. 92—150; "La fonction du lieu et de l'instrument dans les *Topiques*" in Aristotle on Dialectic: The Topics, ed. G. E. L. OWEN, Oxford 1968, pp. 164—188. A statement like the following in Les Topiques pp. 101—102 cannot be defended in the light of any number of passages in the *Rhetoric*: "Selon Aristote, toutes deux [i. e. rhetoric and dialectic] ne sont que des facultés pour fournir des arguments, sans qu'une connaissance spécialisée sur l'objet de l'argument soit présupposée . . ."; *B* 22, 96a 4 ff. is but one example which states the contrary.

clear: the particular topics offer the material for propositional statements (Aristotle's προτάσεις of, for example, *A* 2, 58a 31, *B* 1, 77b 18) about a subject, i. e. what can be said about a subject with respect to its logical comprehension and with respect to its emotional context relative to an other in discussion. The general topics offer forms of inference into which this material may be put so that one may reason by syllogism.

The whole question of particular and general topics is introduced at *A* 2, 58a 2—7. We are told here: "there is a distinction of major importance with respect to enthymemes — although it is almost universally disregarded — a distinction similar to that which is true of dialectical syllogisms. For some enthymemes belong properly to rhetoric, as some syllogisms belong properly to dialectic; other enthymemes are peculiar to other arts and faculties *(dynameis)*, either existent or still to be formulated"[53].

A possible commentary on this passage is, perhaps, *SE* 170 a 20—b 11. The best, as Aristotle himself suggests (*A* 2, 58a 9—10) may be the section which immediately follows in the text: *A* 2, 58a 10—28. Here Aristotle says that the dialectical and rhetorical syllogisms (10—11) are those formed on the basis of the *topoi*[54]. These *topoi* are then divided into the κοινοί (12) which would represent sources for enthymemes κατὰ τὴν ῥητορικὴν . . . καὶ . . . διαλεκτικὴν μέθοδον (5—6), and ἴδια (17) which are the sources κατ' ἄλλας τέχνας καὶ δυνάμεις (6—7). The ἴδια are then specified further: at 27 they are called εἴδη which is repeated at 30, 31 (εἴδη) and 33 (εἰδῶν).

The question is whether or not these ἴδια which are contrasted with οἱ κοινοί, e. g. *A* 2, 58a 12 *versus* 17, are also τόποι as the κοινοί are. By way of introduction let us note that no student of the *Rhetoric*, to my knowledge, has ever questioned the fact that Aristotle is talking about "topics" in *A* 4 to *B* 17. If this is so, then the ἴδια which in our text here are interchangeable with εἴδη are τόποι. For in *A* 4—*B* 17 Aristotle is unmistakeably speaking of what he promises to speak at *A* 2, 58a 32—33, namely "the particular elements, which are all those that come from statements peculiar to each species and class; for example, there are statements about physics from which it is not possible to construct an enthymeme or a syllogism about ethics" (*A* 2,

---

[53] In the interpretation of this text I agree with MAIER, Die Syllogistik des Aristoteles II. 1, Tübingen 1900, p. 497, note 1. SPENGEL in his Commentary (1867 edition) p. 71, and SOLMSEN op. cit. p. 15 note 1 substantially agree. The minor variant readings admitted by SPENGEL together with VATER (Animadversiones ad Aristotelis librum primum Rhetoricorum, Halle 1794, are not substantial, once the correct antithesis of the sentence is understood: μέν setting off 4—6 against the δέ of 6—7. In the light of the context 9—28 this gives the idea of general and particular topics. Such a distinction is also seen in Anonymus, *Commentaria in Aristotelem Graeca*, vol. 21, p. 6. 27 and in Stephanus, ibid., p. 267. 1—23. I would not accept their identification of the general topics.

[54] SOLMSEN, op. cit., p. 15 note 4 appears more correct on the meaning of περὶ ὦν than COPE-SANDYS, Cambridge 1877, I. p. 49.

58a 17—19). Furthermore the statement at *A* 2, 58a 10—11 says that the rhetorical syllogism (like the dialectical) is built upon the topics: i. e. τοὺς τόπους without any qualification. He then introduces a qualification at 12: οἱ κοινοί which is rather senselessly confusing if κοινοί equals τόποι in the sense that the *only* τόποι are κοινοὶ τόποι. In other words if *topos* is a genus without any species there is no need at all to introduce confusion by using κοινοί. One could perhaps accept this idiosyncratic writing if κοινοί were not immediately set in contrast with ἴδια at 17 and both of them brought together in a contrasting statement at 21—28 with κἀκεῖνα (21) of necessity referring to οἱ κοινοί (12) and ταῦτα (23) to ἴδια (17) because the statement at 21—26 so clearly restates that at 12—20. In view of this close contrast and juxtaposition of κοινοί and ἴδια one must attend to the further parallelism in 27—28. Thus there can be little question that if we can understand τόπων with κοινῶν, we can understand it with ἰδίων[55]. And when in c. 22 of book *B* (96a 4—b 21) Aristotle summarizes the analysis he has made of these εἴδη (or ἴδια) in *A* 4—B 17 he concludes at 96b 20—21: "This, then, is one method, the first method of selecting sources — the topical (οὗτος ὁ τοπικός)."

We come, then, to the conclusion of our passage at *A* 2, 58a 10—28 with the understanding that the sources of the enthymeme are "the topics" (e. g. *A* 2, 58a 10—12). At 29—32 Aristotle says that with respect to these sources of the enthymeme (ἐξ ὧν ληπτέον) a distinction must be made in the *Rhetoric*, as in the *Topics*, between the εἴδη i. e. "propositions proper to each subject (31), and the τόπους i. e. "elements common alike to all subjects". It seems quite clear that, while both are *topoi*, the particular *topoi* are called εἴδη and the general *topoi* are given the name τόποι. However, as we will see, he also uses the term τόποι for the εἴδη.

Aristotle then proposes to discuss the εἴδη (32—33), or particular topics, and it is in his presentation of them that a distinction between them and the κοινοί becomes quite apparent[56]. The *eidos*, or particular topic, could be

---

[55] The neuter case, ἴδια, is noted by SPENGEL in his commentary *sub linea*. I do not see any insurmountable problem in it in the light of the neuter κἀκεῖνα (21) referring to κοινοὶ τόποι. See also ROEMER, Zur Kritik der *Rhetorik* des Aristoteles, RhM 39, 1884, p. 506 on similar uses of the neuter at *B* 21, 95a 11 and *A* 2, 55b 35. MAIER's note, op. cit., pp. 497—8 does not appear correct in its exclusion of the idea of τόπος from the ἴδια. This would also be true for SOLMSEN, op. cit. pp. 14 ff.; MARX, op. cit. pp. 281 note 2, 283 and 296 (if I read him correctly) would understand ἐνθυμήματα or εἴδη with ἴδια; the first is not possible; the second is, on the basis of the text, unlikely. More recently DE PATER, Les Topiques pp. 118—122 has attempted an exegesis of this passage. He reaches the conclusion that the passage discriminates between εἴδη i. e. τόποι ἴδιοι and τόποι κοινοί; cf. also his note 266.

[56] Thus Süss, Ethos, Leipzig—Berlin 1910, p. 170 would seem wrong in saying that Aristotle has not given us any sharp and satisfactory division between εἴδη and τόποι.

called a "material topic"[57] in the sense that it offers the matter (ὕλη) for the propositions. It presents one with sources, or focal points, to be examined in order that one may derive all the material pertinent to the subject, i. e. the ὑπάρχοντα of the subject which are necessary for an intelligent statement which carries meaning to the auditor. These εἴδη belong to the subject in itself and in all of its diverse relations. They represent the varied particular aspects of an individual subject which can throw light upon the subject for the audience and for the field of knowledge which it represents[58].

To understand the point of view presented here one has merely to read Aristotle's discussion of the εἴδη for deliberative (cc. 4—8), epideictic (c. 9), and forensic oratory (cc. 10—14) in Book A or those for *pathos* (cc. 2—11) and *ethos* (cc. 1, 12—17) in Book B.

While a detailed analysis of these particular topics in A—B might be valuable in itself it would be neither to the purpose nor particularly helpful to engage upon it here. In order to correct some misunderstanding possibly occasioned by DE PATER's study, however, a further word is necessary. The explanation of the εἴδη (which DE PATER recognizes as particular topics) given by him simply will not explain the particular topics as we find them in the *Rhetoric*. In the *Rhetoric* these εἴδη are all specifics with an occasional principle (usually an accepted general opinion, or a general topic) used from which the specifics, namely, the ὑπάρχοντα, can be drawn[59]. It would be tedious, as I have indicated, to catalogue the process. It begins immediately in c. 4 of book A at 59b 19 where we learn that the deliberative speaker must know — and I am citing directly from c. 4 — the extent of the State's resources, its expenses, its power, the wars it has waged, its conduct of them, the kind of food produced at home, the State's legislation, forms of government. And so it continues in each chapter through c. 17 of book B. Every now and then Aristotle will cite a definition, or a principle which is generally accepted, or a general topic, and from it develop specifics, e. g. in A 5, 60b 14—18: "Let happiness, then, be well-being combined with virtue, or independence of life, or . . ." This, then, enables him to cite the specifics of *eudaemonia*: "noble birth, good friends, wealth, etc.", each of which he then examines in further detail to the end of the chapter at 62a 14. If one wishes to take the statement

---

[57] SPENGEL, Über das Studium der Rhetorik bei den Alten, Munich 1842, pp. 22 ff. makes such a distinction. It may appear a quibble, but "sources for material" seems better than "material proofs" ("materielle Beweise"). For it would appear that the 'proof' is the enthymeme and that the *eide* offer material for inferential argument by syllogism, or enthymeme; whereas the *koinoi topoi* present forms for inference by syllogism. There would be no objection to calling the *koinoi topoi* which are sources for formal reasoning by syllogism, or enthymeme, "formelle Beweise" as SPENGEL does.

[58] See B 22, 96b 11—19 on the use of ἴδια; and Stephanus, *Commentaria in A. Graeca*, vol. 21, p. 268. 12—15.

[59] This process appears remarkably similar to that presented in *Topics* 105b 12—16 (see p. 132 *infra*); cf. also 10—12 on working with accepted statements or principles.

on happiness as a definition, then Aristotle is using his general topic VII (*B* 23, 98a 15) to develop specific aspects of *eudaemonia*. The same procedure is followed in *A* 6 where in the course of his analysis he uses at 62b 30—31 his general topic I (*B* 23, 97a 7) from opposites in order to develop specifics. We have the same kind of particulars in *A* 8, 9. When we turn to *pathos* in book *B* we find that in c. 2 we have descriptions of the angry person, a process which is well expressed at 79a 29: "These, then, are the moods of men who are prone to anger". The same approach takes place in *B* 3 with respect to gentleness. In *B* 12 where he begins the analysis of *ethos* we have simply a detailed statement of the characteristics of the young; in *B* 13 of the old.

In all of these instances it would not be possible to apply DE PATER's definition of the particular topic, the *eidos, e. g.* "le lieu est une formule de recherche et de preuve à la fois. Cela vaut pour la *Rhétorique* non moins que pour les *Topiques*"[60].

There is, however, in a chapter like 7 of book *A*, a use on the part of Aristotle of an assumed general principle (as has been noted), or accepted opinion, or a general *topos*, in order to derive the special elements, the ὑπάρχοντα, of a subject. This is a function which I find the general topics fulfilling frequently in the *Topics* as I mention toward the close of this chapter. This general principle (or accepted opinion, or general *topos*) does function as a "formule de recherche" and can be employed with a force "probatif". Some instances of this in the sections cited above are: *A*: 5, 60b 14 ff. a generalized definition; 6, 62b 30 f. a *topos;* 7, 63b 5 ff. a precisive use of the logical force of "more or less" throughout the section; 9, 66a 33—34 and 36—b1 a generally accepted statement; *B*: 2, 77a 31—33 a statement of what anger is; 3, 80a 7—8 the same for gentleness; cc. 12 and 13 of *B* contain all specific characteristics.

These instances would illustrate the character of the general *topos* as an "acte de l'inventio" and also as "probatif" (Les Topiques, pp. 109, 106) but they are not εἴδη, particular topics. There is certainly no reason to expect *only* εἴδη in *A* 4—*B* 17, particularly in view of the fact that the general topics frequently function as a method whereby one may establish the focal points (particular topics) for an informed understanding of the subject.

Obviously in any intelligent discussion of a subject the bulk of one's argument will be built around the particular topics; and it is this, as far as I can see, and nothing else, that Aristotle has in mind when he says that most en-

---

[60] W. DE PATER, Les Topiques, p. 117; cf. also 106—107, 109, 115. He is speaking of the *eide* and, as he says at 122: "le lieu propre est une proposition probative exprimant une connaissance spécialisée, une formule d'inférence, composée de constantes extra-logiques, et qu'il est, en même temps, une formule de recherche"; or, as he suggests at 124, neither Aristotle's texts nor examples suggest any difference of function between *eidos* and *koinos topos*, they are "tous deux, des formules de recherche et d'inférence".

thymemes will come from the εἴδη (A 2, 58a 26—28). Finally in this explanation of the particular and general topics there is assuredly no reason to conclude that "les lieux propres et les lieux communs . . . *doivent* figurer tous
deux dans le même argument" (Les Topiques, p. 98).

The εἴδη, then, express specific facts or characteristics relative to the subject-matter. As has been said it is difficult to avoid the conclusion that Aristotle considers them τόποι. He sums up his discussion of them with the
words: ὥστε ἐξ ὧν δεῖ φέρειν τὰ ἐνθυμήματα τόπων (B 22, 96b 31—32). The
same idea is repeated at Γ 19, 19b 15—29. And at B 3, 80b 30—31 he says of
the εἴδη that he has been discussing relative to *pathos:* ἐκ τούτων τῶν
τόπων[61]. As particular topics the *eide* are the sources to which one has recourse to develop both an understanding of the subject and the way in which
to present it to a particular audience. Aristotle says quite simply at B 22, 96a
4—b 19: to reason intelligently upon a subject you must reason ἐκ τῶν περὶ
ἕκαστον ὑπαρχόντων (b 2)[62]. As a matter of fact this whole passage at B 22,
96a 4—b 21 illustrates how the *eide* provide information on the subject and
are considered to be *topoi*[63]. Since the material derived from the *eide* as
sources will usually appear as an enunciation on the subject, it follows that
the *eide* supply us with particular propositions which can be used in enthymematic reasoning on the subject. In this sense the *eide* are the sources of particular propositions or statements on the subject under discussion (A 2, 58a 31).
Yet the kind of statement which they provide does not directly implicate the
ultimate and essential truths about the subject, although it may approach
them. The *eide* as used in rhetoric are not concerned with a scientific analysis
of the subject. This is the only conclusion which can be drawn from A 2, 58a

---

[61] MARX admits that there are what he calls *eide* (i.e. *idiai protaseis*) for deliberative, forensic, epideictic oratory, but only *topoi* for the πάθη and ἤθη. This forces him to say on 1396b 28—34 that a
"Redaktor" has confused the words and incorrectly brought them together, op. cit., pp. 287, 299,
307. SOLMSEN, on the other hand, op. cit., p. 170, note 2 with his interpretation of *topos*, has a far
different problem: he cannot understand how any of these εἴδη can be called τόποι by Aristotle: it
is "prinzipwidrig".

[62] The note of COPE-SANDYS, op. cit., II. pp. 228—9 indicates what is had in mind here. These
εἴδη are always specific to the subject but may be particular or general, see B 22, 96b 11—19, with
which compare Isocrates, *Philip* 109. This idea I find present in the *Topics*, e. g. 105b 12—8: one
can discuss the idea of 'good' in itself, or that which constitutes 'the good' in this specific subject.

[63] B 22, 96b 28—34 undoubtedly refers to the section on the εἴδη in Books A and B, and they
are called τόποι here. This is made more probable still by the contrast between τρόπος at B 22, 96b
20 and 97a 1. Here Aristotle contrasts the method already presented in the first two books, of seeking source material for enthymemes (a method called τοπικός, see SPENGEL in his commentary *sub*
1396b 20) with the method which he now intends to take up, namely the method of the κοινοὶ
τόποι (cf. *supra* pp. 40—42). See also RICCOBONO, Paraphrasis in Rhetoricam Aristotelis, London
1822, p. 206, who writes on B 22, 96b 28 ff. and A 2, 58a 12 ff.: "Constat igitur locos accipi aut
latius aut strictius. Primo modo loci comprehendunt etiam formas [his translation for εἴδη] . . .
Secundo modo distinguuntur a formis."

23—26. Here we are told that the more detail with which the *eide* are selected the more will the analysis move toward the first principles of the subject and so toward an *episteme* of the subject; and this is not the domain of either dialectic or rhetoric. Indeed a study of the *eide* in *A—B* will reveal that one could hardly construct a science of government, criminal law, or psychology from the *eide* presented. Rather the purpose of the particular topics we find is to enable one to speak intelligently, but not scientifically, upon the subject under discussion. Enthymematic reasoning based upon the particular topics is valid only for the subject to which the *eide* belong (*A* 2, 58a 17—21).

In this respect the εἴδη differ, as topics, from the κοινοὶ τόποι[64]. The latter transcend the various subjects which rhetoric may treat. They are valid for all subjects (*A* 2, 58a 12—17), and they exemplify in a particular way the nature of rhetoric as *dynamis* in its ability to occupy itself with the suasive in any subject (*A* 2, 55b 31—34 with 25—27).

This brings us to a very fundamental characteristic of the κοινοὶ τόποι emphatically stressed by Aristotle (*A* 2, 58a 2—7), namely, that these κοινοὶ τόποι are universal and transcend all the fields of knowledge to which rhetoric may legitimately apply itself (*A* 2, 58a 10—14); and Aristotle makes his meaning even more specific by referring at a14 to one of the *koinoi topoi* which he later discusses in c. 23 of book *B* at 97b 12 ff. Here, then, we have a kind of topic which is essentially different from the εἴδη. Particular topics are confined to and closely related to their own specific subject-matter (58a 17—18) and are valid sources of information on that matter alone (18—19). The κοινοί, on the contrary, have no such substrate (22) and are valid sources for enthymematic reasoning upon any subject (15—16). Hence it is that, no matter how much a particular topic is universalized, the result will never be a κοινὸς τόπος as Aristotle understands that term in the *Rhetoric*. For an ἴδιος τόπος is always specific in its nature and confined to one subject: general or particular[65].

Any topic, and such are the εἴδη, which is grounded in the particular subject-matter of a specific branch of learning and is productive of knowledge in that area (*A* 2, 58a 17—26) cannot transcend this discipline and include others. But the κοινοί transcend the individual disciplines. This difference in the topics translates itself into what have been called here 'particular topics' (εἴδη), or sources of information upon the subject-matter to be discussed, and 'general topics' (κοινοὶ τόποι), or sources for modes of reasoning by enthymeme: forms of inference most suitable for the enthymeme[66].

---

[64] See Stephanus, *Commentaria Graeca*, vol. 21, p. 267. 34 ff.   [65] See note 62.

[66] E. Havet, Etude sur la rhétorique d'Aristote, Paris 1846, p. 34, expresses the distinction precisely: "En un mot, les τόποι ne sont que des formes logiques, ... τὰ εἴδη, au contraire, ce sont les observations, les faits ou les idées, qui font la matière du raisonnement, et sans lesquels les

A closer study of what Aristotle has to say of these κοινοί in the passage under discussion (*A* 2, 58a 2—7) and in chapter 23 of Book *B* appears to justify this division. In the first place the κοινοί are universal and belong properly to rhetoric (*A* 2, 58a 2—7, 12—17) in so far as rhetoric is a δύναμις περὶ ἕκαστον τοῦ θεωρῆσαι τὸ ἐνδεχόμενον πιθανόν (*A* 2, 55b 25—26) and in so far as it is not ἐπιστήμη[67]. Thus rhetoric does not possess any peculiar ὑποκείμενον (*A* 2, 55b 31—34), and neither do the κοινοὶ τόποι (*A* 2, 58a 21—23). And so we can understand why Aristotle, for whom Rhetoric is a *dynamis* just as Dialectic, lays stress upon the μεγίστη διαφορά in the section *A* 2, 58a 2 ff. which is so frequently discussed by the commentators. This 'difference' resides for him in the fact that there are enthymemes peculiar to rhetoric as a discipline: κατὰ τὴν ῥητορικὴν μέθοδον. If rhetoric possesses no particular subject-matter of its own, such enthymemes could only be syllogistic forms derived from universal propositional statements, which are modes for probable argumentation and reasoning. As he says in the *Sophistici Elenchi* (172a 29—b 1): there are certain general principles common to all the sciences which even the unlettered can use. In themselves they are known to everyone, for they are natural ways in which the mind thinks. Such in a way are the κοινοὶ τόποι. As general axiomatic propositions they are valid forms of inference by themselves. Further, they may also be applied to the subject-matter presented by the εἴδη to permit one to reason by enthymeme with this material[68].

It would appear, then, that the κοινοὶ τόποι are logical modes of inference which generally obtain the matter for their inference from the εἴδη[69]. And as further confirmation that they are general, formal topics, i. e. forms of reasoning, it should be noted that study of the twenty-eight κοινοὶ τόποι

formes sont vides." In essence the idea of a distinction is found in THROM, Die Thesis, Paderborn 1932, pp. 42—6; Jebb in an appendix to book II of his translation of the *Rhetoric* (ed. SANDYS, Cambridge 1909); LANE COOPER, The Rhetoric of Aristotle, New York 1932, p. xxiv.

[67] *A* 2, 55b 25—34; *A* 4, 59b 12—16. SPENGEL's long note in his commentary on 1355b 26 acquires, it seems, a greater significance in the light of this relation between rhetoric as a *dynamis* and the κοινοὶ τόποι.

[68] Aristotle at *B* 23, 97a 23 ff. gives an example. Here we have the κοινὸς τόπος from correlative terms. As we know, in true correlatives what is predicable of one is generally predicable of the other. As a general axiomatic proposition (assuming A and B to be correlatives) we may say: If A is x, then B is x. Aristotle applies this general form to the question of taxes (26—7). But he calls attention to the fact that it cannot be used indiscriminately and that before it can be applied to a subject (justice is his example) one must carefully determine the meaning of the terms (29 ff.). Such a determination must come from the εἴδη before the κοινὸς τόπος of correlative terms can be used.

[69] SPENGEL apparently has this in mind when he writes that the function of rhetoric is to work up the special proofs of the εἴδη and combine them with the formal to make the subject of discussion universally understood, Über das Studium, p. 22 (n. 51): "... ihr [der Rhetorik] liegt ob, die Beweise, welche die einzelne Wissenschaft gibt, zu verarbeiten, mit den formellen zu verbinden, und den Gegenstand zur allgemeinen Kenntnis zu bringen."

in c. 23 of Book *B* shows that they are universal[70] and that they apparently fall into one of three inferential and logical patterns[71].

a) antecedent-consequent, or cause-effect: VII, XI, XIII, XIV, XVII, XIX, XXIII, XXIV.

b) more-less: IV, V, VI, XX, XXV, XXVII.

c) some form of relation: I, II, III, VIII, IX, X, XII, XV, XVI, XVIII, XXI, XXII, XXVI, XXVIII.

One could undoubtedly argue about the terms used for classification, or the distribution of the κοινοί among them. The point of interest, however, is that, no matter how they are classified, these κοινοὶ τόποι reduce themselves to modes of inference[72]. They always assume a form of reasoning which leads the mind from one thing to another. Expressed quite simply they would resolve themselves into the proposition: if one, then the other. And this last statement acquires new significance when, knowing the close relation between the rhetorical syllogism (enthymeme) and the κοινοὶ τόποι[73], one reads: 'All Aristotelian syllogisms are implications of the type "if α and β then γ . . ." '[74]. If, further, consideration is given to Aristotle's identification of these κοινοὶ τόποι with the στοιχεῖα of rhetorical syllogisms, there appears to be no doubt that for Aristotle the general topic is a form of inference and represents the source of enthymemes: κατὰ τὴν ῥητορικὴν μέθοδον.

At *B* 22, 96b 20—22 Aristotle summarizes his discussion of the εἴδη and makes a transition to the section on the κοινοὶ τόποι in chapter 23. He introduces the new subject with the words "let us now speak of the στοιχεῖα of enthymemes." From *A* 2, 58a 31—2 one would expect him to say as commentators hasten to point out: let us speak of the τόπους τοὺς κοινοὺς ὁμοίως πάντων. Having used στοιχεῖα somewhat unexpectedly, Aristotle immediately clarifies the word with στοιχεῖον δὲ λέγω καὶ τόπον ἐνθυμήματος τὸ αὐτό. And lest there be any doubt that by τόπος here he means the κοινοὶ τόποι, he says that these τόποι are καθόλου περὶ ἁπάντων. Thus one can be fairly certain that the τόποι here are the same as the general topics of *A* 2, 58a 32: τοὺς κοινοὺς ὁμοίως πάντων.

---

[70] SPENGEL in his commentary *sub* 1397a 1 maintains that some are not universal, i. e. common to all rhetorical argument; also COPE, An Introduction to Aristotle's Rhetoric, London 1867, p. 129.

[71] The Roman numerals refer to Roemer's numbering in his text.

[72] SOLMSEN, op. cit., p. 163 and note 5 says well: "Die als Beispiele beigebrachten ἐνθυμήματα der Rhetorik sind durchaus in sich geschlossene Gedankengänge . . . und verhalten sich zu den τόποι, die sie illustrieren, in der Tat wie die πολλά zum formbestimmenden ἕν." This idea of the topics as inferential or logical forms has been developed, as I have recently noticed, into a concept of the topics as "inference-warrants", i. e. "rules for constructing arguments once terms are given in some relation" (O. BIRD, The Tradition of the Logical Topics: Aristotle to Ockham, *JHI* 23 (1962) 307—323). [73] Cf. supra p. 124, and *A* 2, 58a 10—17.

[74] J. LUKASIEWICZ, Aristotle's Syllogistic, Oxford 1951, p. 20, see also p. 2.

Aristotle has now specified these κοινοὶ τόποι as στοιχεῖα. But what is meant by calling them στοιχεῖα? At B 26, 03a 17—18 we read: "By *stoicheion* and *topos* I mean the same thing; for a *stoicheion* and *topos* is a general class under which many enthymemes fall." The Greek here, εἰς ὃ πολλὰ ἐνθυμήματα ἐμπίπτει, describes στοιχεῖον (and so τόπος) as a larger category which contains many enthymemes. This at once recalls Theophrastus' definition of τόπος as ἀρχή τις ἢ στοιχεῖον . . . τῇ περιγραφῇ μὲν ὡρισμένος (i. e. of determinate form) . . . τοῖς δὲ καθ' ἕκαστα ἀόριστος (i. e. indeterminate with respect to the individual matter to which it is applied)[75]. Of this definition BOCHEŃSKI writes: "pour Théophraste le τόπος est une formule logique légitime qui sert à former les prémisses de déduction . . ."[76]. But this is precisely what the *koinoi topoi* are: forms of inference by enthymeme, any one of which may offer a form for inference on various subjects. As WAITZ says of a passage in the *Analytics* 84b 21 which is parallel to B 26, 03a 17—18: "In *Topicis* στοιχεῖα vocat quae alio nomine τόπους appellat, universa quaedam argumenta, ex quibus cum veritatis quadam specie aliquid vel probetur vel refellatur"[77].

Before concluding a word should perhaps be said about the *Topics*. First of all it should be noted that this formal distinction between *eide* and *koinoi topoi* is not found, as such, in the work although Aristotle states at *Rhetoric* A 2, 58a 29—30 that the distinction is also present in the *Topics*. Certainly a passage like that at 105b 12—18 strongly implies kinds of particular topics: "we should also make selections from written 'handbooks of arguments' and should make outlines of each and every subject, setting them down under separate headings, as, for example, 'on good', or 'on life'; and the list 'on good' should be on 'all good' beginning with the essence of good". The idea of both the particular and general *topos* appears to be at work in the *Topics*. For Aristotle is concerned with determining as accurately as possible the meaning of things by specifying the various ways in which this meaning can be understood; these specific meanings would be the *eide*. The topics as we generally find them are the principles by which to examine a subject and they frequently employ the same kind of reasoning which we find proper to the *koinoi topoi* in the *Rhetoric*[78].

In the *Topics* Aristotle says that a problem can be considered from four primary aspects: definition, property, genus, accident (101b 15 ff.). The effort

---

[75] And see Alexander, *Commentaria graeca*, vol. II. 2, p. 5. 21—28.

[76] BOCHEŃSKI, op. cit., p. 122. BOCHEŃSKI (and also SOLMSEN) does not think that the Theophrastean τόπος is the same as the Aristotelian. THROM, op. cit., p. 43 and THIONVILLE, op. cit., pp. 30—35 consider it Aristotelian. And BONITZ and ROSS on *Met.* 1014b note that τόπος as στοιχεῖον would be "an argument applicable to a variety of subjects." *Top.* 163b 18 — 164a 2 appears to express a similar idea.   [77] WAITZ, op. cit., p. 362.

[78] I believe that THIONVILLE, op. cit., p. 74 sees this process at work but does not recognize it.

in Books 2—7 is to examine the nature of these categories and what must follow with respect to a thing, if it comes under one of them. This examination is done by the τόποι, and the analysis is determined by the very nature of the category. For example: there are certain ways (τόποι) in which one can further determine the nature of a genus and consequently certain statements which can only be made about it — and they are not valid for an accident. They are ways — determined by reality — in which one must think about the subject. This kind of analysis is a vital, logical one, grounded in the metaphysical reality of the subject, and one engages in it in order to discover as far as possible the true nature of the subject. This was what was meant by saying that these particular topics are not mere mechanical lists of terms to be tried on a subject, no Procrustean bed to which the subject is fitted, rather we have here a method of analysis originating in the ontological reality of the subject[79].

In the *Rhetoric*, however, as I understand Aristotle's effort, he enlarges the methodology of the particular topics owing to his awareness that anything — particularly anything in the area of the probable which is the primary subject-matter of rhetoric — may be conditioned and altered by its situation. In other words, the time, the place, the circumstances, the character, the emotional involvement, may vitally affect the total meaning of a thing in a given situation. Thus he introduced these elements to assist one toward a more precise discrimination of a subject when one is speaking to an other in the area of the problematic. Although the concern of the *Topics* is a methodology directed to a more critical testing and determining of things like substance, genus, relations, opinions, still we find less technical elements such as time (111b 24 ff.), circumstances (118a) which are quantitative and qualitative aspects that alter the meaning of terms like ambition, or covetousness (146b 20 ff.). We also find attention paid to the character of the persons involved in discussion, e. g. their qualities of intellect and emotion (141a 26 ff., 156b 18 ff., 161a 29 — b10). As Aristotle says rather well on this point (141b

---

[79] In the *Topics* many of the *topoi* are principles for analysis, criticism, and evaluation of terms, all within the framework of the four categories. For instance at 132a 22—24 it is by these *topoi* (διὰ τῶνδε σκεπτέον, ἐκ τῶνδε θεωρητέον) that we determine a thing as a property. Another summary expression of the method appears at 153a 6—28, on definition: to be a true definition a *genus* and *differentia* must be present, and to ascertain whether these are present certain *topoi* must be examined. In this regard SOLMSEN's observation (op. cit., p. 156) on the origin of the *topoi* is interesting. He sees the genesis of the Aristotelian *topoi* in the attempt to specify one's subject, and traces their probable origin to the elenctic dialectic of the Socratic-early Platonic τί ἐστι questions. In general it does seem true (and a passage like *Top.* 152b 6 — 153a 5 would appear to strengthen this) that Aristotle is concerned with specifying the meaning of terms, and a meaning grounded in the metaphysical reality. In this sense his method may well have had in mind what HAMBRUCH (op. cit., p. 29) says was the aim of one of Plato's dialectical methods: "die Bildung eines festgefügten und wohlgegliederten Begriffsystems . . ."

36 — 142a 2): "Different things happen to be more intelligible to different people and the same things are not, as it happens, more intelligible to all; consequently a different definition would have to be given to each one, if indeed the definition must be constructed from what is more intelligible to each individual".

As for the *koinoi topoi* they frequently appear in the *Topics* as the method whereby one mays establish the special focal points (particular topics) from which a subject may be studied. In this use they appear in the same form and fulfil the same function, as modes of inference, which they have in the *Rhetoric*. That is to say, they are ways in which the mind naturally and readily reasons, and they are independent, in a way, of the subject to which they are applied, and may be said to be imposed as forms upon this material in order to clarify and determine it further[80]. Thus it is that we will at times find the general topics functioning in the *Topics* as a method to help in the determination of various particular topics to which one should have recourse[81].

It is only in the *Rhetoric*, however, that a clear distinction between particular and general topics appears, and its presence would seem indisputable. This distinction may be ignored, but if the texts cited in this chapter are studied, one is forced either to reject the unity of the *Rhetoric*, or to question the text as one that has been confused by later editors, or to seek an interpretation of the text. The attempt here has been to offer a tentative interpretation which keeps in mind the character of the topics as they are met in the *Topics;* further, it is an interpretation which appears to be demanded by the text of the *Rhetoric* as we possess it, and it seems to express the method Aristotle had in mind when he proposed a way of rational discourse for the whole area of the contingent and the probable. In summary, then, it is proposed:

    a) that the εἴδη are particular topics concerned with the specific content and meaning of the subject under discussion. They enable one to acquire the factual information pertinent to the matter which in turn permits one to make intelligent statement upon the subject;

    b) that the κοινοὶ τόποι are general topics, i. e. forms of inference into which syllogistic, or enthymematic, reasoning naturally falls. As modes

---

[80] In this regard HAMBRUCH's attempt to discover the genesis of the methodology of Aristotle's topics appears valid in its general outline. He finds it (op. cit., pp. 8—17) in the logical-metaphysical rules for Platonic διαίρεσις e. g. ἅμα καὶ πρότερον φύσει, πρός τι ὄντα, μᾶλλον καὶ ἧττον. This last rule is called the κοινὸς τόπος of the more-less in the *Rhetoric* and is set down in this axiomatic form (B 23, 97b 12—24): τοῦτο γάρ ἐστιν, εἰ ᾧ μᾶλλον ἂν ὑπάρχοι μὴ ὑπάρχει, δῆλον ὅτι οὐδ᾽ ᾧ ἧττον. As I see it, HAMBRUCH's rules are the same fundamental sort of rules which were discovered independently to be at work in the general topics (see *supra* pp, 130 ff.).

[81] E. g. in 114b 38 ff. he uses κοινὸς τόπος IV; in 116a—b, XI, XIII, XVII; in 119a 37 ff. I and II are employed, and they are described as: μάλιστα δ᾽ ἐπίκαιροι καὶ κοινοὶ τῶν τόπων; in 124a 15 ff. we find III, and in 154a 12—22 he speaks of the general effectiveness of these topics that are τοὺς μάλιστα κοινούς.

of reasoning they may be used for the εἴδη of various subjects which specifically differ (*A* 2, 58a 13—14: διαφερόντων εἴδει), and when they are applied to the εἴδη they effect syllogistic or enthymematic argumentation[82].

[82] In terms of this distinction it is interesting to note that if a rough analogy is drawn between rhetoric as a part of practical philosophy and *scientia* as a part of speculative philosophy we seem to have something of a parallel between the principal elements leading to ἐπιστήμη in one instance, and to πίστις in the other:

i) ἀρχαί
$\begin{cases} \text{κοιναί — ἀξιώματα} \\ \text{ἴδιαι — θέσεις} \begin{cases} \text{ὁρισμοί} \\ \text{ὑποθέσεις} \end{cases} \end{cases}$
through which syllogism and induction effect knowledge

ii) ἀρχαί
$\begin{cases} \text{κοιναί — τόποι} \\ \text{ἴδιαι — εἴδη} \end{cases}$
through which enthymeme and example effect belief

Furthermore it would follow that there is not in the *Rhetoric* a double enthymeme theory as MARX, op. cit., pp. 281ff. and SOLMSEN, op. cit., pp. 14 f. would suggest, but rather a single theory which considers the enthymeme a unit composed of εἴδη and κοινοὶ τόποι.

CONCLUSION

Any critical study of the *Rhetoric* quickly reveals that Aristotle's analysis develops its form with the enthymeme as the master structural idea. The basic building blocks of the art are the audience, the speaker, subject-matter open to deliberation and judgment, and the source material both logical and psychological which will enable the audience under the informed direction of the speaker (or writer) to attain the truth as best it can be reached on an open problem. For Aristotle these structural elements of rhetorical discourse are subject to a methodology and it is, as has been seen, the methodology of discursive reasoning through induction and deduction. As far as the *Rhetoric* is concerned deduction by means of the enthymeme is the dominant method. In the light of this evidence it is extremely difficult to avoid the conclusion that the enthymeme cast in such a role is totally ineffective as method if it does not incorporate these essential structural elements. The task before us is to discover whether it does or does not do so.

It is more than clear that rhetoric, viewed as Aristotle views it, must be an integrated act in which person speaks to person for this is both the beginning and the end of the whole operation. Furthermore, the very grounds for initiating such discourse, as outlined by Aristotle, necessarily implicate, if the action is to be successful, the three critical areas which he calls the *pisteis entechnoi*. For in discourse on any problem these *pisteis* are the substantial elements which enable a person to lead an other toward belief or conviction. These *pisteis* are *pragma*, the logical and factual presentation of the subject-matter, those rational probabilities, opinions, truths about the subject which translate it to the mind as reasonable; *ethos*, the element of the personal, the person of the speaker and the auditor, his style, so to speak, as it is affected by and flows into the subject-matter; and finally *pathos*, the interplay of feeling, sensibility, emotions in relation to the subject of discourse. These are the intellectual and psychological forces which come into action in the effort to establish conviction. For, as Aristotle says (*B* 1, 78a 7—9), there are other grounds for belief besides the rational argument (ἀποδείξεων). Rhetorical discourse ideally should integrate these three elements which lead to conviction. If the enthymeme is the major methodological instrument for such discourse, then it should integrate them as well.

As a structural form the enthymeme is certainly well adapted to do so. Just as the scientific syllogism organizes the sources of knowledge, so the rhetorical syllogism can organize the sources of conviction. If we ask ourselves what the scientific syllogism is we find that basically it is an instrument for the acquisition of knowledge which takes apparently separate and independent concepts and puts them into a structure which leads to new knowledge. In the same way the enthymeme gives structure to the sources which contribute to belief or conviction. In both instances the scientific syllogism and the rhetorical syllogism, as structural form, stand apart from their sources. They are a technique which utilizes the sources, a method for discursive reasoning. If the speculative reason alone is at work the sources will be concerned with reason alone; if the practical reason is operating the sources will be different. There is a recognition of such a difference at *Rhetoric* Γ 16, 17a 19—20: "Thus mathematical discourses possess no *ethos* since they have no *proairesis*", and *De Anima* 433a 14—15: "mind which calculates to an end, that is the practical mind; it differs from the speculative mind by its *telos*". As has been said previously the only permanent element in "syllogism" is its structure as a form of inference. Its apodeictic, dialectical, rhetorical character is determined by its content, or the source material it uses. In so far as Aristotle usually thinks of syllogism as the apodeictic syllogism, that is to say the inferential form using epistemonic source material, it may be that he calls the enthymeme quite early in the *Rhetoric* (*A* 1, 55a 8) "a kind of, a sort of syllogism".

When Aristotle calls the enthymeme σῶμα τῆς πίστεως (*A* 1, 54a 15) it certainly appears that it is in this sense of inferential form, something which is able to contain and give form to the *pisteis*. Since the *pisteis* as source material are three in number it is clear that the enthymeme as the body must contain all three[1]. There is certainly no ground on which to assume that this phrase refers to the enthymeme as the third of the three *pisteis*, that is to say the logical proof of the subject, with the underlying idea rightly rejected by VATER: "*robur et nervum fidei faciendae*, ut enthymema fit πίστις potentissima, sicuti robur militaris; ceterae autem fidei faciendae rationes sint minus efficaces, ut arma"[2]. This idea is simply not in the Greek word. Rather σῶμα means the body, the whole in which a thing is contained[3]. As

---

[1] A reading of *A* 1, 54a 11—16 together with 54b 19—22 and 55a 3—5, *A* 2, 55b 35—39 with their stress on the entechnic *pisteis* indicates that the enthymeme must be involved somehow with these three sources.

[2] VATER, Animadversiones, p. 5. While he does not appear to say what is being said in this analysis he does discern the import of Aristotle's statements, e. g. "Ad enthymema autem referuntur omnia quibus argumentatio efficitur. Qui versatus est in ταῖς ἐντέχνοις πίστεσι est ἐνθυμηματικός…".

[3] I. CASAUBON, Animadversiones in Athenaei Deipnosophistas, Lyon 1600, on II. 6, p. 54 gives instances of *soma* in this sense. VATER, Animadversiones, p. 5 cites *Meteor.* II. 4 in same sense; he also approves Maioragius' translation of our phrase σῶμα τῆς πίστεως as "ipsa natura et substantia"; in his comments here VATER appears to understand *soma* as I take it, i. e. literally, not metaphorically.

that which incorporates the *pisteis* the enthymeme as structural form should contain and give organization to the material which establishes belief in rhetorical discourse, namely, *pragma* (the logical explanation of the subject), *ethos*, and *pathos*.

Textually it appears impossible to establish the enthymeme as the third *pistis*, i. c. the rational demonstration of the subject. We have already seen that Aristotle never calls the enthymeme the third *pistis*, and, further, that a distinction clearly exists between the sources (the *pisteis entechnoi*) used by the enthymeme and the enthymeme as an inferential form (together with *paradeigma* called the *pisteis apodeiktikai*). Further evidence of that clear separation is found at *Γ* 1, 03b 6—15. Here in a summary of what has been achieved thus far in the treatise Aristotle says that he has discussed the three *pisteis* and he indicates that these are *pathos*, *ethos*, and a probative explanation of the subject (e. g. ἀποδεδεῖχθαι 10—12). He continues the statement with the remark that he has also discussed the enthymeme and its topics (13—14). If one insists that enthymeme is the third *pistis* and consequently that he is referring to enthymeme in the word ἀποδεδεῖχθαι (12) then Aristotle is talking in circles. For he states rather confusingly: "*pathos, ethos,* and 'the enthymeme' have been discussed . . . and the enthymeme has also been discussed".

To rest one's evidence for this identification of enthymeme with the third *pistis* on a phrase at *A* 1, 55a 7 where Aristotle calls the enthymeme κυριώτατον τῶν πίστεων is to forget that *pistis* here refers to the two modes of inferential reasoning, deduction and induction, which he calls the κοιναὶ πίστεις at *B* 20, 93a 24 and the πίστεις ἀποδεικτικαί at *A* 2, 58a 1. There is no question of "logical proof" being the "most decisive, or master, proof", although the statement does have an Aristotelian ring to it and for that reason apparently has an attractive quality. Yet it would indeed be rather foolish for Aristotle to say such a thing of rhetorical discourse directed as it is to move an other toward belief and conviction when he remarks in the *Ethics* (1139a 35—6) that pure reason moves nothing. Further, the tenuous character of such evidence becomes clear when one notes that just a page later in the *Rhetoric* (*A* 2, 56a 13) Aristotle says of *ethos*: σχεδὸν . . . κυριωτάτην ἔχει πίστιν. The enthymeme, then, as "the most decisive" of the proofs means, if anything, that deductive reasoning by the enthymeme is superior to inductive reasoning by *paradeigma*, a judgment completely in accord with his general attitude on the two kinds of inferential reasoning.

As we will see shortly all rhetorical demonstration which is directed toward achieving judgment from the auditor in the area of human action demands specifically a presentation which confronts both the intellect and the appetitive faculties, or *reason, ethos* and *pathos*. Consequently the instruments of such demonstration, whether they be inductive or deductive, must integrate these elements. Since, however, there has been persistent insistence that Aristotle is primarily concerned with rational proof of one's subject and that the enthymeme as the syllogism of rhetoric is the deductive instrument of that rational proof we must carry this matter somewhat further.

As far as I can see the strongest evidence in the *Rhetoric* for the enthymeme as the third *pistis entechnos* is a passage at *Γ* 17, 18a 1—b 4. Here it appears that enthymeme is identified with logical proof of one's statement (i. e. *apodeixis*) and separated from *ethos* and *pathos*[4]. In some ways the text does seem insurmountable, and visions of Marx' editor of *Γ* (see p. 50) begin to take shape before the mind's eye. Unfortunately, however, what is said in part of this passage (e. g. 18a 1—5) was said earlier at *A* 9, 68a 29—33 and the word *apodeixis* was also used, namely, that *paradeigmata* are best for deliberative discourse, enthymemes for judicial. It is of interest to note that this passage at *A* 9 is one of the only three times that ἐνθύμημα is used between *A* 4 and *B* 17 inclusively, a section in which Aristotle discusses the particular topics *(eide)* of enthymemes. His usual phrase throughout is *pistis* such as can be found at *A* 7, 65b 19—21. The other instances are at *A* 15, 76a 32 and *B* 1, 77b 19. In the *A* 15 passage we can see something of the difficulty of making an absolute identification of enthymeme and *apodeixis* to represent the exclusively logical demonstration of the subject. Here (76a 29—32) Aristotle says that in presenting the character of a witness "we must speak from the same topics from which we take our enthymemes". The presumption in this statement is that enthymemes can be derived from topics concerned with *ethos*. There is a somewhat similar difficulty in the *B* 1, 77b 16—24 statement. In the text we are told that from the topics presented (i. e. book *A*) come our "enthymemes" on each genre of rhetoric. This is quite understandable since we are and have been looking throughout the book for the sources of enthymemes. But at b23 Aristotle (in the ordinary interpretation of this passage seems to explain "enthymeme" by the words [λόγος] ἀποδεικτικός . . . καὶ πιστός, and once more the enthymeme appears to be *apodeixis*, or logical demonstration (cf. also 78a 8 ἀποδείξεων). Again, however, it can be asked whether *apodeiktikos* here means anything more than *logos* which arises from the factual presentation of the case. This was the general quest of A, a presentation grounded in the *pisteis pragmatikai. Apodeiktikos* is found in a similar use at *A* 8, 66a 9—10 where we are told that our "*pisteis* come not only δι' ἀποδεικτικοῦ λόγου ἀλλὰ καὶ δι' ἠθικοῦ".

---

[4] It is not possible to refrain from saying here that were we to pursue the not uncommon way of explaining problems in the text we could say that in the light of the evidence already produced Aristotle simply could not have made these statements and that these passages represent the kind of misunderstanding and interpolation characteristic of the *Rhetoric* in general and particularly of the third book. In fact this has been done for the first passage (*Γ* 17, 18a 12 ff.), see SOLMSEN, Drei Rekonstruktionen, Hermes 67, 1932, p. 149.

In other words can we be absolutely certain that in every instance in which Aristotle uses some form of *apodeixis* he necessarily means rational demonstration by syllogism? Can not *apodeixis* mean also the rational character of discourse in the instances cited in contradistinction to the emotional or ethical character? Indeed, in one of the only three passages between *A* 4—*B* 17 where Aristotle uses *syllogismos* (*A* 6, 62b 30; 10, 68b 2; 11, 71b 9), and where he could have used *enthymema* (or *apodeixis* if one insists upon the absolute identity of the two), Aristotle clearly states that the sources of this syllogism in rhetorical discourse are more than merely logical in character. For we read at *A* 10, 68b 1—5: "With respect to accusation and defense one should next state from how many and what kind of propositions the syllogisms must be constructed. It is necessary, in fact, to consider three things, first, for what reasons and for how many reasons men act wrongly, secondly, in what state of mind they are, thirdly, their character and disposition." The presence here among the sources of factual evidence *(pragma)* as well as *pathos* (cf. also 68b 25—26) and *ethos* is more than clear. Equally clear is it that all are the substance for inference by syllogism.

When we turn to our passage at *Γ* 17, 18a 12—17 we read: "whenever you are trying to arouse emotion don't use an enthymeme; for it will either expel the emotion or will be used to no avail. Simultaneous movements expel each other, and they either destroy or weaken each other. Nor must one seek any enthymeme at the moment when making the *logos* ethical; for *apodeixis* has neither *ethos* nor moral purpose". We have here what appears to be an explicit identification of enthymeme with *apodeixis;* and so the enthymeme is apparently the logical proof of one's subject-matter. This viewpoint is presumably repeated at 18a 32—b 2.

Aristotle does seem to speak of the enthymeme as logical demonstration by syllogism of the subject-matter in contradistinction to proof derived from *ethos* and *pathos*. To decide whether or not he is in fact saying this can only be done within the context of his comments on rhetorical discourse as I have just tried to illustrate, not in the study of an isolated statement.

But if we take the statement here does it submit to an explanation? It must be said immediately that there is no problem in the identification of enthymeme with *apodeixis* for Aristotle actually calls the enthymeme the *apodeixis* of rhetoric (*A* 1, 55a 6). *Apodeixis* usually refers to scientific demonstration by syllogism, but in a more extended sense and one met in the *Rhetoric* it means demonstration by syllogism which is for Aristotle a form of rational inference. We should note next that in our passage at *Γ* 17 Aristotle clearly desires to emphasize proof by *pathos*. He separates it distinctly from logical proof. We have already seen in chapter I that Aristotle recognizes that any of the three *pisteis entechnoi (pragma, ethos, pathos)* can be used independently to effect belief or conviction. In our section this acceptance of separate ways of proof is present[5], and with this compartmentalized approach uppermost in his mind Aristotle could readily designate logical proof in our passage by the one word so firmly tied to such proof: *apodeixis* and its rhetorical correlative enthymeme. It is not impossible — though perhaps unfortunate — that when Aristotle wishes to speak of winning conviction by *reason* as opposed to winning conviction by *pathos* or *ethos* he employs the word enthymeme which he has already called ἀπόδειξις ῥητορική (*A* 1, 55a 6). It does not seem that we must inevitably conclude from *Γ* 17 that the enthymeme is, and can only be, the logical demonstration of the subject by syllogistic inference.

In conclusion attention should be directed to the fact that when we find the verb form ἀποδεικνύναι (it is used once between *A* 4—*B* 17 at *B* 4, 82a 17) it can mean simply "demonstration by syllogism"[6]. For example its use in *B* 22, 96a 35 together with δεικνύναι b 2, 10 is at the most "demonstration by syllogism". It would be difficult for it to be *exclusively rational* demonstration by syllogism since *B* 22, 96a 34—b 19 is the conclusion to a 4—34. And in a 4—34 we cannot escape the fact that the "demonstration" includes not simply a knowledge of the facts of the case but of those facts which carry an emotional appeal and reflect the *ethos* of the people addressed, e. g. what is specifically necessary to convince the Athenians that war is necessary. Aristotle is speaking here about the choice of material for argumentation, and as he says *(Topics* 105b 15) such selection should begin with the subject itself (ἀπὸ τοῦ τί ἐστιν). In rhetorical discourse the subject is of necessity specified by something more than its mere logical analysis[7].

However if any corrective to the interpretation of the enthymeme as the third *pistis* and exclusively logical proof is needed it can be found first of all in Aristotle's statements on maxim, γνώμη (*B* 21, 94a 18—95a 34). From his description (94a 22—29) maxim can be called a general truth embodying a moral or practical precept concerning human action[8]. There are four kinds:

---

[5] Our passage appears in a section of the third book which has been said to be from a treatise on "the parts of speech" (μόρια λόγου). This was a fairly traditional approach to rhetoric according to which certain parts of a speech were concerned exclusively with logical proof, others with proof by *pathos*, others with proof by *ethos;* see K. BARWICK, Die Gliederung der rhetorischen τέχνη und die horazische Epistula ad Pisones, Hermes 57, 1922, pp. 11 ff. A number of scholars believe that Aristotle was strongly influenced in this part of the third book by just such an approach, e. g. SPENGEL, τεχνῶν συναγωγή, Leipzig 1828, p. 159, MARX, Aristoteles Rhetorik, pp. 245 ff., Süss, Ethos, pp. 193 ff., SOLMSEN, Drei Rekonstruktionen, pp. 146 ff.

[6] At times cognates of *apodeixis* appear quite similar to uses of δεικνύναι i. e. "universe demonstrandi, exponendi, explicandi vim habet" (BONITZ); the idea of explanation, exposition of the subject-matter rather than its demonstration.

[7] In the area of formal rhetoric a cursory examination of the argumentation of the Attic orators makes this clear; for a general conspectus of such argumentation see M. LAVENCY, La technique des lieux communs de la rhétorique grecque, LEC 35, 1965, pp. 113—126.

[8] There is a perceptive analysis of the word by Planudes in *Rhetores Graeci* (ed. WALZ) vol. 5, p. 422. 3—16 in which he locates its role in the sphere of human action and its purpose "to teach the

(A) maxim with its reason given (e. g. no man is free for he is either a slave of money or chance); this kind of maxim is either (1) part of an enthymeme, or, (2) enthymematic, but not part of an enthymeme; (B) maxim without its reason added (e. g. no man is completely happy); this is either (3) well-known gnomic statement and so familiar, or, (4) eminently clear from the mere enunciation. Our attention naturally gravitates to the first two types because of their relation to enthymeme. It is a very intimate relation since Aristotle says (*B* 21, 94a 26—29): "Consequently since enthymemes are syllogisms concerned with such subject-matter maxims are more or less the conclusions of enthymemes or the premises with the syllogistic form removed"[9]. This statement is general and is true for all kinds of maxim. If it is pressed we can legitimately conclude that premises or conclusions of an enthymeme are often gnomic in character. As such the enthymeme would obviously be something substantively different from bare logical proof. Again, however, from what Aristotle tells us about the enthymeme and maxim there is no need to conclude that maxim *must be* "part of an enthymeme". There can be enthymeme without gnomic statement. The *Anonymi Scholia*[10] explain it well: "the enthymeme differs from the non-apodeictic maxim [i. e. those without the reason added] in that this last is a simple declaration and the enthymeme is a syllogism so to speak; it differs from the apodeictic maxim [i. e. those with the reason added] as the parts differ from a whole, for the enthymeme is contained within the maxim". In Aristotle, however, a close relationship is established between enthymeme and maxim and we read at *B* 20, 93a 25 that maxim is not to be included among the *koinai pisteis* (enthymeme and *paradeigma*) because "it is part of enthymeme"[11]. As an illustration of this relation we have in our section two maxims which become enthymemes (*B* 21, 94a 29 ff.), and at *Γ* 17, 18b 33—38 we have in Aristotle's own words an enthymeme which becomes a maxim with the reason added. This exchange between maxim and enthymeme is also true of maxim which Aristotle says is particularly esteemed by the auditors and which he calls "enthymematic" (*B* 21, 94b 19—20). It is not "part of an enthymeme" but stands by itself. Since it carries in its statement the reason for its truth, e. g. "mortal as you are cherish not an immortal anger" (94b 21—22) it can be easily presented in a

kind of action something is or ought to be"; also in vol. 7, pt. 2, p. 765. 11—766. 4 there is an intelligent discussion of Aristotle's division from the *Anonymi Scholia*. Anaximenes in c. 11 on maxim considers only classes 1 and 2 and his discussion is quite informative about Aristotle's division.

[9] In the light of such an explicit statement there should be no necessity to say that the relationship is *not* based on form, i. e. the enthymeme and maxim are related because they express their thought in a shortened syllogistic form. The relationship is grounded in the subject-matter of each.   [10] See note 8.

[11] This does not mean that *gnomai* cannot be used alone; obviously those without the reason added are so used, and those with the reason given may be. If they do not have the syllogistic form they are not part of an enthymeme but possess the potential to be made into enthymemes.

syllogistic form and so is called "enthymematic"[12]. Such a ready interchange of maxim and enthymeme obviously raises substantial questions about the purely logical character of enthymematic argumentation.

We know from Aristotle's explanation (*B* 21, 94a 22—26) that maxim is a general proposition, or assertion, relative to moral action and human conduct[13]. As such it will of necessity implicate the constituent elements of moral action which includes *ethos* and *pathos*. The maxim is concerned with human action and particularly with *proairesis* in human action (*B* 21, 95a 28 ff.; b12 ff.). In addition to this maxim is an instrument for making discourse ethical (b13) and for the delineation of *ethos* in the speaker (*B* 21, 95a 2—5, 23; b 15—18; *Γ* 17, 18a 17—18). It also is related to *pathos* in discourse, both subjectively on the speaker's part (95a 24—25) and objectively with respect to the audience (95b 10 ff.). A quick glance at the maxims cited by Aristotle reveals, for example, emotional states reflecting fear, patriotism, courage, anger[14]. Maxim functions clearly on two levels: the intellectual and the appetitive. In Aristotle's words the listeners "delight if the speaker happens to express in a general way their specific convictions" (95b 2—5). Thus maxim is a statement of reason together with emotional and associative overtones which influence the person, the appetitive as well as the rational part of him. Aeschines (3.135) expresses it rather well: "I believe that we learn the *gnomai* of poets carefully when we are children for this reason, that we may use them when we are men".

In maxim, then, which is so closely connected with enthymeme, we have argumentation which aims quite directly at the emotional and appetitive side of man. The conclusion which we must draw from this is that the enthymeme cannot be exclusively rational and intellectual. Nor can it be called the third *pistis*, namely the logical proof of the subject. It can not even be identified with the third *pistis* as the rational explanation of the subject-matter. We come back again to the idea that the enthymeme is something which stands apart from the three *pisteis: ethos, pathos, rational explanation*. It gives them form as argumentation incorporating them in rhetorical demonstration. For an assured corollary of Aristotle's comments on maxim is that the enthymeme works not merely upon the intellect but also upon the affective part of

---

[12] Anonymus, *Commentaria Graeca*, vol. 21, p. 127. 5 says as much in a rather vague and elusive comment which leaves his testimony somewhat questionable.

[13] See Gregory in *Rhetores Graeci* (ed. WALZ) vol. 7, pt. 2, p. 1154. 15 who gives the explanation of Theophrastus: "a general assertion in the area of what one must do", or the *Auctor ad Her.* 4. 24, and HORNA, RE suppl. VI (1935) p. 75, on the passage in Aristotle "ihr Zweck das sittliche oder lebenskluge Verhalten des Menschen zu regeln", and RHYS ROBERTS, Demetrius on Style, Cambridge 1902, p. 272.

[14] Anonymus, *Comm. Graeca*, vol. 21, p. 129. 3 ff., grasps the role of *pathos* in *gnome* although he misrepresents Aristotle at *B* 21, 95b 10 ff. in saying that the purpose of gnomologia is to pander to what you suspect the audience's feelings to be.

man. The enthymeme employs both reason, emotion, *ethos*, and directs itself in its argumentation to the whole man. This should not be startling when we realize that it is the primary methodological tool in a *techne* which aims ultimately at effecting in others a judgment and decision with a view to action.

To recall and slightly enlarge upon some of the statements in c. I we know that any kind of argumentation or demonstration which concerns itself with effecting judgment and decision in this area must take into consideration all the factors which make decision possible. Aristotle is always quite clear in the *Rhetoric* that its *telos* is a judgment of some sort, an evaluation to be made by the auditor. When we consider man as someone to be disposed toward *praxis* we soon discover that for Aristotle something more than an informed mind is needed. We learn in the *Nicomachean Ethics* (1098a 3 ff.) that man's nature directed to action involves a twofold element: intellect and appetition. Intellect is directive, appetition is subject to direction, capable of obeying rule. But both are necessary. This nature is more carefully analysed at 1102a 27 ff. and we find that man's soul, as the principle of responsible human action, calls upon two factors in order to act: reason and appetition, *nous* and *orexis*[15]. It is interesting to see this analysis reflected in the *Rhetoric* at *A* 11, 70a 13—27, particularly at 25—27: "rational desires are those men form upon conviction for they desire to see and possess many things after hearing of them and being convinced about them". If we take a closer look at man's nature as the principle of *praxis* we arrive at this general picture of it. From the appetitive side man's soul consists of πάθη (emotions, feelings), δυνάμεις (psychical capacities for experiencing such feelings), ἕξεις (acquired dispositions with respect to the feelings) 1105b 19—21. Fundamentally these are the elements which enter into human *praxis*[16]. If we advance somewhat further there appears to exist in man's soul a dominant appetitive faculty. βούλησις fits the role rather well although Aristotle is admittedly not particularly clear on this. βούλησις is an appetency for the *telos* (1111b 26; 1113a 14—15; b 3) and for the good (1113a 14—24; *Rhet.* *A* 10, 69a 3: βούλησις ἀγαθοῦ ὄρεξις). It is "rational wish" and it corresponds well with that part of the rational soul which Aristotle describes in 1102b 25—6 as λόγου μετέχειν[17].

---

[15] See 1139a 17—b 13; we read at a 21 f.: "what affirmation and negation are in thought, pursuit and flight are in appetition". See *De An.* 432b 26—433b 30; at 433a 9: "these two, then, appear to be the sources of movement, *orexis* and *nous*".

[16] We are not including αἴσθησις (1139a 17—19) since it is not immediately relevant to the problem under discussion.

[17] In cc. 9—11 of the *De Anima* βούλησις is rational wish; on this see R. D. Hicks, Aristotle *De Anima*, Cambridge 1907, s. 432b 5. At 411a 28 (and see 414b 2) βούλησις is a species of *orexis* which is opposed to ἐπιθυμία as rational to irrational desire and this same relationship is present at *Rhet.* *A* 10, 69a 1—3 where βούλησις concerns action which results from ὄρεξις λογιστική as opposed to ὄρεξις ἄλογος.

βούλησις, then, would be the faculty which can exercise control over ἐπιθυμία with which it forms substantially the orectic soul. This dominance by the rational part of the soul, i. e. the part which obeys reason (1102b 26), permits one to understand how intentional habits (ἕξεις) are formed in the soul. For there is definitely something in the orectic soul "contrary to reason and opposed to it" (1102b 24) which can be controlled since ἕξις is that "by which we are well or badly disposed with respect to the πάθη" (1105b 26; see also 1106a 2—3). βούλησις is consistent with this rational control of the πάθη in accord with the rule set by *phronesis*[18]. It is then possible to understand why such ἕξεις when they are "praiseworthy" (1103a 9) can be called "virtues". For *arete* (1106b 36 ff.), as a state of soul apt to exercise deliberate choice under reason, implies a higher rational appetitive faculty controlling first the πάθη, and then action[19]. With this in mind we can understand why such ἕξεις in man may be good or bad, and how it is that these stabile dispositions, dispositions in which βούλησις is the controlling factor, manifest a person's *ethos* or character as we see it in *Poetics* 1450a 5, b 8. *Ethos*, then, would represent the appetitive soul as it is firmly disposed in one way or another, a disposition produced by a dominant appetitive faculty under the control of reason: λόγου μετέχειν[20]. With this understanding of *ethos* it becomes possible to comprehend VAHLEN's translation of ἦθος in the *Poetics* as "Wille", e. g. "Dort sind διάνοια und ἦθος, Intelligenz und Charakter, Verstand und Wille, zusammengefaßt als die beiden Seiten, in denen die geistige Qualität des Menschen überhaupt aufgeht . . .", as well as BUTCHER's interpretation: "Ethos, as explained by Aristotle, is the moral element in character. It reveals a certain state or direction of the will"[21]. Since πάθη play a prominent part in the orectic soul and are capable of influence (1106a 4—5; 1111a 22—25, b 1—3) we can understand that the dominant appetitive faculty seeks to acquire a constant disposition with respect to them. Thus when-

---

[18] *Phronesis* determines the *true* response demanded by the situation; as Aristotle says of the "good" man (1106b 36 ff.): "Virtue is a stabile disposition having to do with deliberate choice consisting in a mean that is relative to us, a mean determined by a rational principle and by that rational principle by which the *phronimos* man would determine it"; see H. JOACHIM, Aristotle, The Nicomachean Ethics, Oxford 1951, pp. 85—89; L. H. G. GREENWOOD, Aristotle, Nicomachean Ethics, Cambridge 1909, p. 37.

[19] Aristotle mentions a number of times that *arete* is concerned with πάθη and πράξεις, e. g. 1104b 13—14; 1106b 16—17, 24—25.

[20] See 1138b 35—1139a 3 where *ethos* is connected with the *aretai ethikai;* and 1138b 18—20 where there is a volitional faculty of some kind (also 1109b 30 ff.); and 1110a 12, 19 where we see some such faculty at work.

[21] J. VAHLEN, Aristoteles' Lehre von der Rangfolge der Teile der Tragödie, Symbola Philologorum Bonnensium, Lipsiae 1867, p. 172, n. 43; S. H. BUTCHER, Aristotle's Theory of Poetry and Fine Art³, London 1902, p. 339; see Isocrates, *Antidosis* 276—280 on the importance of *ethos* as *pistis*.

ever Aristotle speaks of the "good disposition" *(arete)* he tells us that it is concerned with the πάθη.

This, then, is the appetitive part of the psyche concerned with *praxis*. If we now consider the role of reason in *praxis* we may apprehend the final process better. In 1112a 18—1113a 14 Aristotle describes the intellectual process. Reason starts from an assumed or desired *telos* and considers the means necessary to achieve it through deliberation. This activity terminates at the first means necessary and there it stops since neither deliberation nor reason can give the end. Something else must come in to initiate this final action. This is the most damaging criticism of those who would insist that Aristotle identifies rhetorical demonstration with reason alone. Such demonstration would be sterile. When reason has done its work then an evaluation *(krisis)* and a choice must be made. Deliberate choice, *proairesis*, must step in (1113a 2—14). This is the appetitive part of the psyche, "*orexis* assenting to the result of deliberation", or, as Aristotle explains it (1113a 15—b 2; see also 1111b 5 ff.), "deliberate desire of things in our power". Again this is reflected rather well in the *Rhetoric A* 10, 68b 9—12: "men do willingly all that they do with knowledge and without constraint. Thus while all voluntary acts are not the object of deliberate choice (προαιρούμενοι) all that men deliberately choose they do with knowledge; for no one is ignorant of that which he deliberately chooses (προαιρεῖται)".

Praxis, then, is the result of appetition (ὄρεξις) and reason (νοῦς) in two ways: a) remotely in so far as they inaugurate and enter into the process, b) proximately in so far as they constitute *proairesis* which is the efficient cause of action (1139a 31—33). Further the orectic soul, as we have seen, includes feelings, emotions, and stabile dispositions with respect to them. These form the threshold from which the orectic soul steps into action under the guidance of reason[22].

We are thus confronted with the fact that *pathos*, *ethos*, and *reason* are intimately united in *praxis*. In rhetoric which prepares for *praxis* we should expect to find them closely united, particularly in the enthymeme which for Aristotle is the heart of the rhetorical process. Deliberation occupies itself with matters within our power and of consequence to us. In rhetorical discourse

---

[22] GREENWOOD, Aristotle, p. 40, "Action we learn is caused by προαίρεσις or purpose, which is, as the *Ethics* has already shown, a combination of reasoning with ὄρεξις or desire. Therefore the goodness or badness of action must depend on the goodness or badness of both reasoning and desire. The reasoning that has to do with action is, like other reasoning, only a means to an end. But whereas other reasoning attains its end, which is truth, if it is good in itself, reasoning that has to do with action does not necessarily attain its end by being good in itself, but only by also harmonizing with good desire: indeed it cannot in practise ever be called good in itself, because it is in practise inseparable from desire, and the goodness of its relation to that desire is, as it were, an essential part of its own goodness."

the audience must be brought not only to knowledge of the subject but knowledge as relevant and significant for they are either indifferent, opposed, or in partial agreement. They will ultimately decide to act or not after deliberate choice, and *proairesis* is always reason and appetition moving together as Aristotle says at 1113a 11—12: "for coming to a decision after deliberation we desire in accord with our deliberation". The whole person acts and we find this again in the *Rhetoric* at A 10, 68b 32 — 69a 7. Confining ourselves to that part of the text immediately pertinent to the analysis here we read that πάντες δὴ πάντα πράττουσι ... δι' αὑτούς ... δι' ὄρεξιν ... τὰ μὲν διὰ λογιστικὴν ὄρεξιν τὰ δὲ δι' ἄλογον, sc. ὀργὴν καὶ ἐπιθυμίαν: "all men perform all actions ... which are owing to themselves ... through appetition ... some through appetition guided by reason others without the guidance of reason ... in anger and lust". In the *De Motu Animalium* 700 b 15—24 we read in part: "For all living things both move and are moved with a view to some object ... the end in view. We perceive that what moves the living creature is intellect (διάνοια), imagination, deliberate choice, will (βούλησις) and appetite. All these are reducible to mind and appetition (ταῦτα δὲ πάντα ἀνάγεται εἰς νοῦν καὶ ὄρεξιν)". In the *Poetics* 1449b 35 ff. (cf. p. 27 f. *supra*) we are told quite explicitly that drama is an imitation of *praxis* and demands the causes of *praxis*: *ethos* and *dianoia*[23]. Since, as we have seen, *ethos* implicates the play of the emotions *praxis* in drama is the result of the interaction of *ethos*, *pathos* and *dianoia*. It is the externalization of an inward psychical process which develops from the interaction of feelings and reason and is carried forward to its conclusion by the will. "Action, to be dramatic, must be exhibited in its development and in its results; it must stand in reciprocal and causal relation to certain mental states. We desire to see the feelings out of which it grows, the motive force of will which carries it to its conclusion; and, again, to trace the effect of the deed accomplished on the mind of the doer — the emotions there generated as they become in turn new factors of action ..."[24]. It is clear that the emotions qualify and condition man's action both from the appetitive and the intellectual side in so far as they affect reason which is guiding *proairesis*. As Aristotle says at *Rhet.* B 1, 78a 20—21: "The emotions are those things through which men alter and change their decisions". Human action must, then, be determined by *ethos*, *pathos*, and *nous*.

If the whole person acts, then it is the whole person to whom discourse in rhetoric must be directed. One can say *a priori* that anything, such as the enthymeme, which for Aristotle embodies the rhetorical technique must consider *intellect*, *ethos* (that is to say stabile dispositions with respect to one's

---

[23] *De Anima* 433a 1—b 30 explains this in more detail and includes the emotions more specifically.   [24] BUTCHER, Aristotle's Theory, p. 347.

appetitive state), and *pathos* (emotions which enter into and influence human action).

If we return now to the *Rhetoric* and give attention to some statements in the text we find further evidence that Aristotle did not intend the enthymeme, as the rhetorical mode of demonstration, to be exclusively rational, but to incorporate *ethos* and *pathos* as well as *reason*. At *B* 1, 77b 16—24 Aristotle notes that we have been given in the first book δόξαι καὶ προτάσεις (18) which are useful for proving (19). In other words we have at our disposal at the moment generally accepted opinions and propositional statements for logical statements on the subject-matter in each of the three branches of rhetoric (20). From these opinions and propositions enthymemes are formed (19). However, Aristotle continues, rhetoric is directed toward judgment (21) and this demands that the *logos* (23) present not merely the logical aspect of the subject-matter but also give attention to *ethos* and *pathos* (23—24), since they, too, affect judgment (25 ff.). It is not unnatural to expect that he would now present us with such "generally accepted opinions and propositions" on *ethos* and *pathos* and this he tells us (78a 28—30) is his plan: "and so just as we drew up a list of premises in the case of the earlier material, let us now also do this on the material before us and analyse it in the same way". When we come to the conclusion of the analysis of *ethos* and *pathos* in the second book we read at *B* 18, 91b 25—29: "and with respect to all the kinds of rhetoric generally accepted opinions and propositional statements have been selected from which those who engage in deliberative, epideictic and forensic rhetoric take their proofs, and further still those opinions and propositions have also been determined from which it is possible to make the *logos* ethical"[25]. Even were the advocates of the enthymeme as exclusively rational demonstration to confine themselves to cc. 4—14 of book *A* together with the summation of these chapters at *B* 1, 77b 16—24 their argument would be incomplete and inadequate. For in the course of these chapters Aristotle manifests an awareness of the role of *ethos* and *pathos* in demonstration. For example he explicitly remarks of judicial oratory (*A* 9, 68b 1 ff.) that with regard to the number and nature of the premises of rhetorical syllogisms we must not only consider the reasons why men act but also their emotional attitudes and their characters. These elements also enter into the rhetorical syllogism. In view of the fact that as yet there is no formal discussion of *ethos* and *pathos* one would rightly expect such a discussion and Aristotle promises it at 68b 25—26.

These text statements on δόξαι καὶ προτάσεις coalesce and we can see a larger meaning when they are taken together with the seminal statement

---

[25] It is not usual to take *B* 18, 91b 27 in this way with δόξαι καὶ προτάσεις as the antecedent; in the light of *B* 1, 77b 16 ff., 78a 28 ff., *B* 22, 96b 28 ff., however, it is more than justified.

which is the preface to the entire discussion. At *A* 1, 59a 6—10 we read: "It is clear from what has been said that we must have first of all premises on such matters; for *tekmeria*, *eikota* and *semeia* are the premises of rhetoric; while in general a syllogism is built upon premises, the enthymeme is a syllogism built upon the premises just mentioned". This statement is a preface to a study of precisely such particular premises from c. 4 of book *A* to c. 17 of book *B*. At the end of the study we find the same statement substantially at *B* 18, 91b 24—29 and again at *B* 22, 96b 28—34. This last immediately precedes his discussion of the general sources for the enthymeme and states in part: "for premises have already been singled out with respect to each branch of rhetoric so that the sources from which one must draw enthymemes on the good or bad, honorable or dishonorable, just or unjust are on hand, and in like manner the sources for *ethos*, *pathos* and the habits have been selected and are on hand for us"[26]. We cannot forget that Aristotle refers in these last two passages to his discussion from *A* 4 to *B* 17 which presents the particular topics. These topics are the sources for *eikota*, *semeia*, and *tekmeria*. The *eikota*, *semeia*, *tekmeria*, however, are the premises which form rhetorical enthymemes.

It appears rather difficult to escape the fact that the enthymeme as the primary instrument of rhetorical argumentation and demonstration brings together reason and appetition in its effort to make a judgment possible. This understanding of the enthymeme was not entirely unknown to the ancients. Planudes in a discussion of enthymeme in which he defines it as a condensed syllogism, incomplete with respect to one of its propositions, goes on to cite Neocles: "Neocles says that the syllogism is put together from premises and a conclusion; but the enthymeme as compared with the epicheireme is

---

[26] The Greek itself seems clear; a check on a few translations reveals the following. SANDYS and FREESE agree; SANDYS translates: "so that we have already ascertained the topics from which enthymemes are to be drawn about good or evil, ... characters, feelings, moral states". BONAFOUS, La Rhétorique d'Aristote, Paris 1856, p. 249 concurs. SCHRADER in his third edition of the *Rhetoric* (1672), whom MURETUS apparently follows in his edition of 1685, puts a period after ἀδίκου (b33) and starts a new sentence. This, however, does not change the meaning from the above translations. On the Greek itself COPE, Commentary, vol. II, pp. 233—234 has a note. SOLMSEN, Die Entwicklung, pp. 233 ff. acknowledges that the discussion on *pathos* in book *B* cc. 2—11 parallels the discussion in *A* cc. 4—15 in its concern for what SOLMSEN calls the *idiai protaseis* of enthymemes which in this study are called the *eide*. SOLMSEN also calls attention to *B* 1, 78a 28 (p. 148 above) and claims that here Aristotle wishes to emphasize the parallelism. It is unclear whether SOLMSEN would draw the conclusion from this that since *pathos* is a source for his *idiai protaseis* of enthymeme *pathos* should be as much a part of enthymeme as *reason*. He does make note of, but also rejects (p. 224, n. 1) BRANDIS' theory of the "πάθη-Lehre ... als einen Teil der Enthymemtheorie". Those who maintain that the *Rhetoric* as we have it represents a conflation of two theories: purely rational demonstration, *ethos-pathos* argumentation which did not succeed too well, must ask themselves in the light of a passage like this (*B* 22, 96b 28—34) whether or not the synthesis of *reason—pathos—ethos* was not Aristotle's starting point.

produced in a condensed form with one proposition of *ethos* and *pathos*, and sometimes *ethos* and *pathos* are commingled"[27].

Aristotle's achievement is expressed well by Cicero *(De Orat.* 2. 160): *"Atque inter hunc Aristotelem, cuius ... legi ... et illos, in quibus ipse sua quaedam de eadem arte dixit, et hos germanos huius artis magistros hoc mihi visum est interesse, quod ille eadem acie mentis, qua rerum omnium vim naturamque viderat, haec quoque aspexit quae ad dicendi artem, ..."*. The major difference between the Aristotelian analysis and that of others is that Aristotle recognized the organic character of discourse. Knowing that men are moved to judgment by the concomitant action of reason and appetition he argued that discourse must be unified in both its argumentation and its language. *Reason, ethos*, and *pathos* not only permeate the language of discourse but are also unified in its argumentation, particularly in the enthymeme. The movement toward conviction *(pistis)* and so toward judgment *(krisis)* is an integral action and implicates reason *(nous)* and appetition *(orexis)* working together. The *logos* in both its expression and argumentation must fuse these elements. Aristotle's view of discourse is organic not separatist. This last which we can find in a statement attributed to Theodectes: "to make the exordium with a view to winning good will, the narration with a view to plausibility, the confirmation with a view to persuasion, the peroration with a view to anger or pity" (cf. H. RABE, Prolegomenon Sylloge, Teubner 1931, p. 216) is an interpretation which has come down into modern rhetorical theory where we find parts of the discourse given over to logical proof, parts to emotional appeal.

With some qualifications Aristotle's attitude toward discourse is more correctly represented in an article of F. SOLMSEN, "Aristotle and Cicero on the Orator's Playing upon the Feelings". SOLMSEN believes that he has recovered the Aristotelian theory of rhetoric in Cicero's *De Oratore* 2. 27. 115, where Cicero's view of rhetorical discourse is that of a unified *logos*. With a slight change of the schema given we have Aristotle's theory well expressed. The *ratio dicendi* (the discourse) represents in itself a concurrence of (a) *ratio probandi (pragma*, i. e. logical analysis of subject), (b) *ratio conciliandi (ethos)*, (c) *ratio commovendi (pathos)*. SOLMSEN concludes that Aristotle "rather thinks of the λόγος as a whole and thinks of it as being made πιστός and becoming effective by the combined and simultaneous application of the three πίστεις: ἀπόδειξις, τὸ ἦθος τοῦ λέγοντος and τὰ πάθη"[28].

---

[27] Planudes in *Rhetores Graeci* (ed. Walz) vol. 5, pp. 403. 10—404. 2. Neocles is probably the technographer of the first-second century A. D. The Greek reads: Νεοκλῆς δέ φησιν, ὅτι ὁ μὲν συλλογισμὸς ἐκ λημμάτων καὶ ἐπιφορᾶς συνέστηκε· τὸ δὲ ἐνθύμημα παρὰ τὸ ἐπιχείρημα συνειλημμένως ἐκφέρεται καθ' ἓν ἀξίωμα ἤθους καὶ πάθους, ἐσθ' ὅτε συναναμεμιγμένων.

[28] See p. 393 of the article in Classical Philology 33, 1938, pp. 390—404. What has been said in this study of the enthymeme and the idea of *praxis* lends strong confirmation to this interpreta-

Aristotle has created a superb synthesis. He has fully justified rhetoric for the most Platonic Platonist. Rhetoric is not philosophy nor is it a mere technical game. It is the use of language in an artistic way, language which brings together in its effort to communicate knowledge and understanding to an other the elements essential to that understanding: reason and appetition.

tion. At the same time it would be difficult to make the correlation which SOLMSEN makes, i. e. *ratio probandi (apodeixis* which is then subdivided into *pisteis atechnoi* and *pisteis entechnoi)*. For it seems clear that *ethos* and *pathos* are *pisteis entechnoi*.